How To

FIRE
The IRS
A Plan To Eliminate
The Income Tax And The IRS

———⊳∘⊲———

A
NATIONAL SALES TAX
THE ONLY FAIR, SIMPLE AND ECONOMICAL
REPLACEMENT TO OUR TAX SYSTEM

Daniel J. Pilla

WINNING Publications, Inc.
450 Oak Grove Parkway, Suite 107C
St. Paul, Minnesota 55127

First Edition: October 1993

Printed in the United States of America

Library of Congress Catalog Card Number 93-094197

ISBN: 1-884367-00-3

Notice from the Author and Publisher

This book is designed to provide the author's findings and opinions based on research, analysis and experience with the subject matter covered. This information is not provided for purposes of rendering legal, accounting or other professional advice. It is intended purely for educational purposes.

The author and publisher disclaim any responsibility for any liability or loss incurred as a consequence of the use and application, either directly or indirectly, of any information presented herein.

Because the United States currently operates under an evolutionary legal system, the reader bears the burden of assuring the principles of law stated in this work are current and binding at the time of any intended use or application. Caution: The law in this country is subject to change arbitrarily and without prior notice.

Dedication

"The tree of liberty must be refreshed from time to time
with the blood of patriots and tyrants."

–Thomas Jefferson ,1787

––––––––––––

*This book is dedicated to the many Americans
who gave their lives in the true service of our nation;
that is, in the defense of the Constitution
and the great liberties it protects.
It is our responsibility
to preserve and protect
the liberties they died to defend.*

––––––––––––

For freedom Christ has set us free;
Stand fast therefore, and do not submit
again to the yoke of slavery.
–Galatians 5:1

CONTENTS

Introduction

My battle against IRS abuse began in 1977. At that time, my father was deeply embroiled in a conflagration with the IRS which resulted in the seizure of the family business. The agency closed his small printing business in 1974. In 1976, the IRS turned its attention to the family home. With its usual abandon, it moved against the home, seeking to have all of us relegated to life on the streets.

I became involved more out of desperation than anything else. At the age of 18, I surely knew nothing of the IRS, tax law, court procedure or any of the other necessary lessons of legal self-protection. However, the action was purely a matter of survival as my father had no money for an attorney. As I later came to understand, that was certainly a blessing. For my experience since has shown me the majority of attorneys know only that they wish to *stay away* from the IRS, not how to successfully fight them.

My father was in trouble with the IRS for a number of reasons. Many of the factors fueling his debate with the authorities shaped what would become my attitude toward taxation in general, and the IRS in particular. His battle centered around employment taxes. These are the burdens Washington imposes upon business for the privilege of hiring workers. I have since come to know these taxes are the undoing of countless entrepreneurs nationwide, year after year.

My father owned and operated a small printing business in St. Paul, Minnesota. With barely a high school education, he began printing business cards in a tool shed behind his father's (my grandfather) house on the east side of town. My father is the son of Italian immigrants who came to the United States from southern Italy in the 1920's. They settled in St. Paul only because a cousin found his way there several years prior.

The east side of St. Paul, where my father grew up, started his business and raised his own family, was populated with nothing but Italians. Italian was the language of choice in the neighborhood, and the best restaurants in town were located just blocks from where I grew up. Each small yard hosted a vegetable garden featuring plump tomatoes, romaine lettuce, and fresh herbs of every description. Fruit trees and grape vines were found everywhere. This was a place where wine making was utilitarian and the aroma of simmering spaghetti sauce and frying peppers and sausage always filled the air.

These people were fiercely independent. Those of my grandfather's generation were poor. The house I grew up in was purchased by him for $3,000. Those of my father's generation were lower middle class, at best. Most worked in the factories or brewery near the neighborhood. My father began his printing business as a very young man. It was the only available means he saw to improve his condition.

The printing business grew with time. He moved the shop out of the shed into a two car garage adjacent to the house where it operated for years. By the late 1950's, the business specialized in engraved high school graduation announcements. The work was seasonal, but the money was good. Within five years, my father moved his business downtown, occupying 10,000 square feet of a warehouse. It was steadily growing and by about 1964 he employed 22 people. It was at this time his trouble with the authorities began.

The 1960's was a time when urban renewal, a Department of Housing and Urban Development (HUD) program, was demolishing buildings and homes throughout America. St. Paul was not spared the wrecking ball as the need was determined by faceless Washington bureaucrats. In 1964, the building which housed the printing business was targeted for destruction. All building occupants would have to move.

The City of St. Paul, administering the program for HUD, assured all the tenants their costs of relocating would be covered under the redevelopment program. Letters of confirmation were sent, along with deadlines for vacating the premises. All the grumbling in the world did not help, so dutifully, my father, along with all the other businesses relocated.

Perhaps you can imagine what it takes to move heavy equipment, machinery, paper and supplies that occupied some 10,000 square feet. Special machinists were required to disassemble then reassemble huge engraving machines, linotypes and bindery equipment. The new facility had to be rewired to accommodate the equipment. Offices and other subdivisions had to be built in the new space. A moving company was hired which specialized in moving industrial equipment.

For weeks, the entire operation was shut down as all employees participated in the adventure. By the time the move of one block was complete, my father incurred costs of approximately $45,000.

The real shock came in the fall of 1964, after the dust had settled from the move and things were back to normal. It seemed the City did not plan to pay for the move after all. How could this be? All the meetings, letters and discussions with city planners left all involved with the assurance their costs would be reimbursed. But it was not to be. However, my father's Italian spirit would not allow him to merely acquiesce as many of the others did. He found a lawyer and sued the city.

After lengthy litigation and a trial, the city was forced to pay $27,000 to compensate for the move. That was barely half the costs incurred and the experience and financial loss left a great distrust in my father's heart for city officials. Ironically, the city block which was demolished stood vacant for *over 20 years.* All that time, the entire city block featured nothing but a hole in the ground which functioned as a parking lot. A wooden fence was built around the hole to prevent passers by from falling in. This is what Washington and the City of St. Paul referred to as "urban development."

My father's attitude toward government in general was galvanized by not one experience with urban renewal, but three. In 1968, city fathers decided to reroute a road, under the urban renewal umbrella, right through the middle of our neighborhood. Three city blocks, including the one we lived on, would be levelled by wrecking crews to make way.

Once again, meetings were held, letters issued and promises of compensation poured forth. All the assurances of city officials rang quite hollow in my father's ears. He voiced loud opposition at the many community meetings on the issue. Nevertheless, the plan went ahead and our neighbors began to move out. One by one, the houses of our oldest friends were destroyed and the remaining holes covered with dirt. My father, however, refused to move. By the end of 1968, our house was the only one left. Dozens of others were destroyed.

We lived one year in that house as if we were in the middle of a farm field. Eventually, the city pushed, and we too moved. However, our house was not destroyed. We elected to move it to a new location, about six blocks away. This was done in early 1969. The house was remodeled and we moved back in the summer of 1969.

This situation turned out to be a repeat of the 1964 industrial move. The city again welshed on its promise to pay. My father retaliated with a lawsuit and a settlement was reached at a fraction of the costs he incurred. As if to rub salt in the wounds of all those displaced by the "development," in early 1970, the city *changed its mind* about rerouting the road. As a result, the three city blocks laid waste by a bulldozer in the name of progress stood vacant for over 20 years.

Virtually the same scenario was played out with respect to a parcel of commercial property my father owned, just to the west of our home. He bought the property during the negotiations with the city in 1964, believing it may be more beneficial to build his own building rather than continue to lease space. The costs being prohibitive, he opted to lease. As luck would have it, the property was located on the western edge of the area which was to encompass the new road. You remember. The one the city changed its mind about.

While he certainly did not incur costs of moving and remodeling the land, he was paid substantially less for the land than it was worth at the time.

These experiences left my father bitter with the local authorities. He became involved in local government, became an activist against urban renewal and other myopic bureaucratic undertakings. As he spent more and more time on civic issues, he spent less and less time on his business. More of his resources were poured into his battle against encroaching local government, including, at one point, financing his own campaign for the State Legislature. As a result, business productivity went into a death spiral.

Gradually, the number of employees began to drop off. By 1974, when the IRS problem was thrust to the fore, he had just seven remaining. He also had an employment tax problem to go along with those seven employees.

As the employment tax delinquencies began to grow, my father was exposed to the tax protest movement. This was a loosely organized group of citizens spread throughout the United States. They were opposed to the income tax laws on moral, ethical, religious or constitutional grounds. They advocated non-compliance with those laws.

Their anti-government message rang true in my fathers ears, having been well groomed to receive it through his experiences with the City of St. Paul. He saw the tax protest movement as a potential answer not only to his tax problem, but the problems of encroaching government in general.

Given his frustration with the system, he became a willing disciple of tax protest teachings and a leading proponent of its philosophy. Unfortunately, the tax protest theories did not solve his tax problem. In my opinion, they exacerbated it. In July of 1974, the IRS seized the print shop and later sold off the equipment. A total of two dozen printing and engraving machines of various descriptions were sold at auction for a mere $3,100. Of that money, just $900 was applied to the tax debt. The remainder went to cover the "costs of the sale."

By this time, my father had an openly defiant attitude toward the IRS and a hefty distrust of government. Shortly after the property was seized, but prior to its being sold, he surreptitiously re-entered the building, contrary to the advice given on the IRS' posted seizure notices. As it happened, the IRS had the premises under surveillance. He was arrested at the scene. He was later charged under federal tax laws with "rescuing seized property." After a trial in 1976, in which he was convicted, he spent nine months in a federal correctional institute (that's bureaucratic lingo for jail).

While in prison, my mother was left with the care of myself and three brothers. Of the four boys in our family, three of us were out of high school. We all helped out as much as possible. In 1976, prior to his going to prison, the IRS filed a civil lawsuit against my father, seeking to foreclose and sell our home to settle the lingering employment tax debt.

I knew nothing of the suit when it was filed, but along with the rest of the family, got a rude awakening in the fall of 1977. At that time, my father was in prison. In the mail one day came a notice from the local federal court. My mother handed it to me, asking, "What do you make of this?" It was a notice of trial. It indicated the case against the house would be brought to court within 90 days.

In an effort to find out more about the matter, I went to the federal court house the next day. I obtained the case file, made copies of relevant documents, brought them home and studied them. Thus began my research into the federal tax laws. In the ensuing several weeks, I spent many hours of the day and night in the library of the local law college searching for a way to head a sure tragedy off at the pass.

What I found was an entire body of tax law which addressed the rights of citizens and the limitations of the IRS. Using what I learned, I crafted a crude petition, filed it with the court and behold, won an injunction against the IRS' further pursuit of the home. The court order was entered in December of 1977. I mailed a copy of it to my father in prison at Christmas time that year.

What began as an act of holding my finger in the dike, evolved into a dissertation of taxpayers' rights, IRS abuse prevention and cure, and problems resolution that spans 16 years and seven books. I have been involved in thousands of tax audits, hundreds of civil court cases, and dozens of criminal prosecutions. Through this, I have seen human nature at its worst when it comes to financial matters. And, I have seen government at its worst when it comes to illegal tax law enforcement and abuse of citizens.

I have learned many important lessons along the way. Among them is the lesson that traditional tax protesting is an extremely expensive and largely ineffective way to challenge improper IRS actions. By traditional tax protesting, I refer to the individuals and groups which advocate the non-filing of tax returns and non-payment of taxes as a means of protest. I learned this lesson from the first hand experiences of my father as well as the early tax protester cases in which I found myself involved. It did not take long for me to recognize that there had to be a better way to combat IRS abuse.

Each of my books, beginning with *The Naked Truth* in 1986, discussed IRS abuse in terms of the individual. Only theoretically did I address eliminating it in a broad, institutional sense. My theory is simple. If you educate citizens as to their specific legal rights and the IRS' express limitations, you reduce the available pool of potential victims who can be abused by the agency. In this way, you slow down the runaway train in the hope it can later be brought under control.

There is no question about the fact that this approach has met with staggering success. Through my books, radio appearances, seminars and monthly newsletter, thousands of people have been able to solve abusive tax problems which otherwise may have destroyed them. I and my publisher, Winning Publications, Inc., and its president, David M. Engstrom, receive testimonial letters each week decrying the effectiveness of the material and its value.

Based upon these letters and major changes that have occurred within the IRS in the past year, changes which I shall address in this book, I can declare that we *have* brought the train under control. I can confidently declare that IRS abuse cannot occur if you understand your rights.

But that brings us to the next part of the equation. How do we stop the train entirely? Without a doubt, as long as the IRS lives, the potential for abuse lives with it. As a result of the IRS and its pervasive influence upon the courts and Congress, most of the constitutional rights we hold dear have been seriously eroded or completely stomped out. We live in a nation whose rich past is grounded deeply in the doctrine of liberty, but in whose present those fundamental rights are nearly extinct. And the IRS is largely responsible for this reality.

Last fall, we were in Dallas to present my seminar entitled, *Stairway to Freedom*. The seminar was sponsored by KVTT Radio in Dallas, and my publisher, Winning Publications, Inc. After the seminar, while taking questions, I was approached by a young man. He acknowledged the value of my presentation, recognizing the important role each individual plays in keeping the IRS at bay. Still, he wanted more. He demanded to know what could be done to eliminate, once and for all, the IRS' threat to individual liberty and our national heritage, not to mention the enormous drain of resources occasioned by having to deal with the rogue agency.

He, like many others, was seeking an alternative to the IRS and all it implies. He pointed out that since I have been so vocal in opposing the tactics of the agency, surely I must have an idea or two for a better system. As so many observe, it is easy to criticize. It is not so easy to come up with a better idea. He demanded of me a better idea.

This book is my response to that young man's demand. In short, I do have an idea for a better system. I have an idea which I am certain will all at once eliminate the greatest threat to individual liberty the United States has yet faced, as well as stimulate economic growth and opportunity to levels never before seen in this country.

There is much work to be done, however. While great strides have been made in bringing the IRS under control, the beast yet breathes. Therefore, the concept of this book is to, quite literally, *Fire the IRS.*

This book is presented in three parts. I outline them here.

Part I - Keep the IRS Out of Your Life. Part I of this book addresses techniques for *preventing* problems with the IRS. Through my many years of experience in solving tax audit and collection problems, I have developed techniques for avoiding such problems altogether. The techniques have proven quite successful over the years. They are equally simple and inexpensive to implement. You do not need an accounting degree or a Harvard attorney to insulate yourself from potential IRS abuse. What you need is guidance you cannot obtain any place else.

Part II - Get the IRS Out of Your Life. The most crushing IRS problems begin as simple ones. The vast majority of Americans still do not understand how to solve those simple problems. Consequently, they grow into monsters which threaten to destroy them. In this regard, I have distilled the thousands of pages of tax code and regulation into what I consider to be the most important rights a citizen has when dealing with the IRS. I am satisfied if you understand these rights, know how and when to implement them, you will never fall victim to IRS abuse. And taking it one step further, you will never pay a tax you do not owe.

Part III - Fire the IRS! The final part of this book addresses itself to my master plan for eliminating the IRS and regaining control of government. Any responsible observer of the federal legislative process agrees that government tax and spend policies must change if all our citizens are ever to have a meaningful opportunity to realize the American dream. My plan to eliminate the IRS and control spending has never before been proposed. It is entirely unique and unlike most tax proposals, is completely consistent with the Constitution. In that sense, it is sure to protect the life, liberty and property of all our citizens. At the same time, it will ensure sufficient revenue to fund the legitimate functions of the federal government.

Just as important, it is *simple.* I do not mean "simple" in the Congressional sense. I mean it in the sense that you think of the word. That is, easy to understand and implement.

My belief is you cannot have both freedom and an income tax coexisting within one society. One must go if the other is to succeed. My vote is to eliminate the IRS and the income tax as we know it. By doing so, we will restore individual liberty, limit the power and reach of the federal government, and restore economic prosperity to all within our borders.

It is time to go to work. It is time for real change. Change which will help real people – people like you.

Daniel J. Pilla
St. Paul, Minnesota

1

KEEP THE IRS
OUT OF YOUR LIFE

A Personal Program
For Financial Privacy

Why Fire the IRS? After all, any reasonable person recognizes the need of the federal government to collect revenue. Is not the IRS and the income tax the most efficient and effective way of doing that?

The answers are not as simple as the establishment would have you believe. In the first place, the IRS is far from efficient or effective in collecting taxes. Second, the mechanism of a personal income tax as the primary means of raising revenue has grown into a behemoth; the tentacles of which stretch into every aspect of your business and private affairs. Third, the reality of dealing with the IRS has caused legal and economic repercussions of a staggering magnitude.

All these issues are examined in detail in this book. The conclusion we reach after reasonable analysis of all factors is the IRS must go. The income tax must go. If we are to survive as a free society, we must implement major changes to the manner in which we collect taxes. Without such changes, our legal system, grounded in the concept of a constitutional, limited government is at grave risk. Without such changes, our system of free enterprise, a system which established the highest standard of living in the world, is at serious risk of being unable to support an adequate level of employment.

Changes must be made and they must be made quickly. In the meantime, the IRS continues on a pattern of legal and economic domination of the nation. Its powers grow each year. With them grows the agency's ability to squeeze the public.

In my first book, *The Naked Truth* (Winning Publications, Inc., 1986), I put forth a number of projections concerning the future of the IRS. In examining a document entitled *IRS Strategic Plan*, IRS Document 6941, released on May 9, 1984, I exclaimed the agency's intention to audit every taxpayer for every year. I declared the IRS intended to eliminate the paper income tax return by the year 2000 and replace it with an electronic filing system. Under the system, I predicted the IRS would gather mountains of information from third party sources. The broad nature of the data would allow it to know every nickel of income you earn and where you earn it. It would allow the IRS to know every nickel you spend and where you spend it.

I also pointed out the IRS intended to greatly increase the number of computer generated contacts for a very ominous purpose. According to the plan, such contacts were designed to "create and maintain a sense of presence" in the lives of all Americans. IRS Plan, page 61.

Beyond that, the Plan declared war on self-employed Americans. As justification, it referred to them as a "soft-spot" in the "voluntary compliance" system. Stated another way, self-employed persons are, according to the IRS, more likely to cheat than pay. The result is, stepped up enforcement programs directed at the self-employed. (IRS Strategic Plan, page 69.)

Since the Plan was issued in 1984, the IRS has made great strides toward achieving the goals expressed. Most notably, improvements in computer power are at the top of the list. The IRS has already spent over $8 billion upgrading what it regularly refers to as "stone age" computers. What is shocking, however, is the revelation the agency will spend another $21 billion before it is all over. I discuss this more in detail in Part II of this book.

The point is clear. With respect to the ability to track each citizen individually, to know what he earns and where he spends his money, the major upgrades in computer power go a long way toward achieving that goal.

Significantly, with each tax law change, we see added requirements for information reporting. It is now required that virtually every financial transaction to which you are a party be reported to the IRS on an information return, such as forms W-2 or 1099. The reporting requirements allow the IRS to know instantly, by accessing a computer file known as the Information Returns Master File (IRMF), exactly what you earned and where. To a large extent, the IRS also knows what you paid and to whom. These advancements spell a virtual end to your financial privacy.

To illustrate, the IRS' 1992 Annual Report explains how far the IRS has come in its ability to spy on Americans through computer technology and information returns. Consider this statement:

> "* * *More than 90 percent of all income individuals report and more than 40 percent of deductions they claim are reported to the taxpayer and the IRS on an information document. About 45 percent of the 115 million individual returns filed in 1992 are based solely on data from information documents.* * *" –1992 Annual Report, page 12.

Those who yet believe there is no way for the IRS to know all you do financially need only re-read the above statement. Information returns now account for 90 percent of all income reported to the IRS, and 40 percent of all deductions claimed. Forty-five percent, virtually one-half, of all individual income tax returns filed are based *entirely on information returns*. This allows the IRS to audit the returns entirely through the computerized process.

The increase in reporting requirements has caused an explosion of paperwork finding its way into IRS computers. In 1988, the IRS received and processed *913 million* information returns of every description. By 1992, the number grew to *1.035 billion* documents. To put that in perspective, this amounts to four pieces of paper for every man, woman and child in the United States! As I explain in Chapter Two, the IRS uses these documents to perform computerized audits of every return filed. This, of course, represents success in achieving the goal of auditing every return filed each year.

Electronic filing of income tax returns began in earnest in 1986. That year, just 25,000 returns were filed to the Cincinnati Service Center via computer modem. By 1992, 11 million returns were filed in that fashion nationwide. IRS expects 14 million to be filed in 1993, and 100 million to be filed within the next 8 to 10 years. 1992 Annual Report, pages 17 and 23.

The IRS suggests electronic filing is a way to greatly reduce the "compliance burdens" placed upon citizens. I do not see how this is true, since one still must make and keep all necessary records, organize those records at the end of the year, read and try to make sense of dozens of tax preparation booklets and hundreds of pages of instructions, or hire a professional. Ultimately, the return must be prepared, regardless of the manner in which it is filed. The fact is, the simplest part of the process is transmitting the return to the IRS once completed. In that respect, electronic filing does little or nothing to reduce the burden of compliance. Of course, there is no reduction in the burden of *paying the tax*, a burden which grows every year.

I assert the electronic filing system is merely a means of indoctrinating the public with the idea of having the IRS "do all the work" of the preparation process. It is merely a stopping off point on the road to a system which eliminates the citizen from the tax preparation loop entirely. When the agency reaches the 100 percent point with information documents on both income and deductions, it can and will prepare your return for you. All you will receive is a bill stating what you paid or what you owe.

You may ask, "What's wrong with that?" The idea of having the IRS do all the work becomes more attractive as the tax laws become more complex.

The notion is based upon a fundamental misconception. The misconception is that the IRS could possibly "get it right!" The truth is, the agency cannot get it right when it comes to ascertaining income tax liabilities. As I prove in later chapters, the IRS is wrong 48 percent of the time with computerized notices it mails to the public. These notices are generated through the computer systems which assimilate the information documents received. Under the present system, which is certainly no gem, at least the citizen has a right to challenge the notice and is entitled to a hearing on the matter. With the wave of legislation granting the IRS more power, I doubt a new system would preserve this important right.

In addition to the reporting requirements mentioned, the IRS has, since 1984, embarked upon multiple courses of ensuring its ability to know everything about everyone. One law passed in 1986 requires reports be made to the IRS by persons receiving cash in the course of business. The requirement, imposed by Code section 6040I, mandates that cash transactions in excess of $10,000 be reported on Form 8300. During 1992, more than 140,000 such forms were filed with the IRS, up from just 1,200 in 1986.

This requirement is imposed in addition to that which commands banks to report currency transactions in excess of $10,000. The currency transaction report, Form 4789, is completed and mailed to the IRS whenever you add or subtract currency in that amount to your own bank account.

Another law passed in 1986 is pointed at children. The law requires children claimed as dependent exemptions on their parents' income tax return to have social security numbers. Under the terms of the statute, when a child reaches the ripe old age of one year, he must have a social security number if he is to be claimed as a dependent. Much more is provided on this topic in Chapter Three. Can you imagine any system which mandates the effective federal registration of our children?

Ostensibly, this rule was imposed as a means of combating supposed exemption fraud. While it certainly is true that exemption fraud existed, it is not fair to say the only effective method of dealing with it was to impose a *registration* requirement upon *minor children*. Whatever the merits of the arguments, pro or con, one thing is clear: the IRS' power to know is growing every day. Nobody, not even tender children, seem exempt from its purported reach.

The key, of course, to the IRS' power to know is the information returns nexus. Without a direct link from one citizen to another through an information document of some nature, the IRS' main information supply line is interrupted. It is precisely for that reason the IRS has been so relentless in its attack upon small businesses since 1984.

I pointed out earlier the IRS considered self-employed small businesses to represent a "soft-spot" in the voluntary compliance system. More specifically, the IRS views small business as being outside the "safety net" of the information reporting system. Self-employed persons do not receive W-2 forms reporting their annual earnings. Those forms are restricted to employees. Further, many small businesses do not receive 1099 forms, since those are required only when annual payments exceed $600 from any one source. Consequently, much of the income paid to small businesses is not reported to the IRS by third parties.

Viewing this reality as a threat to the collection system, the IRS has set out to eliminate as many self-employed persons as possible. In the agency's view, there simply are too many of them for the system to work up to expectations. If, for example, the IRS is to increase to 100 percent the number of returns which report income and deductions verified by third party statements, they must *ensure* that all income paid is reported either on a Form W-2 or 1099. The easiest way, from the agency's view, to accomplish this goal is to convert to employees as many self-employed's as possible.

Since 1984, the agency has been aggressively pursuing just such an undertaking. Employment tax audits are examinations of the employment tax returns of businesses large and small. They are designed to detect payments to self-employed persons which, in the opinion of the agency, should be converted to employees. When the conversion occurs, the agency scores twice. First and most importantly, it brings more people under the thumb of the information reporting system. Secondly, additional tax, penalty and interest assessments grow from these conversions.

In just one year, the IRS increased the number of employment tax audits from 58,000 to 73,000 in 1992. In that same year, the IRS reclassified 90,000 workers from self-employed, independent contractors to that of employees. Since 1988, the IRS' aggressive attack, based largely on administrative fiat and the arbitrary application of ambiguous guidelines, has *eliminated 400,000 self-employed persons*. 1992 Annual Report, page 9.

As you can plainly see, the IRS is embarked squarely upon a course calculated to eliminate most self-employed persons, eliminate paper income tax returns, and, create an electronic system of taxation which it alone controls. But it does not end there. In order for the system to be truly ubiquitous, the agency recognizes it must also eliminate cash. The agency believes as long as cash circulates in the economy the "potential" for fraud exits. Therefore, the Treasury has been pursuing an equally aggressive approach to eliminate currency. Of course, with the elimination of cash comes the extinction of any financial privacy rights which might yet exist.

For years, various financial newsletters have reported on an alleged Treasury plan to replace our existing currency with a new currency. The new currency, it was claimed, would sport high-tech features allowing the government to actually trace its course through the marketplace. In this way, the IRS could actually detect tax evaders by decoding the currency itself, thereby learning the names and social security numbers of those who handled the bill.

In past issues of my newsletter *Pilla Talks Taxes*, I scoffed at this notion. The number of common sense reasons why such an idea simply would not work far outnumber any possible benefits such a program would promise for the IRS. I even suggested it was "ludicrous to think government would go to so much trouble."

However, in February of 1992, I learned something much different. I learned that new series 1990 US currency notes, manufactured beginning in October of 1991, contained a strip physically embedded in the fabric of the paper. The strip is visible only when you hold the note up to a light source. The strip is located on the left edge of the note, about one and a quarter inches from the end. The strip itself runs from the top to the bottom of the note. The markings on the strip read, "USA 100." Those markings repeat over and over across the entire length of the strip.

My newsletter report revealed the markings were metallic and capable of being encoded. It seemed the new technology enables banks and other major currency issuers, such as casinos, to encode the notes with various identifying information such as name, address and social security number of the recipient. That information can then be deciphered when the bill resurfaces at any bank.

The information I reported was an eyewitness account from one of our many associates. He had a firsthand demonstration of the technology given him by a banker friend. Using technology in the hands of only banks and the government, he provided information on the source of the bill used in the demonstration. I discovered, however, the authorities are not admitting the notes are capable of such a feat.

In the spring of 1992, I spoke with Ira Polikoff, an official spokesman from the Treasury department. I asked Mr. Polikoff why the Treasury placed metallic, encodable trips within the paper of $100 currency notes. Mr. Polikoff responded that to his best knowledge, the "polyester strip," as he called it, was not encodable. Rather, it was placed within the currency notes solely as an anti-counterfeiting measure.

Specifically, he pointed out the strip "will be virtually indistinguishable when held down on a flat surface but when held up to a light source, you can, in fact, see the strip and read in the inscription."

Mr. Polikoff went on to explain that because modern copiers were so effective, currency notes could be counterfeited by the photocopying process. Because the strip could not be picked up by copiers, it would be impossible to effectively duplicate a bill using that process. If a store clerk wanted to authenticate a bill, according to Polikoff, all he would have to do is "hold it up to a light source." By doing so, you can plainly see the strip. If there is no strip, then it follows, the bill is counterfeit.

Seems reasonable, doesn't it?

The problem with Mr. Polikoff's explanation is if the Treasury Department really wanted store clerks to identify counterfeit bills by holding them up to a light source, it seems only logical that store clerks would have to *know about the strip!* If a given store clerk had no idea bills contained these strips, how could they possibly be used to verify the legitimacy of any bill?

To test whether the Treasury publicized the move, I talked with John Clemens, Director of News at the USA Radio Network in Dallas, Texas. I asked if his news department received any notification from the Treasury that such strips were placed in new currency notes. Keep in mind, the USA Radio Network is one of the nation's *largest news networks*, providing news and information to over 950 radio stations nationwide. It seems to me if the Treasury Department wanted store clerks to know how to identify bogus bills, it would distribute news releases to the nation's news sources for dissemination to the public.

John explained, however, his news department never received such a release. In fact, John *never heard* of the fact that these strips were added to the currency until I told him so! Strange, isn't it? The Treasury Department spends millions printing new currency with this foolproof anti-counterfeiting measure built right in, but *forgets* to tell anyone about it?

In a second effort to determine whether store clerks could utilize the strip, I went to Macy's department store located in a major mall in the north Dallas area. One would think if the Treasury chose not to notify the media of the new device, they might instead communicate directly with major retailers.

I spoke with several personnel in the Customer Service department at Macy's, including the manager on duty. Customer service is where folks go to get refunds, cash checks and apply for store credit. That office operates much like a bank and always has plenty of cash on hand. One would think at least the manager of the department would know a little something about the anti-counterfeiting measures his government employed to protect his store.

The fact is, nobody there, or at any other store I questioned, had any idea about the strip I was describing. In fact, they looked at me sideways until I asked for a $100 bill, *which was provided from their cash drawer.* I then pointed it out. With surprised looks, they said they had no idea the strip was in the bills.

So the question is simple: if this strip is indeed an anti-counterfeiting device, why has the government kept this tool from the people most likely to run across counterfeit bills?

When I pressed Mr. Polikoff about the encodability of the metallic strip, he insisted on two things. First, the strip was a *polyester* strip, not metallic. Second, it "absolutely was not encodable." Where had I ever gotten such a notion anyway? What I did learn from Mr. Polikoff, however, proved interesting.

I discovered that in addition to the strip now embedded within the fibers of most currency notes, there are two lines of *micro printing* on their face. The micro printing, according to Polikoff, was also added to deter counterfeiting.

If you have a series 1990 $100, $50 or $20 currency note, look carefully at the outer edge of either side of the portrait. There you will see printing that stretches from near the bottom to near the top of the portrait. At first glance, that printing appears to be scroll work. But upon closer examination, you see those tiny markings are actually printed words. Under magnification, the words read, "The United States of America."

I learned this printing - *micro printing* - is so small there is no photographic equipment capable of reproducing the image with sufficient clarity to pass for a genuine bill.

Okay, I thought. No cloak and dagger there. That seems reasonable enough. In fact, what could be easier and less expensive than to include micro printing on the note, *if* the task is to deter counterfeiting?

So why go to all the trouble and great expense of the polyester strip if its purpose is merely to deter counterfeiting? Would not the micro printing do the job at a fraction of the cost? Keep in mind, this strip is imbedded within the fibers of the paper. Surely it is no easy task to accomplish and with the U.S. Government picking up the tab, you can bet it's not cheap either!

Also keep in mind that counterfeiting is *no great problem!* According to the Treasury Department, just $14 million in counterfeit bills were passed in 1991. Treasury officials report that 90 percent of all counterfeit currency is seized before it is passed, primarily because counterfeiters produce poor copies at best, without regard to any polyester strip. Measured against the billions of dollars in circulation at any one time, $14 million in bogus bills is not bad.

In response to my continued pressing for answers on the characteristics of the strip, Mr. Polikoff suggested I speak with the manufacturer of the paper. Good idea, I thought.

I phoned Crane and Company of Dalton, Massachusetts. Crane and Company manufactures top grade paper, including the paper on which US currency is printed. When my call was taken, I asked to speak with someone in authority and to my surprise, I found myself speaking with Chris Crane, the owner of the company. After a few questions and no answers, Mr. Crane kindly directed me to the company's spokesman, Mr. Jim Manning, whom he was sure could answer all my questions.

Jim was a very professional, easy-going man who seemed perfectly willing to help me in every way he could. In fact, within three minutes I had information which directly contradicted what Mr. Polikoff of the Treasury Department told me. Polikoff, you will recall, insisted the article imbedded within the currency was a "polyester strip" with no metallic or encodable characteristics whatsoever.

Jim Manning, on the other hand, explained the term "polyester strip" was, in his words, "merely the nomenclature we've assigned to the strip." He pointed out the phrase had "nothing whatsoever to do with the strip's actual physical characteristics."

Now we're getting somewhere. While I still did not know what the strip *was,* I did know what it *was not.* It is *not* a "polyester strip" as the Treasury led to me believe.

I then asked Jim the question you are likely asking me: "If it's not polyester, what is it?"

"I'm not sure," Jim replied in the voice of honesty I could hardly challenge. I specifically asked whether it was metallic and whether it was encodable. He could not be certain but insisted that to the best of his knowledge, the ink on the strip was non-metallic. He did recall, however, some "talk in the industry about using magnetic ink" on currency notes. He could not be sure they ever did it.

When I asked him who would know what the strip was made of, he kindly directed me to "the subcontractor" who manufacturers the strip. "They might be able to tell you what it's made of," he explained. In his polite, kind and helpful manner, he gave me the name of a company called Technical Graphics, located in Milford, New Hampshire.

I phoned Technical Graphics and spoke with a very abrupt, skeptical man who not only would not give his name, he would not answer *question one* about the polyester strip. I shyly explained that Mr. Manning of Crane and Company directed me to Technical and asked if he would please talk to me. In a huff he said he could not answer any questions. He did say, however, *Manning* was the man with all the answers. In fact, he added, since Technical Graphics was *owned* by Crane and Company, I should just talk to Manning if I wanted any information.

Now the plot thickens. If Crane owns Technical, and if Mr. Manning is Crane's official spokesman, why would he send me off to talk to someone at Technical? Was he trying to steer me off the trail?

When I again phoned Crane and Company, I spoke with the polite, kind, Mr. Manning. "I called Technical," I said. "They wont talk."

"Gee," said Manning, in an apologetic tone, "I'm sorry."

"They sent me back to you," I explained. "In fact, Jim, I was informed that Technical Graphics is owned by Crane and Company and you are the guy with all the answers. Is that true?," I asked pointedly.

"Yes it is," he said flatly, with a smile in his voice.

"Then you've been holding out on me," I accused.

"Yes I have," he said without hesitation.

"I just want to know two things," I insisted. "What is this thing made out of, and how is it encodable."

His response was rehearsed. He explained the manner in which the strip was manufactured was proprietary and he was not at liberty to disclose any specific procedures. Coming at him from another direction, I said, "I don't really care how it's made, I just want to know if in fact it's encodable."

Now back to his very pleasant, very courteous demeanor, Jim explained he honestly didn't know whether it was metallic, but to the best of his knowledge, it was not.

"Well, who knows," I asked.

He explained that Tim Crane (a son?) holds the *patent* on the strip, but Chris Crane, the company's owner, was the *one man* who knew what the strip was or was not, and he *was not* talking. "You can call Chris if you like, but he'll simply send you back to me and I've told you all I can." Jim made it clear the information well had run dry.

After hanging up the phone, I thought, *"A patent? This thing is patented?"*

Why would a simple polyester strip, or whatever it is, used solely to prevent counterfeiting, employ technology so sophisticated it is worthy of a *patent?* Exactly what is this modern day wonder currently imbedded within the very fabric of all currency made since October of 1991? More important, why isn't anyone talking about it? If indeed the strip is nothing more than a simple anti-counterfeiting device, as Polikoff insists, why the secrecy?

Two things are certain: *it is not polyester and it is not simple!* Otherwise, why the patent?

In early January of 1993, I learned more fascinating information concerning our currency. My friends at *Monetary and Economic Review*, an economic newsletter published in Ft. Collins, Colorado, reported to me some very interesting developments. It seems they took several bills to their friends at Checkmate Electronics, Inc., for testing. CEI is the company which manufacturers the technology used by banks for reading the magnetic codes imprinted on your check blanks.

Those codes allow for machine sorting of the thousands of checks handled by banks every day. The specific line of equipment manufactured by CEI tests the quality of magnetic ink printed on checks and is used by banks and other check printing companies. CEI also produces a point of sale recognition device that reads the magnetics on checks just as on credit cards.

CEI used its technology to read a 100, 50 and 20 dollar currency note. According to CEI, "they all produced a Signal Level Histogram with a recognizable bar graph." According to Harry Grow, of CEI, "The new currency holds a distinct and readable pattern."

In case you missed it, the bills that the Treasury Department and manufacturer insisted are non-encodable, are not only *encodable*, but are in fact *encoded.*

With this new information I went back to the Treasury Department in January of 1993 with more questions. Looking for Mr. Polikoff, I found he was replaced by Norma Upgrand, Chief of Public Affairs in the Treasury Department's Bureau of Printing and Engraving. In asking pointed questions of Ms. Upgrand, she restated the polyester strip (she was now referring to it as a nylon or mylar strip) was "non-encodable."

She did say, however, that "other areas of the bills are encoded." She referred to the codes as "covert anti-counterfeiting measures." So what my banking source found on the bill he tested, and what was discovered by CEI with its technology, was not imagined by some wild-eyed conspiracy buff. No, the bills are in fact planted with top secret codes. And, according to Ms. Upgrand, the Treasury Department has not and "will not discuss them with the public."

Ms. Upgrand confirmed what I have already said about the letters on the strip. She explained the letters "USA" were printed with metallic ink, something Mr. Polikoff denied.

I asked Ms. Upgrand how the encoding process worked, and what information was contained in the code. She explained the Treasury Department is making no public statements whatsoever concerning the codes, their nature, or the manner in which they operate. She did say they were present to allow banks and the Federal Reserve to "authenticate" the bills they handle.

She also explained the codes were placed on the bills in the manufacturing process. She said they can be read, but not re-recorded. She would not tell me, in terms of quantity, how much information, or for that matter, the nature of the information within a given code.

After speaking with Ms. Upgrand, I phoned Ira Polikoff to confront him with my latest findings. After all, he expressly denied the bills had any encoding feature whatsoever. Further, he denied that the polyester strip contained any metallic features or that metallic ink was used to print the notes.

Mr. Polikoff seemed to recall our conversation. When I confronted him about his statements regarding encodable notes, he defended himself by saying, "You asked about whether the strip was encodable. It is not. That's what I told you. I didn't give you incorrect information."

When I pressed him about my inquiries concerning general encodable features of the bills, he said, "I must have misunderstood your question. If I understood your question properly, I would not have given you deliberately incorrect information."

Then I pressed him about the metallic features of the strip itself. I learned from him the letters "USA" are imprinted on the strip with *aluminum*. That certainly seems to be metallic to me. I asked why he did not explain that to me in 1992, when he insisted the strip had no metallic qualities whatsoever. He answered that he must have misunderstood my questions.

In the meantime, Polikoff and the Treasury continue to insist this measure and all other are solely for anti-counterfeiting purposes. "We have an obligation," Polikoff explained, "to insure the public is protected from any losses due to counterfeiting. Our bills contain several features to ensure this protection. As the techniques of sophisticated counterfeiters catch up with our measures, we will develop new ones."

I asked what the various anti-counterfeiting features are, and he provided an impressive list. They are:

1. The engraving technique;
2. The red and green security threads within the paper;
3. The serial numbers;
4. The Federal Reserve seal must have clear, sharp points;
5. The letter within the Fed seal must match the first letter in the serial number;
6. The micro printing around the portrait. Under magnification, the apparent scroll around the portrait actually reads, United States of America;
7. The portrait must be life-like, featuring lines and shadows in the face;
8. The Treasury seal features sharp, saw tooth edges,
9. The Treasury seal must be the same color as the serial number;
10. The new security strip, otherwise known as the polyester strip we have been discussing;
11. The denomination of the bill must be the same as is written over the Treasury seal;
12. The boarder must be web-like, featuring clear detail; and
13. The character of the paper itself.

These thirteen specific measures were identified by Polikoff as those of which the public should be aware. But in addition to these thirteen, he stated the Treasury Department also uses *"covert features."* These features are those of which the public is not only unaware, but of which the Treasury *will not speak* or answer any questions. The encodable device identified here is one such "covert feature." I learned, however, it is not the only one.

Polikoff said there is more than one, but probably "not more than two or three" covert features, *all of which* involve encoding of some magnitude. Polikoff said he did not know precisely how many were involved. "Why isn't the public informed of these features?" I asked.

"Because they have no need to know," he answered. "They are for the benefit of banks and the Federal Reserve only. We have no reason to inform the public because they can't read them anyway," he concluded.

Norma Upgrand also stated bills contain other "covert features," but she too refused to discuss them in any particular. She did say only banks and the Bureau of Printing and Engraving were privy to the codes. She assured me "the IRS and Customs Bureau do not have access to them."

Maybe they do. Maybe they don't.

After Polikoff listed the 13 anti-counterfeiting measures mentioned, I asked why the security thread (the polyester strip) was not disclosed to the public. I pointed out to him that it was impossible for the public to employ any anti-counterfeiting feature if they had no idea it existed. He insisted the Treasury went to great lengths to publicize the information. He stated that all Congressmen and Senators were notified, as well as all three networks through a formal news conference hosted by then Treasury Secretary Brady and Fed Chairman Alan

Greenspan. He also stated a detailed news release was sent nationwide to radio, television, newspaper and other media outlets.

I can only speak of my personal experience on the issue of publicity. Please recall my discussions with merchants in the Dallas area shopping mall. None of them, including those in customer service rolls with a major retailer, had any idea of the strip.

After my story in the April 1992 newsletter was released, Herbert Lockwood, a financial reporter for the *San Diego Daily Transcript*, picked up the ball and did a similar survey of local merchants. His findings were much the same. None of the local merchants he spoke with had any idea new currency notes contained the polyester strip. Lockwood's story ran in the *Daily Transcript* on April 21, 1992.

Lockwood went one step further than I. He contacted local banks. A spokesperson for the Bank of America said they have no education program on anti-counterfeiting features, and hence, would not disseminate any information to the public. Another banker, of San Diego Trust and Savings, did confirm they received an information packet from the Federal Reserve, but noted "the information was only for the bank's protection." From this I conclude it discussed only the covert codes.

I make one further note concerning the Treasury's apparent effort to inform the public of the polyester thread. We have been receiving the *Treasury News*, the Department's official newsletter, for years. I read it religiously. No statements were made there, that I can recall, concerning such a strip. Certainly no statements were made concerning any "covert features" involving encodable currency.

While it seems we have answered a few questions concerning encodable currency, we certainly have raised a few more. After my last encounter with the Treasury, I feel I can summarize exactly what we know and do not know.

WHAT WE KNOW:

1. Contrary to the Treasury's earlier statements, we know series 1990 Federal Reserve Notes are absolutely encodable. Such notes include the 100's, 50's, 20's, and as of 1993, 10's and 5's.

2. Contrary to the Treasury's earlier statements, the polyester strip is absolutely metallic. The letters are stamped in aluminum.

3. Contrary to the Treasury's earlier statements, all currency notes are absolutely printed in metallic ink. Specifically, the material used contains high concentrations of iron oxide. Rust to be exact. The same material used to coat computer diskettes to allow them to record and re-record your data.

4. The currency notes are encodable in at least two ways; maybe more.

WHAT WE DO NOT KNOW:

1. We do not know how the process works. I was told the coding was placed on the bill in the manufacturing process. That cannot be confirmed.

2. We do not know what the codes tell the reader. The Treasury and banks

certainly know, but they are not talking. They insist the IRS and Customs do not know either, but I am not so sure.

3. We do not know how many different codes or families of codes are used. We know there is more than one.

4. We do not know with certainty which portion of the bill contains the code. Polikoff and Upgrand both insist the polyester strip is not one of them. However, Polikoff also insisted the strip was not metallic. We now know it is stamped with aluminum. It is interesting to note that aluminum probably would not be subject to simple or inadvertent demagnification, such as often occurs with credit cards.

5. We do not know if the data on the bills can be updated or in any way revised. Polikoff insists the bill in no way contains any information on where it has been, who has it, or where it is going. Our source in the banking industry indicates otherwise, but both Polikoff and Upgrand adamantly deny it.

6. Most importantly, we do not know *why*. They tell us the codes are, ultimately, for our own protection from counterfeiters. That does not seem to stand the test of reason, however. Polikoff himself points out counterfeiting is not a major problem to begin with. Of the approximate $3 billion in currency circulating at any one time, barely $10 million in counterfeit bills surface in an average year.

Even at that, Polikoff admitted most counterfeit notes are "crude." That is to say, they do not pass muster on the most basic of the thirteen features listed. In fact, Polikoff pointed out much counterfeiting is accomplished with a color copy machine. Such equipment is hardly capable of producing a bill even remotely close in quality and detail to a genuine US currency note.

So why the super-sleuth, cloak-and-dagger features involving codes and metallic lettering? Polikoff insists they are present for nothing more than authentication purposes. I am not so sure.

In any event, it seems the IRS is certainly achieving the goals set for itself in the 1984 Strategic Plan. This includes the goal of eliminating its problems with the cash economy, apparently by introducing encodable currency into the marketplace.

The realities expressed here make it clear one must take steps to *Keep the IRS Out of Your Life*. As the agency grows in size and power, it can be expected to assault more and more of your liberties - and money. That is one compelling reason why it is so important for America to adopt the rebuilding goals expressed in the latter pages of this book.

What follows are simple yet effective techniques for *preventing* problems occasioned by an over zealous tax collection agency. They center around the proposition that you need not roll over when faced with IRS audit demands. If you take the steps I outline here, the result is full compliance with the tax laws, but in a manner which actually affords you a level of financial privacy which does not now exist. In truth, I offer a program to win at least some measure of personal financial privacy. When dealing with the IRS, anything is better than what you have now.

1

STRATEGIC
RECORDKEEPING
CONTROLLED COMPLIANCE

When illustrating the extent to which citizens are burdened by the federal income tax system, there is no topic more salient than that of the tax audit. The notion of an audit strikes fear into the hearts of most Americans. Citizens are terrified at the idea of placing their financial security into the hands of tax auditors sure to light upon some indiscretion.

The audit raises one's anxiety level for several reasons. Chief among them is that we recognize the fruits of an audit are usually increased tax debt. Virtually all are surprised at the extent to which IRS collects additional revenue through the audit process. They are not surprised, however, that the overwhelming majority of audits lead to increased tax bills.

In fact, the 1992 average increased assessment due to face-to-face audits is in excess of $5,800! Since roughly 12 of 100 audits resulted in no change the additional tax burden placed on the remaining 88 audited individuals is even more staggering. (1992 IRS Annual Report, Table 11) The next reason the audit raises such consternation is the trauma of the experience. Whether real or imagined, Americans believe the audit process is a fate worse than death. Perhaps it is only because of the financial ramifications of losing. The fact of the matter is the IRS has expended much effort in sowing the idea the agency is unbeatable. They carefully cultivate the proposition that whether the agency is right or wrong, one cannot prevail in a dispute with it. The fruit of this campaign is simply that the public is terrorized! They want nothing whatsoever to do with the IRS, especially in any environment presenting such immense exposure.

The IRS maintains tax audit assessments are high for the simple reason that most citizens either cheat or make mistakes on their returns. In fact, this presumption drives the IRS to throttle its tax audit machine and drives Congress to fund it. Not long ago, the GAO called upon the IRS to increase by *five times* the number of face-to-face tax audits conducted in a given year. GAO views the process as a fruitful profit center.

I explain the deficiencies in a much different way. My explanation is based upon over 16 years of experience dealing with audits and appeals. My explanation is also based upon intensive study of the tax code during this period of time.

I attribute the substantial tax audit deficiencies to the fact that auditors routinely and systematically bluff and intimidate taxpayers into agreeing to pay more taxes than are owed. Tax auditors regularly employ tactics of misinformation and disinformation in the audit process. In many cases, they outright lie to taxpayers. If this were not the case, I hardly suspect citizens would prevail, on average in 1992, 69 percent of the time when challenging auditor decisions. Yet, this is the success rate according to the IRS itself.

The fact of the matter is the tax laws are so confusing, it is functionally impossible for any person to accurately prepare a return. In the decade of the 1980's alone, the tax laws were changed *more than 100 times*. Many of those changes were broad, sweeping amendments to the code which altered the tax landscape much the way a hurricane does.

Examples are the *Tax Equity and Fiscal Responsibility Act of 1982*, the *Economic Recovery Tax Act of 1984*, the *Tax Reform Act of 1986*, *The Omnibus Budget Reconciliation Act of 1990*. Of course, the hail storm of change has not subsided. With the passage of the *Omnibus Budget Reconciliation Act of 1993*, the Clinton tax increase package, the pot has been stirred yet again.

The quagmire of confusion created by constantly changing tax laws is best illustrated by *Money Magazine's* annual survey of tax preparers. Each year since 1987, the year magnificent tax simplification took effect, *Money* prepares a hypothetical family financial profile based upon its average reader. The profile is submitted to 50 different tax preparers, both large and small, with instructions to determine the tax liability for this family.

In each of the surveys conducted since 1987, 50 different preparers came up with 50 different tax bills. The results of the 1992 study were particularly telling. That year, just 48 preparers participated because the only two with any sense dropped out before the test began. Of the remaining 48, each reported a different liability.

Most poignant, however, is the range of difference between the high tax and low tax. The lowest tax liability was found to be $16,219. The highest tax bill was fixed at $46,564. This evidences a spread of almost 300 percent. It is apparent from this that even tax professionals are lost in what has become a 17,000-page maze of hopeless confusion.

Money editors emphasized a point which I have made time and again. This statement, in my opinion, fully explains why the average audit assessment is so staggering. It has nothing whatsoever to do with cheating or errors. Consider this:

"While there were no perfect scores, a dozen returns were exemplary. Because of the tax code's *ambiguity*, the target tax of $26,878 *was not the only acceptable answer.* * * *" *Money*, March, 1992, page 90 (emphasis added).

Each tax law change brings more confusion. Confusion naturally leads to uncertainty. Uncertainty breeds doubt. These factors all weigh heavily upon a citizen facing an audit. They, more than anything else, account for the fact that large assessments are made in the process. After all, any citizen so unsure whether he has done the right thing almost automatically accepts the auditor's view that he did not. This dynamic is compounded when you consider that most people have no idea they may appeal an auditor's decision.

The reality is, the IRS auditor generally has no better idea than you whether or not the return is correct. What he has is the apparent *authority* to make his view stick. As I expose in Chapter Five, however, this tactic is merely a bluff. The auditor has no power over you. He cannot change your tax return without your consent.

My experience with tax audits leads me to declare that the majority of examination changes are supported by the fact that citizens either have insufficient records, or were convinced by the agent they had insufficient records. The tax code's failure to prescribe objective standards for recordkeeping requirements enables this phenomenon to occur regularly. That is why I have developed a strategic recordkeeping program calculated to defeat the major attack experienced in the tax audit.

WHY STRUGGLE WITH RECORDS ANYWAY?

The short answer to the question is very simple. Adequate records optimize your ability to claim deductions, allowances, credits and exemptions. These operate to reduce your tax bite. Naturally, all things being equal, one is directly compensated for the time it takes to keep adequate records by a reduction in his tax burden.

Furthermore, the law places an affirmative obligation upon each citizen to keep records necessary to determine the extent of this liability for tax. See Code sec. 6001. Stated another way, the courts have held repeatedly the citizen bears the burden to prove the claims made on his tax return are correct in all respects. Absent adequate records, the IRS is at liberty to—and regularly does—add additional income to your tax return and disallows deductions claimed. See Code sec. 446(b).

The effect of either action is to increase your tax liability. The effect of both combined is to increase your tax liability to a level at or near the gross amount earned during the entire year. Left unchecked, the IRS' power to add income and disallow deductions translates in practical reality to a 100 percent tax bracket. This recordkeeping system can prevent this from happening to you.

OKAY, OKAY! BUT WHAT ARE "ADEQUATE" RECORDS?

In 17,000 pages of law and regulation, one would hardly think it likely the tax code is deficient in any particular. Nevertheless, it is. The deficiencies often operate to the advantage of the IRS. The most glaring absence of regulation occurs in the area of audits. You see, the tax code, in all its gory detail, *does not* define what constitutes adequate records in any but a precious few circumstances. No general rules, guidelines or standards exist to guide one in ascertaining whether his year-long recordkeeping sojourn is worth the scraps of paper it is written on. Tax auditors know this. They deliberately and premeditatedly take advantage of the situation.

Consequently, proving the validity of certain deductions is often akin to entering an accounting black hole. Citizens unaware of what constitutes adequate records almost certainly end up owing more taxes. Yet, the hassle and expense may be entirely avoided if one understands what the courts have determined to be adequate records.

Follow closely as we now examine my complete recordkeeping system. The system, when fully implemented, allows you to keep proper records of all deductions. It can lead to a reduction in the taxes you pay. It will, as illustrated in Chapter Two, impart to you a new level of financial privacy.

1. RECORDING YOUR INCOME

The power of the IRS to wreak havoc on your financial life is not limited to the ability to disallow deductions. In fact, an even more potent weapon is the agency's ability to "determine" your income based upon "available information" or by using statistical data.

Tax protesters theorize that by not filing tax returns, they thereby prevent the IRS from obtaining any assessment of taxes. That in turn, makes it impossible to collect a dime. However impressive this theory is to the citizens who place it into practice, it ignores one very important legal remedy available to the IRS. We explore tax protester arguments in more detail in Chapter Four.

In the absence of a return, or even adequate records of income, the IRS is permitted to determine one's income based upon available information. The IRS can establish your income using the total of all deposits to your bank account. It can compute changes in your net worth, or use statistical data compiled either by the agency itself or other agencies of government. The most favored source of statistical data utilized by the IRS is Bureau of Labor statistics. The data set forth the average income earned by individuals within a particular element of the work force, and within a given geographical location.

One example of how the IRS uses statistics gathered by the agency itself occurred in Atlantic City during 1984 and 1985. During that period, agents of the Criminal Investigation Division conducted surveillance of all gambling casinos in operation at the time. The Atlantic City Tip Project, as it was called, was specifically designed to fetter out alleged unreported tip income earned by casino employees. The project focused on waitresses, bartenders and gaming dealers.

After completing surveillance of the casinos, the IRS audited a targeted group of employees to determine whether they reported the "correct" amount of tip income. On the average, the IRS claimed tip income in the amount of about 13 percent was earned by the casino employees. If that amount was not reported on their tax returns, the IRS added it to the employee's return and demanded taxes and, of course, penalties. Later in this chapter, we explore the casino case in more detail. (See *Case Study Number One*.)

Similar programs operated in Nevada casinos. This led to a continuing, heated battle between the IRS and casino employees. The reason for the heated dispute is simple. Despite the trappings of a highly controlled and scientific statistical survey, the employees claim the findings are wrong - high to be exact. More specifically, one waitress involved in the dispute contended her tips were more accurately in the eight percent range, nearly half what the IRS claimed.

Still, the court ruled in favor of the IRS due to the citizen's failure to keep accurate records of her tip income.

In Chapter Two of *How Anyone Can Negotiate with the IRS - And Win!* (Winning Publications, Inc., 1988), I discuss at length how the IRS uses four different audit methods to increase one's reported income. I refer to this practice as adding *phantom income* to one's return. Phantom income is earnings which seem to exist only on IRS accounting ledgers, but not in your pocket.

There are two specific techniques for avoiding a phantom income determination. Let us address them here.

a. Bank Records. Bank account information is perhaps the number one tool used to add phantom income to one's return. For example, suppose a dishonest citizen claims he earned $20,000 during the year. However, he deposits $30,000 to his bank account. The IRS quickly draws the conclusion that $10,000 was earned but not reported.

Conversely, bank account records can operate to the honest citizen's advantage. When all one's income is deposited to his bank, the bank itself makes clear and indisputable records of each deposit. The IRS is fond of claiming citizens often receive cash from the "underground economy" which they in turn fail to report. Countering such a claim with bank deposit records showing check and cash deposits prevents the IRS from sustaining such a claim.

In addition, carefully document, through independent records, deposits to a bank account that do not constitute taxable income. Examples include gifts or loan proceeds. Bank records make no distinction between the source and nature of the funds. Bank deposit records show merely the deposit of checks or cash, and the amount.

Thus, if your total deposits exceed declared income, the IRS' tendency is to scream "unreported income." Be prepared to demonstrate the source of the deposit as a non-taxable source.

b. Ledgers or Log Books. Ledgers or log books are contemporaneous records of income (or expenses). They are without a doubt the best weapon against the assault on the veracity of your tax return. Contemporaneous ledgers or logs are made at the time of the occurrence of the events being recorded. When done properly, they are unassailable.

Ledgers or logs used in conjunction with bank records allow you to file an accurate tax return, insofar as the issue of income is concerned. More importantly, they provide the basis for audit-proofing the income claimed in your return. We discuss audit-proofing in detail in Chapter Two.

2. How to Make Foolproof Records of Income

Begin immediately to log all income. Do not rely on third parties to make your records. By making your own records, you eliminate the potential that third party errors will haunt you. Let me give you an example.

Tim, a citizen of Chicago, worked for a local radio station. He received a Form W-2 as an employee of the station. In addition, he did independent production work for other companies. Those companies issued a Form 1099 to report payments to Tim. However, one company failed to submit the form on time. Because Tim relied solely on third party records as his only recordkeeping system, he did not report the income on his tax return when filed.

Approximately 18 months after filing, the company discovered the oversight then issued a late 1099. The IRS received the form and as they do with all information returns, cross-checked it with Tim's 1040. Tim under-reported his income by the amount shown on the 1099. He did not intend to deceive the IRS. He merely failed to keep his own records of income.

The IRS made a correction to Tim's return based upon the Form 1099. Within a short period of time, the IRS levied Tim's paycheck for the additional tax, interest and penalty. The entire ordeal could have been avoided if Tim made and kept his own records of the income he earned during the year.

Create an income log for each source of your income during a given year. Each log should show the date of the income, the nature of the payment, the payor, and the amount of withholding for state and federal taxes, if any. The following examples illustrate more specific income logs.

a. Wages and Salaries. Make an entry in your Wages log each and every time you receive a paycheck. Transfer all data shown on the check stub to the wages log. If you receive tip income during the year, create a separate log for tip income. Your tip income log should have an entry for each day you work, rather than for each payday. The reason is tips are earned on a daily basis and therefore should be recorded as such.

Keeping a log of wages and earned income, to some, may seem redundant. However, as I illustrate later, this process precludes the IRS from adding phantom income to your return.

b. Rents and Royalties. Create a separate log for rents or royalties income. Make the entries as payments are received. Be sure to indicate the source of the income, such as from a particular asset or property. Generally, rent and royalty payments are not subject to withholding. However, certain royalty payments may be subjected to 31% backup withholding if your social security number has not been verified to the payor. If this is the case, indicate the amount of any withholding from the payment in the appropriate column. Also, your estimated tax payments should be noted in an appropriate column.

c. Interest and Dividends. Make all entries in this log as payments are received. In the Payor column, note whether you were paid interest on a bond or checking account, etc., or dividends on stocks or mutual funds, etc. Indicate the specific source of the payment. In an appropriate column, indicate whether any backup withholding was taken. Last, note whether the payment is taxable or not. Certain interest payments on federal, state and local bonds are not taxable. Determine whether your payments are subject to taxation and note accordingly.

d. Stock Transactions. A Stock Transactions Log is a means of simplifying the data transmitted in your monthly brokerage statement. These statements can be difficult to read. My format allows a convenient way of tracking all stock purchases and sales. This enables you to quickly determine the gain or loss incurred in connection with any stock transaction. From left to right, the entries should be, Buy date; Sell date; name of stock; number of shares; price each; total purchase price; gain or loss.

Because you purchase and sell a specific block of stock just once, you can record all stock transactions in a continuing format, running the log from year to year. The gain or loss on a stock is computed and entered after you sell.

e. Pensions and Annuities. In the Payor column, indicate the company making the payment and the type of plan under which it is made. Also note the amount of the payment and record any withholding.

f. Estates and Trusts. In the Payor column, indicate the source of the payment. Make a note as to the purpose of the payment, whether, for example it was an inheritance or trust distribution. This enables you to later determine whether that particular payment constitutes taxable income. Be sure to note any backup withholding or estimated tax payments withheld from the payment.

g. Self-Employed, Partnerships and S Corporations. If you derive income from self-employment, partnerships or through an S corporation (other than wages or dividends paid), maintain a log reflecting such payments. Express the payments in terms of gross amounts. This is because any deductions, such as for costs of goods or operating expenses, are shown in a corresponding expense ledger. We examine expense logs presently. With self-employment income, there is a firm duty to make estimated payments against your tax liability. Record the quarterly payments as made. Also, if you earn income from a variety of sources or customers, you may wish to create a log for each source or customer. In that manner, you can track receipts more specifically.

Cases studies more fully explain the effectiveness of using logs to report income. In the examples, one can easily appreciate the tax savings experienced through the use of logs.

Case Study No. One - *Krause v. Commissioner*, T.C. Memo 1992-270 (May 11, 1992).

Earlier, I discussed an IRS surveillance project of Atlantic City casino employees. The Atlantic City Tip Project was patterned after similar efforts carried out in Nevada casinos. These undercover efforts were designed to determine the amount of tip income earned by employees working in gaming casinos.

In the Atlantic City project, teams of two IRS agents observed cocktail servers within the casino for periods of 30 minutes in length. The agents went to locations chosen at random by computer and observed the tips given to a server. They were instructed to make certain conservative assumptions during the operation. For example, if they could not clearly see a bill, they were to assume is was a dollar. If they could not clearly see a coin, they were to assume it was a quarter.

During the years 1984 and 1985, there were 63 half-hour periods of surveillance conducted at each of the 10 gaming casinos in Atlantic City. During 1987 and 1988, 42 half-hour spying sessions took place at each of 12 casinos.

Based upon the surveillance, IRS statisticians developed a series of figures said to represent the average tip income of servers in the slot machine and gaming areas. These figures varied according to work shift. The evening shift, for example, was said to earn more tips per hour than the day shift. By 1988, the IRS concluded cocktail servers earned as much as $23.27 per hour.

In case after case, the IRS audited casino employees and hit them with tax on unreported tip income. The determinations were based solely upon the statistical analysis generated by the undercover operation. The additional tax was hotly contested by the employees but the Tax Court rubber stamped the IRS' ruling because the citizens were *without records* to prove them wrong.

Judy was a bartender at the Sands hotel in Atlantic City. She was swept up in the IRS' Atlantic City Tip Project drag net. Judy ended up in Tax Court for 1985 over the tip income fight. The case went to trial and Judy lost. The Court found that what few records of her tips she bothered to keep were not sufficient to overcome the IRS' assumption that her tips were equal to $6.77 per hour worked. That assumption was supported by the surveillance project described above.

Judy claimed her tips were about half that amount. However her records did not clearly reflect her income so Judy was stuck paying taxes on tip income she probably never earned.

Judy learned a valuable lesson from her bitter experience. She determined never again to be in a position of being unable to challenge a decision by the IRS concerning tip income.

She began keeping contemporaneous, detailed records of her tip income using a log. Judy carried a small notebook in her pocketbook. She brought it to work with her every day. In the notebook, she filled in the amount of tips earned by her that day, either immediately after work or when she arrived home the same evening. At the end of each pay period, Judy reported her total tips to her employer. The tip income was then reported to her, on her weekly pay stub, with the appropriate income and social security tax withheld. On Form W-2, the amount of tips reported by Judy to the Sands was in turn reported to the IRS as tip income.

When the IRS took another crack at Judy, she was ready for them. Judy claimed $6,473 in tip income in 1986. According to the statistics developed by the IRS' undercover operation, Judy should have claimed $12,324. The IRS determined Judy had unreported income of $5,852. While this is precisely the problem she faced in 1985, this time she could prove they were wrong!

At trial, Judy presented the contemporaneous log she kept of her tip income. She testified about her habit of carrying the log with her to work each day and recording her tips in the log that very day. She also explained she made a report of those tips to her employer so the amounts were included in Form W-2. This way, she also provided for income and social security tax withholding.

The IRS, on the other hand, argued that their statistical analysis showed Judy in fact earned $12,300 in tips, not $6,400 as she reported. The agency hung its case on the analysis and refused to back away from its finding.

However carefully the IRS may have observed the casino employees, and however scientific its analysis may have been, it does not change the fact the IRS did nothing more than *guess* at Judy's tips. They had no way to know what those tips were and neither did the employer. That is precisely why the employee is required to keep contemporaneous records of tips. The IRS is not free to reject contemporaneous records merely because they disagree with the conclusions.

This time around, the court agreed with Judy. It specifically found the IRS' otherwise valid statistics "do not reflect (Judy's) income in tax year 1986 as accurately as *her own daily records.*" The court went on to stress that Judy complied with all the reporting requirements by keeping a daily log and reporting to her employer the amount of tips she earned. The count concluded by saying, "we hold that (Judy) fully reported her tip income on the Federal income tax return she filed for the year 1986."

By keeping a contemporaneous log of her tips and reporting them in the proper fashion, Judy avoided paying taxes, interest and penalties on income she never earned.

Case Study No. Two - *Portillo v. Commissioner,* 91-1 USTC 50,304 (5th Cir. 1991).

Ramon was a self-employed painter from El Paso. He contracted with builders all over town to paint both residential and commercial projects. General contractors paid him on a weekly basis so he could pay the crews doing the work.

Each payment was recorded in Ramon's ledger. He kept careful records of his income in precisely the manner illustrated here. Each time Ramon received a check from a contractor, he recorded the gross amount in his ledger. Ramon was careful to record the check *upon receipt.* That way, his records were contemporaneous in nature.

Ramon did not have a bank account. Consequently, after recording the contractor's check in his contemporaneous ledger, he cashed it. He used the proceeds to pay his employees and to purchase supplies. All payroll records were maintained by Ramon in a separate ledger.

At the end of each year, Ramon used Forms 1099 issued by the contractors to confirm the gross receipts shown in his ledger. He then handed his ledgers to a tax preparer. The preparer used the ledgers to complete Ramon's federal income and employment tax returns. In 1984, however, the preparer did not have a Form 1099 from a particular contractor when preparing the return. Consequently, gross receipts from that contractor were determined strictly from Ramon's ledger.

In mid 1985, the contractor filed a Form 1099 with the IRS. In 1987, Ramon was audited for tax year 1984. When the agent reviewed the form and cross-checked it with Ramon's tax return, he discovered an important discrepancy. Copies of checks paid to and cashed by Ramon totalled $13,925. However, the contractor's Form 1099 reported Ramon was paid $35,305 during 1984. The difference was $21,380. What do you suppose the agent concluded with respect Ramon's income?

If you said the agent claimed $21,380 to be unreported income, you are *exactly* correct. The final audit determination held Roman responsible for tax, penalties and interest on the alleged unreported income. The agent took the hard-line position that Form 1099 was presumed correct and Ramon had the burden to prove otherwise.

Ramon appealed the decision. On appeal, he testified he did not receive $35,000 from the contractor in question. He presented his ledgers showing what actually was received. This established the factual premise that the Form 1099 was false. In addition, the contractor produced his own records showing he paid Ramon just $13,925. No proof whatsoever existed for any amounts above that. Yet, the auditor continued to insist Ramon received unreported income.

Ramon challenged the IRS' decision on precisely the grounds I outline in *How Anyone Can Negotiate with the IRS - And Win!* (Winning Publications, 1988.) When the issue is unreported income, the burden of proof rests with the IRS, not the citizen. The IRS' burden is to establish a foundation of evidence upon which the determination of unreported income can securely rest. Without such a foundation, the courts have universally held any subsequent determination concerning unreported income is "naked" and does not enjoy the presumption of correctness.

"Several courts, including this one," reads the decision in Ramon's favor, "have noted that a court need not give effect to the presumption of correctness in a case involving unreported income if the Commissioner cannot present some predicate evidence supporting its determination."

More to the point, the court laid an affirmative duty at the feet of the IRS. The agent must support its claim with hard evidence. The court demanded the IRS "engage in one final foray for truth in order to provide the court with some indicia that the taxpayer received unreported income." The "final foray for truth," translates to the responsibility to investigate the facts and determine whether indeed the citizen received the income he is accused of earning.

Here, the IRS found no records to prove anything beyond what Ramon reported. That should have told the agency an error was made. Apparently the obvious conclusion never entered the auditor's mind. Then again, such a conclusion would have made the agency no money! Consequently, the IRS charged ahead, completely lacking any evidence other than an incorrect Form 1099. It made no further effort to engage in the final foray of truth required to support its claim.

When properly confronted, the IRS lost the issue. Ramon's ledgers, made as outlined here, provided the basis upon which the court ultimately held the IRS' position bogus. Without ledgers, surely Ramon would have paid tax, interest and penalties on income he never received.

3. RECORDING YOUR DEDUCTIONS

Each tax return contains two elements. Both must be proven by the citizen signing the return. The first element is that of *income*. We addressed above the aspects of proving one's income. The second element is a bit more tricky. It is the element of *deductions*. The citizen bears the burden to prove each deduction claimed is both legally permissible and, in fact, paid in the year claimed.

I began this discussion with reference to the difficulty most citizens encounter concerning their deductions during an audit. The reason for this difficulty is most citizens simply do not keep adequate records of deductions. Those who have records are bluffed by pushy agents into believing the records are not adequate. The result in either case is citizens pay more taxes than are owed. By understanding what type of records constitute adequate proof of deductions and keeping accurate records in the first place, you virtually eliminate the threat of having deductions disallowed.

4. STRATEGIC RECORDS OF DEDUCTIONS

There exist six legally acceptable ways a person can prove his deductions. Four of those six methods involve contemporaneous records. Those are records made at the time of the occurrence of the event being recorded. Contemporaneous records provide the most sound means of proving deductions. Here are six methods of proving deductions.

a. Cash Receipts. Cash receipts must contain a date, a description of the items purchased, the amount of the purchase and the name of the vendor from whom purchased. You may add to the receipt comments to allow a potential auditor to see at a glance how the item relates to a deductible expenditure. For example, if you purchase bolts from a hardware store for use in your business, make a note indicating the business use to which they are put.

b. Canceled Checks. Canceled checks must contain precisely the same information as shown above. Use the "memo" portion of the check to record descriptive information and make further notes if necessary in the check register. Resist the temptation, brought on by a desire for expedience, to fail to complete the check blank and register as fully as possible.

c. Year-end Statements. Year-end statements are summaries of expenditures made by third parties and issued to the citizen. Examples of year-end statements include statements issued by mortgage companies indicating the amount of interest paid during the year, statements by churches showing the amount of contributions, and, statements of county tax assessors reflecting real estate taxes paid. These statements are perhaps the best method of proving a deduction. The reason is they come from third parties and contain all the necessary information in a single document.

Take time to seek third party statements from as many persons or businesses as possible at year's end. For example, a letter to a supplier seeking a statement reflecting purchases during the year will surely result in a year-end statement. This greatly aids your ability to prepare and file an accurate and audit-proofed return.

d. Log Books. I already explained what log books are and how they work. Log books can be utilized effectively to prove deductions as well as verify income. Any expense which you incur on a regular basis should be recorded in a log. This is particularly true if the expense is paid in cash. The log book, coupled with cash receipts, nails down your burden of proof with respect to that deduction. Examples of expenses where log books should be used regardless of how the expense is paid are mileage, lodging, meals, and entertainment. Log books are not used very often. If you place them in service in your recordkeeping sojourn, you are miles ahead of the average citizen and more importantly miles ahead of the IRS.

e. Reconstructions. Reconstructions are used where there are no supporting documents upon which a claimed deduction is based. It is perhaps the least known method of proving deductions. The IRS has been successful in convincing us that without a piece of paper supporting the claimed expense, the expense is simply not allowed. This is not true. When done correctly, reconstructions are every bit as valid as the other methods of proof.

Here is an example. Kathy was a traveling sales representative for a clothing firm. For three years, she traveled across five Midwestern states. Often using her American Express card, she went from town to town peddling her wares.

As an independent contractor, she was responsible to pay all of her own costs of doing business, including her travel and related expenses. These expenses climbed into the tens of thousands of dollars for each year she was on the road. For some reason, her personal records were lost. When called in for an audit of her returns, she did not have one scrap of paper to document a trip around the block.

Without sympathy, her business travel and other expenses were disallowed. After pursuing her appeal rights, Kathy was in a position to negotiate a settlement. She began the process of reconstructing three years of her life. The starting point was her address book in which she recorded the names and addresses of the various retailers who purchased her wares and upon whom she called. She used her American Express card quite often while on the road. She mailed a letter to American Express requesting copies of the monthly bills.

As you may know, charge card slips are itemized with the name, address and date of the item charged. Most hotel and meal charges, it was reasoned, could be shown via the slips. Upon receipt of the American Express material, Kathy undertook the process of retracing her steps.

The first charge slip showed she spent a night in Fargo, North Dakota. Looking then to her list of actual and prospective customers, she determined and listed on a separate sheet each of the retailers she called upon in Fargo and the immediate area. When she was able to pin down the specific amounts spent on food and fuel, they were noted. When she was unable to do so, she estimated the amounts based upon reason and common sense. She followed this process for each of the 36 months at issue. It enabled her to document most, if not all, of the expenses incurred during the periods in question.

On appeal, the IRS allowed the reconstructions—to the penny!

WARNING: By their nature, reconstructions are estimates. To the best extent possible, they attempt to recreate a picture of reality as it was in years past. Because they are not self-contained as are canceled checks or cash receipts, they must be supported with oral testimony.

For example, in many cases, Kathy's charge slips showed a hotel expense evidencing she spent the night in a distant town, but did not show any cost of food. Common sense dictates one must eat on a daily basis. For that reason, she carefully provided testimony to the effect that food was purchased on those days when no food charges were shown.

When used in conjunction with oral testimony, reconstructions are an effective method of proving deductions.

f. Testimony. Testimony is nothing more than oral representations and assurances by the citizen to the effect that the amounts claimed were in fact paid. When such proof is offered to an auditor, the most common response is something such as, "Well, I am sure you are telling the truth, but I cannot take your word for it. I must have some kind of proof."

This statement assumes your word is not "proof." However, courts regularly allow deductions when the only proof offered by the citizen is testimony, i.e., his word. How is that so?

Provided the testimony is plausible, believable and credible, the court cannot refuse to consider it. Testimony which meets these criteria is just as valid as any piece of paper you can name. Let us prove it.

Tom was a regular churchgoer. Every Sunday, he and his family attended weekly services at the local church. Every Sunday, Tom deposited money in the collection basket. He gave cash, usually $40, each Sunday. At the end of the year, Tom deducted $1,980 from his income tax return as a charitable contribution.

He was later audited. As you may have guessed, the auditor requested to see proof of the $1,980 contribution. He did not have any substantiation as he gave only cash. But he did explain to the agent what his practices were, why he engaged in the practices and without a doubt, he did give the money.

The auditor was not impressed. After resolution of all other issues, Tom took an appeal on the question of his deductions. His case ended up before the Tax Court. During the trial, Tom testified to the judge as to his practices and the reasons for them. The judge kindly asked Tom questions about his habits and how he was able to determine the amount he gave. Tom's answers were direct and to the point. They were sensible and believable. All in all, Tom was honest and forthright with the judge during the trial.

In addition to his own testimony, Tom presented the testimony of the church pastor who corroborated the fact Tom was at church each Sunday. The pastor backed Tom's position that he always tithed with cash rather than by check. The pastor's attitude and demeanor was equally forthright.

At the conclusion of the trial, the court ruled in Tom's favor. Specifically, the court held that the deduction was supported by his testimony and that of the church's pastor. As a result of this and other successes like it, your case will not likely go to court. You may face an administrative appeal, as explained in Chapter Five, but such an undertaking is far from expensive and is far less stressful than the typical audit.

WARNING: To be effective, oral testimony must be specific. Qualified claims and vague recollections will not carry the day. Be sure all explanations are seasoned with as many hard facts as possible. Specificity leads to believability.

Oral testimony must be presented in the form of an affidavit. An affidavit is a sworn statement explaining the facts and circumstances of your claim. Your affidavit must explain just exactly how your reconstructions were prepared. It must clearly and plainly describe the expenses shown in your reconstruction worksheets. Lastly, it must declare that you in fact paid the expenses in the year claimed. Without contemporaneous records to back up your claimed expenses, reconstructions and affidavits provide all the proof needed to settle the audit dispute favorably. The book *41 Ways to Lick the IRS with a Postage Stamp* provides detailed examples of affidavits and guidance on how to draft them. See *41 Ways*, Chapters Four and Five.

5. How to Make Foolproof Records of Deductions

All the hassles which grow from inadequate records, including the need to create affidavits, are avoided when you make contemporaneous logs of your expenses. Begin immediately to record your expenses in an organized fashion. Much of the April paper war can be avoided if you organize yourself at the beginning of the year and carry that organization with you throughout the year. When faced with the April deadline, the lion's share of the work is done.

The log formats we are about to review are not designed to replace any accounting system installed by a competent accountant. However, they can augment any system, allowing you to keep careful track of where you spend your money. In each case, the log calls for an entry of a check number if the expense was paid by check. Enter the number to later recover that check quickly. When expenses are paid in cash, keep the receipt. If for some reason the receipt is unavailable, be careful to verify the logs. We discuss this in more detail later. Following this procedure ensures the strength and stability of your logs.

Let us examine log formats which enable you to install an effective recordkeeping system to optimize deductions in every area.

a. Rents and Royalties. Persons deriving income from a rental business or royalties naturally incur expenses associated with operating that business. Record those expenses in a log. I suggest the following columns at a minimum: date, payee, check number, taxes, repairs, insurance, utilities, legal and professional fees, and, interest. Also record any expense directly related to earning rent or royalty income. You may wish to add a Miscellaneous column to record expenses which do not fall directly into one of the above categories.

Please note that mileage incurred with rental or royalty income is deductible. If you incur mileage in connection with the operation of more than one business, create a mileage log for each business.

b. Interest and Dividends. Expenses associated with earning interest and dividends can be recorded in a log virtually identical to the one outlined above. You may wish to drop a particular column, such as Repairs, and add a column, such as Commissions.

c. Estates and Trusts. It is not likely you have expenses directly related to earning income from an estate or trust. In most cases, the estate or trust has an administrator or trustee whose job is to conduct the business of the trust. However, if for some reason you do incur expenses on a regular basis relative to an estate or trust, create a log to record them. Use the categories set forth above.

Certain adaptations may be in order based upon your circumstances.

   d. Self-Employed, Partnerships and S Corporations. A log of expenses related to the operation of a business must contain many more columns than those shown above. The reason is a business incurs a much wider range of expenses. Among the entries such a log must contain are: date, payee, check number, advertising, bad debts, car and truck expense, commissions and fees, depletion, depreciation, employee benefit programs, insurance, interest, legal and professional fees, office expenses, pension and profit sharing programs, rent or lease payments, including lease of business equipment, repairs and mainte-nance, supplies, taxes and licenses, utilities, wages, postage, and miscellaneous. Maintain a separate log for business travel, meals and entertainment. Use the mileage and travel logs discussed later.

   e. Cost of Goods Log. It is not uncommon for small, part time business operators to fail to keep track of their business inventory purchases properly. Your business deduction for cost of goods sold will not be allowed unless you properly document purchases of inventory items made during the course of the year. The reason is the IRS has created a formula for arriving at the cost of goods deduction shown on the Schedule C. An integral part of the formula is total purchases made during the year. See IRS Schedule C, Part III (not shown here).

   Those who will benefit from a cost of goods log are those involved in direct sales of one kind or another. It is common for such persons to maintain a small inventory of items which they turn regularly. Preparing a log optimizes the cost of goods deduction. The log described here is not designed to enable you to control inventory. Such a task is aptly performed by any number of PC software packages on the market. The sole purpose of this log is to record in one place all inventory purchases needed to compute the Schedule C cost of goods expense. Your cost of goods log should contain columns for the date, check number, payee, description of the goods purchased, and the amount.

   f. Residential Improvements Log. The sale of your residence may or may not constitute a taxable event. If you reinvest in another primary residence within the allowable time period, all gain on the sale is deferred. You are taxed only on the capital gain realized from the sale of the house. In computing the gain, you are allowed to take into consideration all the capital improvements made while you owned it.

   For example, if you purchase a house for $50,000, make $20,000 worth of capital improvements (i.e., new siding, new furnace, new roof) then sell it for $70,000, you realize no gain on the sale. Hence, you are not taxed on the proceeds, whether or not you reinvest in a new home.

   Most of us would have a record of a $2,000 roofing job or a $4,000 kitchen remodeling job because they were probably paid by check. The question is whether we would *remember* the expense when it comes time to compute the gain (or loss) from the sale. More importantly, most of us *do not* keep track of the more subtle improvements. Though they may be of a lesser amount, they are nevertheless deductible at the time of sale. For example, $50 worth of boards and $10 in nails to repair a deck are capital expenditures. Whenever you make a trip to the home improvement center or hardware store, be sure to make an entry in your Residential Improvements Log. You will be surprised how fast the deductible expenses mount.

Data in the Residential Improvements Log should include the date, check number, type of improvement, to whom the money was paid, and the amount.

g. Travel, Meals and Entertainment. List all travel, meals and entertainment expenses on a separate log. In fact, I recommend one segregate these expenses by business or activity. For example, if you incur expenses as an employee of a company, and at the same time have your own small side-line business, maintain two travel logs. This enables you to more easily organize your figures at the end of the year. Claim employee expenses on Form 2106 and business travel on Schedule C.

Data in such a log must include the date, purpose of travel and cities visited, amounts for fares, meals and lodging, and, entertainment expenditures. As to Entertainment expenditures, you must include the name of the persons entertained, their relationship to your business, the business purpose of the entertainment and the bona fide business discussions had before, during or after the activity. Without such supplemental information, no type of record is adequate to prove entertainment expenses.

h. Mileage. Mileage expenses can be deducted under one of two methods. One may either deduct his actual expenses for auto depreciation, fuel, oil, maintenance, etc., or he can claim the IRS' standard mileage allowance for business miles travelled. Careful records, including odometer readings, are needed to support actual expenses. However, just a simple mileage log is needed to support the standard allowance claim. In either event, maintain a thorough log.

If you intend to deduct your actual expenses, including auto depreciation, record the total miles driven during the year. This is done by keeping odometer readings. Your mileage log should include start-mileage stop-mileage columns for this purpose. In a business miles column, note the portion of total miles driven which were business related miles. These figures allow you to determine the percentage of driving which is business versus that which is personal. If the percentage is 65 percent business, you are entitled to deduct 65 percent for all actual auto expenses.

When utilizing the standard mileage allowance, one need not record expenses associated with operation of the vehicle. To earn the deduction, you need only maintain an accurate log of business miles driven. Multiply the number of business miles by the IRS' standard mileage allowance (it increases each year) to determine the amount of the deduction. If you operate more than one business, or have a day job which requires the use of your auto, and a sideline business in which you incur mileage expenses, I recommend you maintain two separate logs.

i. Employee Business Expenses. Ordinary and necessary expenses incurred on behalf of your employer in the performance of your duties as an employee, and which are not reimbursed by the employer, may be deducted. A log should provide for such additional expenses as work clothes, safety equipment, education, dues and fees, medical expenses related to your job.

j. Asset Purchases. Assets placed in use for business may be depreciable. I draw back to the individual who operates a small business out of his home. He may not realize purchases of shelving, calculators, etc., used exclusively for the business are depreciable assets. If he does know it when the purchase is made, he may forget the fact, or the amount, come tax time. Therefore, make a log of asset purchases contemporaneously with the purchase. This ensures you claim the full amount of your deduction. An Asset Purchases Log must include the date, check number, type of asset purchased, from whom purchased, whether it was new or used, and the cost.

k. IRA and KEOGH Plan Contributions. A log reflecting deductible payments to an IRA or KEOGH retirement plan should be maintained to optimize your deduction. This log must include the date of the contribution, check number, payee, type of plan, nature of the investment, and amount.

l. Itemized Deductions. Itemized deductions are those which can be claimed on Schedule A. They include medical expenses, interest on your principal residence, state and local taxes and charitable contributions. A log recording these expenses should be made for each category. The four logs should be organized as follows: *Medical* - date, payee, check number, prescriptions, doctors, hospitals, etc.; *Taxes* - date, payee, check number, state and local income taxes, real estate taxes, other taxes; *Interest* - date, payee, check number, mortgage interest, deductible points; *Gifts to Charity* - date, payee, check number, cash contributions, non-cash contributions.

The Clinton tax measure added a provision pointed directly at verifying charitable contributions. The measure is specifically designed to inhibit charitable contributions by making the verification process more difficult. The law, Code section 170, requires contemporaneous written acknowledgment by the donee organization of contributions in excess of $250.

Congress expressly declared it is no longer sufficient for a citizen to rely upon his "canceled check as substantiation of a donation of $250 or more." Congress is deliberately making it more cumbersome to claim a charitable contribution because Congress does not like charitable contributions. However, it has not yet mustered the guts to eliminate the deduction.

Under the new law, it is incumbent upon the citizen to obtain from the donee organization, i.e., church, etc., a statement verifying the contribution. The substantiation is considered contemporaneous if obtained by the citizen either before filing the return for the year in question, or, by the filing due date, including extensions.

The written acknowledgment must contain, (1) the amount of the cash and a description, but not the value, of any property other than cash contributed; (2) whether the donee organization provided any goods or services in consideration, in whole or in part, for any property contributed; and (3) a description and good-faith estimate of the value of any goods or services so provided, or, if the contributed goods and services consist solely of intangible religious benefits, a statement to that effect.

An "intangible religious benefit" is any benefit provided by an organization organized exclusively for religious purposes and that is not generally sold in a commercial transaction outside the donative context.

As a result of the Clinton attack on charitable contributions, logs become more necessary. You should include the above information in your log form. It can then be independently verified by your church or other charitable organization. This new provision applies to contributions made after January 1, 1994. Under the new law, no other method of proof is valid for charitable contributions.

m. Moving Expenses. Certain moves of your residence can be deductible. If you are planning a move, start with the creation of a log. That way, all of your moving expenses can be recorded contemporaneously to avoid missing the smaller items. A moving expenses log should include the following categories: date, payee, transportation of goods, travel, lodging, temporary living expenses, meals, and mileage.

n. Alimony. Alimony and separate maintenance payments pursuant to a divorce decree or settlement are generally deductible. A log helps to ensure recording all of the expenses as they occur. Such a log must include the date, check number, payee, type of payment and amount.

o. Miscellaneous or Non-Business Expenses. Expenses not covered above, which are deductible on Schedule A, are considered Miscellaneous expenses. They include, tax preparation, legal fees paid in connection with audits or other tax disputes (See Chapter Eleven), accounting fees, and safe deposit box rental.

6. ADAPTING THESE LOGS

As we know, each person's facts and circumstances vary. Therefore, employ these logs on a trial basis before making any changes to accommodate your individual needs. After some experience, make whatever alterations are necessary. In my *Stairway to Freedom* program, we provide reproducible log blanks which meet the criteria I set out above for recording both income and expenses. The *Stairway to Freedom* reproducible log kit has proven extremely effective for recording both contemporaneous expenses and in reconstructing expenses. The program consists of a 96-page workbook and two 60-minute audio cassette tapes. It is available from Winning Publications, Inc.

7. VERIFYING CASH EXPENDITURES

Whether your expenses are paid by check or cash, using logs to augment the records process virtually eliminates the IRS' latitude to disallow deductions due to insufficient records. However, one faces a potential problem when he incurs cash expenditures but does not have receipts to back them up. Under such circumstances, a contemporaneous log helps greatly, but is not guaranteed to work.

Cash expenditures for which there is no receipt need verification beyond a contemporaneous log. In my judgment, *testimony* must be offered to support such expenses. But when you are not directly questioned concerning those expenses, how do you create testimony to support your claims? The answer is quite simple. Your logs should be maintained on a monthly basis. That is, you should begin each month with a blank log and new entries. At the close of a given month, type a verification clause onto your log and have it notarized.

The verification clause should read as follows:

"The entries in this log were made contemporaneously during the month of _____, 19_____, and reflect ordinary and necessary expenses of the kind described. Each and every entry in this log is true, correct and complete in all respects, and is an accurate reflection of expenses incurred by me (or by _____ business) and paid by check or in cash on the date and for the purpose indicated."

_____
Your Signature

_____
Signature and Seal of Notary

_____
Dated by Notary

When notarized, this log not only provides details of cash expenditures, but provides *contemporaneous sworn testimony* to support them. This procedure eliminates the IRS' capacity to claim the logs are not truthful or accurate, or were made in a last minute effort to deceive the agency. Verified logs made in this fashion can then be used to audit-proof your tax return as explained in the next Chapter.

Logs are easy to create by adapting simple columnar or ledger sheets. My own customized log sheets can be found in my *Stairway to Freedom* workbook. Those found in this workbook are reproducible and contain a pre-printed Verification clause. You need only sign the verification in the presence of a notary public and have the notary sign and seal the completed log. It is a good idea to have income logs verified in this manner. This is true especially if the income reflects cash receipts. Your income verification should note that all cash received during the period stated is reflected in the log. This contemporaneous record goes a long way to defeat any IRS claim that you had unreported income.

8. UTILIZING LOGS TO MAXIMUM BENEFIT

Properly followed, the strategic recordkeeping program allows you to actually audit-proof your tax return. The logs made during the course of the year form the basis of an audit-proofed tax return.

Do not be concerned that the number of example logs may seem overwhelming. Not every citizen has income in each of the categories mentioned. Certainly not every citizen has expenses in each of the categories mentioned. You need only concentrate on those categories applicable to you. For example, a person with only W-2 income needs just a wage income log. Similarly, if his expenses are limited to charitable contributions, he need keep a log only of those expenses.

At this juncture, I want to expand upon the use of logs in recordkeeping to demonstrate more specifically how they may be utilized to maximum benefit. Thereafter, I illustrate the manner in which those logs are employed to ensure an audit-proofed and penalty-proofed tax return.

I believe utilizing these techniques frees you once and for all from the dread, anxiety and turmoil of not only the tax audit itself, but much of the return preparation process. No longer will you labor over the nagging question whether or not to claim a particular deduction. "Will it cause an audit? Will I be penalized if it's disallowed?" The answer is, "If the deduction is legitimate, claim it - period." Whether or not it raises red flags, my recordkeeping and return filing techniques help to insulate your return from potential damaging backlash of audits and penalties.

Another, most tangible benefit of this system is the feature of "controlled compliance." You see, without this system, tax auditors in the course of an examination often demand production of every scrap of paper a citizen has. They demand to see all canceled checks, whether or not relevant to a deduction. They demand to see all bank records, whether or not relevant to the receipt of income. They also tend to ask a myriad of probing and intrusive questions which seem to have no relevance to anything. They may even ask you to complete income and expense estimates to use against the figures shown in your own tax return.

By using the recordkeeping system, you comply with the legal mandate to prove your income and expenses, but avoid the necessity of jumping through all the ancillary hoops created by the tax auditor. Controlled compliance implies that you comply with the law regarding your tax return and necessary proof, but control the agency's ability to push you around during the audit process.

9. EXPANDING LOGS FOR RECORDKEEPING

The general log forms shown earlier can be expanded to very specific uses. Such uses enable you to accurately record, and hence, claim with confidence items you never before claimed. The example I use relates to charitable contributions. However, as I explain, specific logs can be applied to any situation where you incur regularly recurring expenses. The focus of these logs is to document cash expenditures. The reason is simply most people do not record in any meaningful way their cash expenditures. Thus, their otherwise fully deductible expenses fall through the cracks.

Considering specifically the charitable contribution deduction, I heard it said many times one may claim up to $200 in charitable contributions without supporting proof. Stated another way, the theory suggests the IRS simply "gives" you $200 worth of itemized deductions without the need of supporting documentation. In a word, the suggestion is nonsense.

The IRS gives you nothing in the way of deductions, charitable or otherwise. If you wish to claim the item, you must prove, through one or more recognized means, the legitimacy of the claim. By keeping logs of cash expenditures you will no doubt discover the amount you give exceeds $200 per year. Consider the following:

a. Kiddie Cash. I know of no small child who does not thrill to dropping cash into the collection plate on Sunday morning. Often, a quarter or a dollar is handed to the child (or children) just prior to the basket reaching your seat. Once gleefully deposited, the money is forgotten. This goes on week after week. If you have just one child, you are likely to have dropped $50 into the collection plate over the course of one year. Now multiply that amount by the number of children you have.

Often parents of older children teach the law of tithing by providing more substantial funds for the child to control and give on his own. Under these circumstances, the funds given to your church each Sunday go well beyond merely the amount of your own check. Based on my own limited experience as a father of small children, I believe the average family will find an additional $200 to $250 in cash contributions to their church each year.

Before you suggest recording these transactions are much ado about nothing, consider this. If I freely handed you $100 bill, would you accept it? That is what you stand to gain in tax savings by logging cash contributions of just $250. By using a log and obtaining substantiation of it by the church as required under the new law, the fact of your contributions will be unassailable by the IRS.

b. Cookie Cash. How many times have you purchased cookies, candy or some other product from neighborhood children? It may be the Girl Scouts, a playground booster club, a school program, the Y.M.C.A., or a church fund raiser. If your neighborhood is anything like mine, last year it was *all those things!* Another common "hit" comes in the form of sponsorships: You are asked to sponsor a child in the "Walk Against Drugs" or the "Bike Ride for Hope." By agreeing to sponsor a child, you contribute the agreed upon amount, say 50 cents per mile, to the charity promoting the event.

My guess is you donated money to one or more of these causes and you did so in the form of cash. Contributions to these organizations are usually tax deductible. But there is no way you will remember to claim them unless you make a record of the gift at the time it is made.

My suggestion is to create a log and keep it handy. When the inevitable knock at the door comes and you fall victim to another flawless sales pitch, make a contemporaneous record of the transaction for use at tax return preparation time. You may be entitled to claim an additional $25 or $50 in contributions you otherwise would overlook.

c. Christmas Cash. Do you give money to the Salvation Army during the Christmas Season? Do you contribute to local food shelves or toy drives. In my area, such causes solicit funds in full force during the holiday season. Certainly, many millions of citizens across the United States contribute. Just as certainly, they do so, in large measure, in cash.

I am willing to guess the vast majority of the millions of dollars collected by Salvation Army "bell ringers" is not deducted. The reason is simple. The money is placed in the collection pots in the form of cash. Just because you give in cash does not mean you cannot deduct the contribution. The contribution is fully deductible whether given in cash or not. However, you must prove you gave the cash. Under the new law, you must have your contribution acknowledged by the charity when the separate contribution exceeds $250.

Keep a log of cash contributions. Include not only the coins dropped in collection pots, but the canned corn donated to the food shelf and the Barbie Doll given to a toy drive. Have your contribution acknowledged by the charity if it exceeds $250.

d. Clothes Cash. Do you dispose of used clothing or other household items by conducting a garage sale? Or, do you donate them to the Salvation Army, Goodwill or your own church rummage sale? If you donate them to any of the latter causes, your contribution is tax deductible.

Unfortunately, millions of citizens who do contribute goods to charity do not claim the benefits they are entitled to. Folks regularly unload boxes of used clothing at Goodwill centers without bothering to create a log of the items contributed. Your log should list the specific items donated together with a declaration of their fair market value on the date of the gift. Have your list signed by a representative of the charity to whom given. Make sure the signed statement meets the requirements discussed above to constitute an acknowledgment of the contribution. The log constitutes proof of the contribution and its value.

Bear in mind that under the new charitable contribution verification law, the donee organization must acknowledge your contribution when it exceeds $250. Your notarized logs become a mandatory part of the verification process.

Each of the examples given above apply to *just one* category of deduction item — charitable contributions. My discussion was intended to be exemplary only. I did not intend to limit the use and application of logs for verifying deductible expenses. The general rule for utilizing logs is very simple. Any payment made in cash on a recurring basis which is ordinarily deductible should be recorded in a contemporaneous log. The verified log constitutes your ticket to the tax deduction. It also forms the basis for audit-proofing your deduction as discussed in the next Chapter.

10. CREATING SPECIALTY LOGS

Each of the logs discussed thus far is pointed at recording very objective occurrences. The occurrences are, of course, the expenditure of a sum of money on a specific item for some particular purpose. However, the deductibility of many business expenses depends not only on the amount of the expenditure, an *objective* consideration, but the business purpose of the expenditure. The latter consideration is entirely *subjective.* One person's view of what constitutes a necessary business expense is not always in agreement with the next person's (a tax auditor, for example) view.

Add now the fact that the deductibility of certain expenses is dependent upon *intangible* aspects. For example, your ability to deduct a portion of your home as office expenses depends upon, among other things, whether your home office space is used "regularly and exclusively" for business purposes. The so-called "exclusive use" test is an intangible item. It is intangible because under no circumstances can you obtain evidence, such as a canceled check, to prove "exclusive use." You cannot, for example, obtain a receipt from your children indicating they are not allowed to play in the den.

Safely proving your entitlement to a home office deduction necessitates the use of specialty logs. When employing such logs in other areas, you greatly increase the scope and value of your business deductions. Consider these items:

a. The Home Office. The tax code allows a deduction for a home office when a portion of the home is used regularly and exclusively as the principal place of business. See Code sec. 280A. In the past, the home office deduction has been the source of much abuse, both by citizens *and* the IRS. Citizens abuse the deduction by claiming a space in their home which is not legitimately used for business, or used so randomly it does not fairly meet the standards of deductibility.

The IRS abuses the deduction by disallowing legitimate home office expenses based upon harsh application of a rule known as the "focal point test." The focal point test attempts to ascertain whether a person's home office indeed constitutes his "principal place of business." Under the focal point test, if income is earned and services performed in the home office, the home is the principal place of business. However, when the services are delivered and income is earned outside the home office, the focal point test holds the home office is not the principal place of business. Thus, no deduction is permitted.

On January 12, 1993, the Supreme Court issued a decision greatly impacting the home office deduction. The decision was that of *Commissioner of Internal Revenue v. Soliman*, 113 Sup. Ct. 107 (1993). The court was called upon to determine, once and for all, whether the IRS' harsh "focal point test" was appropriate for determining the deduction. The court's decision failed to establish clear guidelines on the matter. But, the Supreme Court did provide what appears to be two guides. They are referred to by the court as the "two primary considerations in deciding whether a home office is a taxpayer's principal place of business."

The two guidelines are: 1) The relative importance of the activities performed at each business location (that is, both inside and outside the home office) and, 2) the time spent at each place.

Beyond this, the court makes what I consider to be a deliberately convoluted stab at justifying its pre-determined notion to kill Soliman's home office deduction. Consider this legal reasoning by the Supreme Court:

> ". . .the place where the contact (with customers, etc.) occurs is often an important indicator of the principal place of business. . .but as we have said, no one test is determinative in every case. We decide, however, that the point where goods and services are delivered must be given great weight in determining the place where the most important functions are performed."

After recognizing that not all businesses are *capable* of meeting with clients in an "office environment," (i.e., salesmen, contractors, etc.) the court noted:

> "We agree with the ultimate conclusion that visits by patients, clients, and customers are not a required characteristic of a principal place of

business, but we disagree with the implication that whether those visits occur is irrelevant."

Concerning all the other "essential tasks" necessary for the success of a business, the court stated:

"Whether the functions performed in the home office are necessary to the business is relevant to the determination of whether a home office is the principal place of business in a particular case, but it is not controlling."

So what is the court saying? Let us summarize the court's observations:

1. The location where one meets with clients is very important, i.e., "it must be given great weight." On the other hand, "no one test is determinative in every case." Furthermore, the court explained that visits by patients and clients "is not a required characteristic of a principal place of business." Therefore, simply because you do not happen to meet with clients or customers does not mean you are precluded from claiming the home office deduction.

In that respect, the IRS' austere view of the focal point test is dead. Remember, however, the standard (if you can call it that) is, where are the business's most important activities preformed?

2. In determining what are the "most important activities," the court observed that necessary functions performed in the home office are relevant, "but not controlling." That is to say, one must consider the nature of the tasks performed in the home office, but standing alone, they do not control the outcome of the case. This is true unless such tasks are more important than those performed outside the home office.

Why did the court attack the home office deduction, leaving us with such an obscure view for the future? I believe the reason is found between the lines of the closing remarks of Justice Stevens' *dissenting* opinion. The final sentence of his dissent reads, "Given the growing importance of home offices, the result is most unfortunate."

In Part III of this book, I point out the courts and Congress hand the IRS more power and authority for one reason only. That reason is - *To Get the Money!* I have little doubt such is the case here. On two separate occasions in his 10-page dissent, Justice Stevens observes the growing financial importance of the home office deduction to many citizens. If Justice Stevens recognizes its importance to taxpayers, you can be sure the IRS and the remaining members of the court recognize its importance to the *federal coffers.* The court is trying to kill the deduction because the government needs the money - period! It has nothing to do with law or justice.

Through its convoluted reasoning, the Supreme Court killed Soliman's home office deduction for two reasons. They are:

1. The actual treatment of Soliman's patients "was the most significant event in the professional transaction." It occurred outside the home office, at the hospitals where Soliman worked. The home office activities, such as recordkeeping, professional study, etc., "must be regarded as less important to

the business of the taxpayer than the tasks he performed at the hospitals."

2. A comparison of the time spent in the home office versus that spent at the various hospitals "supports a determination that the home office was not the principal place of business." The 10 to 15 hours per week Soliman spent in his home office studying, etc., "measured against the 30 to 35 hours per week at the three hospitals are insufficient to render the home office the principal place of business in light of all the circumstances of the case. That the office may have been essential is not controlling."

Exactly what is controlling, we still do not fully know. The court contradicts itself too often to be clear. Whether you meet with customers and clients, well, that is important, but not controlling. Whether you perform important tasks in the home office, that too is important, but not controlling.

What I glean by sifting through the mud is this: The principal place of business is ascertained by determining what the most important tasks of the business are and where they are performed, and, the time spent at each place performing them.

The time factor seems to be the key, for the court says:

"This factor assumes particular significance when comparison of the importance of the functions performed at various places yields no definitive answer. . .to the inquiry."

In other words, the court seems to be saying, if all else fails, just figure out where you spend most of your time and that is where your principal place of business is found.

In light of this "court decision," a log evidencing the use of your home office is vitally important. It alone enables you to prove what you are doing in your home office and the amount of time you spend doing it. Without such a log, you have no reasonable chance of prevailing in your claim for a home office deduction. The *Stairway to Freedom* program contains a specialty log entitled *Home Office Use Log*, which I strongly recommend.

The home office log is completed on a daily basis. The log has columns for each of the following entries: date, task performed, time in, time out, total. For each task performed, list the date, a general description of the job and the time spent. For example, you may spend 35 minutes each day reviewing sales orders. You might spend two hours prospecting for customers or clients. You might spend 20 minutes ordering product. The remainder or your time may be spent in the field.

b. The Home Computer. In the past five years, the use of office equipment in the home has grown by leaps and bounds. We have computers, copiers, sophisticated telephones, fax machines, etc. Many people purchase home computers for use in a mix of business and personal reasons, but do not claim the deduction to which they are entitled. I find the IRS challenging the deduction of home computers because citizens often lack the proof to establish the business use of the machine. You may ask, "How does one prove business use of a computer?" The answer is, with a log!

A log dedicated to equipment usage allows you to make a record each time you use your computer. (Why not computerize it!?) The log reflects the date of use, the function performed, whether business or personal, and the time spent. After maintaining the log for a 30-day period, you are able to ascertain the percentage of time spent on business functions and that spent playing Space Invaders.

The percentage of business use established over the entire tax year determines the deductible percentage of the total cost of the computer. For example, suppose your logs for all of 1993 reveal you spend 65 percent of your home computer time performing business related functions. If you paid $2,000 for your computer, you are entitled to a business deduction of $1,300 ($2,000 x .65 = $1,300). The key to establishing the deduction is to faithfully keep the log. Only with the log are you able to unequivocally prove 65 percent business use of the home computer.

c. Other Business Equipment. The idea we just explored is not limited in scope to a personal computer. Any piece of equipment which has at least some business use is subject to the allocation shown above. Remember, you do not have to be self-employed to claim these deductions. If you purchase equipment for use in your job and are not reimbursed by your employer, you may be able to claim a deduction for the expense on Form 2106, *Employee Business Expenses.* Do not be afraid to make logs covering the following:

i. Video Cassette Recorder. Many people employed in direct marketing companies use VCR's to make sales presentations. Make a log using precisely the same form illustrated for the computer. Indicate at the top of the log which article the log covers.

ii. Telephone use. Be sure to note whether the call was long distance. Long distance business phone calls are not subject to any allocation rule. If the call has a business purpose, it may be deductible. Record business use on a log.

iii. FAX use. While I cannot imagine owning a FAX machine for non-business purposes, I suppose there are those who do. Nevertheless, if the FAX is used partially for business purposes, a log enables you to deduct the correct percentage as a business expense.

4. Meals and Entertainment. Entertainment expenses must be given careful consideration. The reason is the IRS and Congress have established stringent rules regarding the deductibility of such expenses. Earlier in the discussion, I touched on the rules, but let us elaborate.

Entertainment and meals are deductible when they constitute an ordinary and necessary business expense, and they are: 1) directly related to the operation of your business, or, 2) they directly precede or follow a bona fide and substantial business discussion.

The entertainment can take place at a restaurant, sporting event, theater or other non-business environment. The entertainment can be for the benefit of existing or potential clients or customers, suppliers, dealers, professional counsel, or employees.

The key to deductibility of any meal or entertainment expense is a log. The log must carefully note the persons entertained, the business purpose of the entertainment, the bona fide and substantial business discussion had before, during or after the entertainment, the date, and of course, the amount of the expense.

Proper logs carry your meal and entertainment expense deduction well beyond the charge card slips we generally fall back on. Consider this:

a. Entertaining at Home. When you conduct bona fide and substantial business meetings in your home, the cost of entertainment associated with such meetings is deductible. Your log must record the date of the entertainment, the persons in attendance and their affiliation to your business, the purpose of the entertainment and a description of the substantial and bona fide discussions had either before, during or after the gathering. The purpose of the entertainment must be commercial and not merely social. Of course, you should have records of the costs of food, beverages, etc., served at the gathering.

b. Entertainment Facilities. You may already know it is not legal to deduct the cost of maintaining or operating so-called "entertainment facilities." Entertainment facilities include such assets as boats, vacation homes, swimming pools, etc. However, it is possible, under the rules discussed above, to deduct entertainment expenses incurred while using such facilities. Entertainment expenses include food, beverages, supplies, etc., related to providing business entertainment at or with the facility.

For example, if you own a boat, the cost of maintaining and operating the boat is not deductible. However, if you entertain business associates on your boat from time to time, the cost of such entertainment (apart from operating the boat) is deductible. Those costs include the food, beverages, etc., supplied for the entertainment. You must maintain logs just as you would for home entertainment. The logs must reveal precisely the same information as shown under *Entertaining at Home.*

CONCLUSION

I am the first to confess that recordkeeping requirements and the IRS' appetite for information has gone far beyond the bounds of reason. But keep in mind the point I made early in this chapter. The lack of proper records is what often enables the IRS to take advantage of citizens. I pointed out the tax code is 17,000 pages of jumbled mess nobody understands - including (or, especially) IRS auditors. Therefore, when you properly understand your burden with regard to the tax return, you are in a substantially better position to *assert* deductions than any agent is to *deny* them.

The recordkeeping requirements speak loudly of the need for sweeping change. The system we now have must go. As you witnessed in this chapter when examining the *Soliman* decision, the Supreme Court has allowed tax law administration and enforcement to degenerate into a frenzy of convolution designed only to separate you from your money. Such a system is intolerable in a free society. It is time to rebuild our system based upon the changes I recommend in Part III of this book.

2 AUDIT- AND PENALTY-PROOFING YOUR TAX RETURN
PREVENT MORE TAXES & PENALTIES

Each year, we file millions of tax returns with the IRS. During the 1992 filing season, Americans filed almost 115 million individual income tax returns. Businesses and corporations filed another 34.75 million returns, including employment tax returns. In all, the total number of tax returns filed with the IRS during 1992 was a record high *203.075 million*. This does not include the over one billion information returns submitted for 1992.

Each year, the IRS electronically audits 100 percent of the returns filed. Computers perform much of the task. Only three percent of all returns are subjected to a grueling face-to-face audit.

On the mind of each citizen about to file his tax return is the question, "How do I avoid an audit?" The typical answer, offered by many tax experts over the years, always disturbs me. The suggestion is to forego claiming various deductions to which he is entitled to reduce the chances he will be selected for examination. Stated another way, the prevailing "professional" opinion is one should *buy* audit protection. He does so by failing to claim legitimate deductions to which he is entitled. This, of course, has the direct impact of increasing your tax liability.

Another "professional" technique for limiting the bite of an audit revolves around the same principle. Citizens often intentionally "hold back" deduction items at filing time. The theory? If audited, they can later throw them on the table to negate the effect any anticipated disallowances. This too amounts to the purchase of audit protection insurance at the price of increased taxes.

Unfortunately, the IRS' audit statistics reveal that neither of those techniques is worth the professional paper it is written on. In the first place, accept the fact that 100 percent of all returns filed are examined by the IRS' computers — period. There is nothing anybody can do to prevent that. Merely failing to claim legitimate deductions does nothing to preclude computerized scrutiny.

Furthermore, statistics reveal that 88 percent of all citizens audited are found to owe more money. The average amount due after face-to-face examination is more than $5,800. Therefore, "holding back" deductions at the time of filing in order to spring them upon the auditor later, simply does not work.

Both the foregoing techniques for "avoiding an audit" are based upon two fundamental misunderstandings. The first is uncertainty about how returns are selected for audit. Second is misgivings about what it means to be audited.

Here, we closely examine both questions. Ultimately, we answer once and for all, what can be done to avoid being dragged through the hot coals of a face-to-face tax audit *without* losing one dime of deductions in the process. These techniques allow one to claim with confidence all legitimate deductions. Further, you gain the confidence to claim legitimate deductions you never before thought (or dared) to claim.

Lastly, a valuable by-product of my recordkeeping and returns filing technique is the introduction of a new level of financial privacy. Following these techniques enables you to rest assured you have met your legal obligation to prove the correctness of your tax return. At the same time, you minimize the extent to which you must bear your financial soul to the IRS. Truly, this system allows you to close the IRS' spying eyes in its attempt to criticize each detail of your financial affairs.

How Returns are Selected for Audit

None of what I say in the following pages holds any significance unless you understand how the IRS selects returns for audit. Learning the audit selection basics will allow you to fully appreciate my audit-proofing techniques.

The IRS uses four basic systems to select tax returns for audit. Let us briefly address each of them.

1. Mathematical Errors. Upon receiving a return, Service Center computer programs compare all computations for mathematical accuracy. If an error is found, the computer generates a correction notice, then mails the notice to the citizen. It demands payment of the additional taxes, with penalties and interest. Each year, millions of these notices are generated through the computer process. In an average year, about 3.5 million such notices hit the streets.

In 1986, I claimed most of these notices, including others discussed below, were simply bogus. I claimed the IRS mailed them under the terms of the 1984 Plan solely as a means to "increase presence." In 1986, a GAO study of such notices confirmed my claim. The GAO found IRS' computer generated notices to be "wrong, incorrect, incomplete or incomprehensible" in 48 percent of the cases. I discuss this issue in greater detail in Chapter 10 of this book.

2. Mechanical Errors. The same computer program searches for mechanical errors in return preparation. Such errors might include failure to attach a necessary supporting schedule or failure to carry a total from a schedule to the tax return itself. When such errors are detected, correction notices are mailed to the citizen. The GAO study encompassed these correction notices as well. They too are discussed in Chapter 10 in more detail.

3. Unreported Income. Over the years, the IRS developed a program known as the Information Returns Program (IRP). Under the program, IRS compares all information returns filed, such as Forms 1099 and W-2, with all tax returns. If the computer reveals the presence of an information return showing payment of income, but such income is not reported on a tax return, the computer issues a correction notice. The notice adds the unreported income to the return then computes the additional tax due. In turn, it demands payment of the additional tax, with interest and penalties. This is precisely what happened to Tim as we discussed in Chapter One.

The IRP is designed to detect non-filers in the same manner. For example, suppose the computer detects a Form W-2 showing receipt of $20,000 in wages during 1992. However, in cross-checking for a tax return, it finds none was filed for tax year 1992. Considered a non-filer, you are mailed a notice demanding you file a return or explain why none was filed. If you fail or refuse, the IRS computes your liability based on available information and bills you accordingly.

4. The Discriminant Function. The Discriminant Function System (DIF) is a sophisticated computer program. It compares each entry of your tax return with national and regional statistical averages for persons within the same income category and profession. If any line of your return is out of sync with those averages, your return is flagged for review. The DIF program is the system past "professional" audit-proofing guidance was designed to beat. Theoretically, if one merely reduced the amount of deductions claimed, those deductions would then fall below the averages. That way, you would be assured your return would not be selected for examination.

The problem with this theory is two-fold. First, we do not know the DIF scores. Therefore, any effort to place your claims below those scores is purely speculative. Secondly, even if we did know them, in order to place one's self below the threshold, he would have to forego claiming deductions to which he is lawfully entitled. This practice is like throwing the baby out with the bath water!

The philosophy behind "professional" audit-proofing techniques is all wrong. Those who exercise the practice of reducing claims in order to avoid an audit do not understand an audit. The audit is nothing more than the process by which the IRS determines the correctness of a tax return. The fact that your return may be selected for audit is no indication whatsoever of an *error* in the return. Rather, it indicates only that there is a *question* raised by one or more claims within the return. The audit is the process by which IRS obtains answers to those questions. If you understand your rights and can demonstrate the accuracy of your return, the audit should hold absolutely no hidden danger or financial risk.

How My System Works

Having examined the many facets of recordkeeping logs and the audit selection process, let us answer the question I raised earlier. The question was, in essence, how can we take what we know about the audit selection process and use it to our advantage in audit-proofing tax returns? The answer lies partially with logs. We know the IRS selects the vast majority of returns for audit, not based upon known errors in the returns, but based its upon statistical variance with stated parameters.

I know from studying the IRS' audit referral system that returns selected by the DIF program are first assigned for review at the Service Center. Only after a reviewer finds a need for a face-to-face exam is the return formally referred to a local tax auditor. My audit-proofing techniques are designed to take effect at the point of Service Center review to prevent the return from being forwarded for personal exam. The result is to avoid the hassle, anxiety, and trauma of a face-to-face audit, not to mention the $5,800 tax bill that accompanies it.

I know from experience when sufficient information is provided with the return *at the time of filing*, there is no need to forward the document for full-scale examination. Therefore, we effectively short-circuit the audit process by simply providing sufficient information with the return at the time of filing. The information must answer any potential questions raised by the return itself.

Let me offer an example. Suppose your logs reveal you are entitled to claim 20,000 business miles during the year. Suppose further, however, you are advised by your tax preparer or your inner voice that claiming 20,000 business miles will send a red flag sky high. Rather than reduce your claim to something less, my techniques allow you to claim the full amount of the deduction.

To audit-proof the claim, make a copy of your verified mileage log and attach it (never send originals) directly to the tax return at the time of filing. In this fashion, you have both claimed every deduction you are entitled to claim, and have provided information with the return sufficient to answer any potential questions regarding the claim. If your return is kicked out by the DIF program because of the apparently high mileage claim, IRS examination personnel at the Service Center will find all needed supplemental information attached directly to the return. At that point, why will the matter be pursued any further?

Keep in mind, over 200 million returns of all kinds are filed each year. At the same time, just two to three percent are ever assigned for face-to-face examination. When the subject is individual income tax returns, Form 1040, the average is more in the nature of one percent. If your return is audit-proofed in this fashion, do you suppose your return, or an undocumented one, will be assigned for full-scale audit? My guess is the file on your return will be closed at the point of Service Center review.

Do you wish to be absolutely safe concerning all claims on your return? If so, audit-proof each and every deduction or entry made!

Complete audit-proofing is done not just by providing copies of your verified logs. Indeed, the logs are a means of enabling you to capture all of your expenses, particularly those which generally fall through the cracks. But there is more. Full scale audit-proofing is accomplished by attaching to your return copies of all information necessary to prove a claim. This includes logs, canceled checks, cash receipts and year-end statements.

A fully audit-proofed return provides copies of all the information which otherwise would be provided to a tax auditor in a face-to-face environment. In this manner, you completely eliminate the need to see an auditor, even if there is an incorrect claim on the return. You and the IRS may act strictly through the mail. Since all documentation and details are provided with your return, a face-to-face meeting is entirely unnecessary. This is consistent with the right to a so-called correspondence audit. In a correspondence audit, you never enter the lion's den. Rather, you operate out of your home or office and through the mail. For more on the correspondence audit, see Chapter Nine.

To summarize, a completely and properly audit-proofed return contains the following line-by-line attachments:

1. An explanation of the nature of the claim. IRS Form 8275, *Disclosure Statement* can be used for this purpose. *(See Exhibit 2-1 in this chapter.)*

2. A full and complete explanation of the purpose of the expense (if a business expense, your explanation should include a statement as to why the expense is "ordinary and necessary" to the operation of your business);

3. Copies of all documentary evidence available to support the deduction, including logs; and

4. If the IRS has a particular form covering the deduction, such as Form 4684 for Casualty and Theft Losses, or Form 8283 for Non-Cash Charitable Contributions, complete the form and attach it to the return.

When a return is supplemented with this kind of complete proof, you eliminate the need of an audit. Even beyond that, should a claim be disallowed for some reason, you avoid being penalized. The reason is when "full disclosure" of all facts, supporting documents and reasonable justification for the claim are presented with the return, the law does not permit assessment of penalties. A case study illustrates my point.

Case Study No. One - *Stein v. Commissioner*, T.C. Memo. 1992-651 (Nov. 5, 1992).

In 1988, Hester received a lump sum distribution of $44,000 from her employer. The distribution was part of an early retirement incentive package. According to documents provided by the employer, the source of the distribution was a pension plan. Both Hester and her employer believed the distribution did not constitute severance pay.

When the employer issued a W-2, however, it identified the $44,000 distribution as *wage income*. Hester filed her 1988 income tax return on time. She did not, however, treat the distribution as wage income. Rather, she called it a *pension distribution*. She elected to income average the payment over 10 years as allowed at the time by pension distribution rules.

On the face of her Form 1040, Hester added this language, "Lump sum Distribution erroneously reported by employer on W-2 and reportable on Form 4972 (relating to pension distributions)." In addition, she attached directly to the return a copy of a statement prepared and issued by the employer. It described the payment plainly as a pension distribution.

The IRS audited Hester's return and determined she received severance pay, not a pension distribution. As it turned out, they were right according to the fine print in her contract. She should have reported the payment as wage income not subject to the 10-year income averaging right. As a result, she owed more income tax. However, the IRS' claim did not end there. They ordered Hester to pay the sum of $2,244 as a penalty under Code section 6662. That penalty applies when one substantially understates his income tax liability.

Hester challenged the IRS' proposed penalty. She claimed she was not liable for a penalty because she made full disclosure to the IRS of the facts surrounding her claim on the face of return. The IRS was on notice of the nature of her claim. At the time of filing, she provided documentation sufficient to allow the IRS to pass upon its merits. Please recall Hester included a written explanation of the issue and attached a copy of the written statement issued by her employer.

Revenue Regulation 1.6662-4(b)(1) provides disclosure is adequate if a statement is attached to the return which includes, (a) a caption identifying the statement as a section 6662 disclosure, (b) identification of the item to which disclosure is made, (c) the amount of the item in question, and (d) the facts affecting the tax treatment of the item that reasonably may be expected to apprise the IRS of the nature of the potential controversy concerning the tax treatment of the item.

The IRS created a form which meets all the above requirements. I refer to it as the *penalty-proof form.* Though the IRS does not like to discuss it, it is available for all to use. The form I speak of is Form 8275, *Disclosure Statement.* (This form is reproduced on the following page as Exhibit 2-1.)

In this case, Hester *did not* use Form 8275. Rather, she simply added her explanation to the return and attached supporting documentation. The IRS argued that her failure to use the form meant the $2,244 penalty should apply. The Tax Court rejected the IRS' argument. The Court stated:

> "(Hester) did not use Form 8275. Yet, our inquiry does not end there. According to the Joint Committee's (Joint Committee on Taxation, U.S. Congress) explanation of section 6662, 'disclosure is adequate if the taxpayer discloses facts sufficient to enable the IRS to identify the potential controversy, if it analyzed that information.'"

After analyzing Hester's disclosure, the Court held:

> "We conclude that the disclosure on (Hester's) return was adequate to disclose the controversy. (Hester) did not try to hide the position she had taken on her 1988 tax return as is often done by those attempting the 'audit lottery.' (Hester) not only made a notation on the tax return that indicated the position she had taken, but also attached a copy of the explanation of the payment which indicated the potential controversy. We, therefore, hold that (Hester) is not subject to the (penalty) under section 6662."

In the above example, Hester saved $2,244 by penalty-proofing her tax return as I suggest. While she did not use Form 8275, her effort was nevertheless successful. The key to avoiding penalties is simple. Do not attempt to hide your claim from the IRS. When making a claim which is potentially controversial, disclose the facts to the IRS to allow them to pass upon the merits of the claim.

By doing so, if it transpires you are not entitled to the tax treatment elected, as was the case with Hester's distribution, you avoid penalties associated with the claim.

You may be thinking the 8275 is a way to call attention to yourself. "Why file the form," you ask, "if all it does is trigger an audit?" The form itself does not trigger an audit. An audit is triggered when the computer flags a potential trouble spot in your return. Please review our earlier discussion on the manner of selecting returns for audit. By not using Form 8275, you are virtually assured the return will be handed off for a face-to-face examination if a complex or questionable item appears.

Using Form 8275 and providing supporting documentation as outlined here assures there is no need for face-to-face scrutiny. By providing supporting material with the return, IRS need only pass upon the merits of your claim. That is exactly what happened in Hester's case. Of course, if they disallow your deduction, you have the right to appeal the decision. The important key is, even if you lose on the merits of the deduction, you *prevent the assessment of very costly penalties.* In Hester's case, the extra few minutes she spent penalty-proofing saved exactly $2,244!

Exhibit 2-1

Form **8275** (Rev. July 1992) Department of the Treasury Internal Revenue Service	**Disclosure Statement** ▶ Attach to your tax return. ▶ See separate instructions.	OMB No. 1545-0889 Expires 5-31-95 Attachment Sequence No. **92**
Name(s) shown on return		Identifying number shown on return

Part I **General Information**

Caution: *Do not use this form to disclose items or positions that are contrary to Treasury regulations. Instead, use Form 8275-R, Regulation Disclosure Statement.*

(a) Detailed description of item (or group of similar items) being disclosed and the location of the item(s) on your return, including schedule and line (e.g., Schedule A, line 20).	(b) Amount of disclosed item described in column (a)
1	
2	
3	

Part II **Detailed Explanation**

1 ....

....

....

2 ....

....

....

3 ....

....

....

Part III **Information About Pass-Through Entity.** To be completed by partners, shareholders, beneficiaries, or residual interest holders.

Note: *A pass-through entity is a partnership, an S corporation, an estate, a trust, a regulated investment company, a real estate investment trust, or a real estate mortgage investment conduit (REMIC).*

Complete this part only if you are making adequate disclosure with respect to a pass-through item.

1 Name, address, and ZIP code of pass-through entity	2 Identifying number of pass-through entity
	3 Tax year of pass-through entity / / to / /
	4 Internal Revenue Service Center where the pass-through entity filed its return

For Paperwork Reduction Act Notice, see separate instructions.	Cat. No. 61935M	Form **8275** (Rev. 7-92)

A NEW WRINKLE IN PENALTY-PROOFING REQUIREMENTS

My penalty-proofing techniques have been extremely effective over the years. As you can clearly see from the above case study, they work! You can be sure this little fact was not lost on the IRS. Penalties are big business for the IRS. Each year, tens of millions are assessed against individuals and businesses, netting billions in increased revenue. Penalties have become a revenue enhancement tool; no longer considered a mere deterrence to abhorrent taxpayer behavior.

Chapter Seven of this book discusses in general the terms of Clinton's plan to squeeze more money from the public through penalties. One provision of the new Clinton tax bill addresses itself squarely to penalties. It impacts the penalty-proofing techniques discussed here. Frankly, in light of the present administration's desire to collect substantially more penalty revenue in the four years of its term, it is imperative to use these techniques to the fullest.

The provision of which I speak altered sections 6662 and 6694 of the tax code. Under the terms of the old law, one avoids a penalty if his claimed position was disclosed on the return as outlined above, *and*, if the position was not "frivolous." A position is "frivolous" only if it is "patently improper." See Revenue Regulations, sec. 1.6662-3(b)(3). A claim that is arguable–whether or not correct–but not patently improper, is not "frivolous."

In other words, you avoid penalties for understanding your tax and or for negligence or disregard of the tax code's rules and regulations when, 1) the facts relevant to the treatment of the issue were disclosed on the return (i.e., Hester's case); and 2) the position was not "frivolous."

At Clinton's request, Congress tightened the belt on this rule. The new rules take effect with regard to tax returns due after December 31, 1993. Under the latest revenue enhancement scam, you avoid penalties only if your position has "at least a reasonable basis." This standard is *higher* than the not "frivolous" standard previously applicable. The Conference Committee report on the Clinton tax plan describes the difference in these terms:

> "* * *The conferees intend that 'reasonable basis' be a relatively high standard of tax reporting, that is, significantly higher than 'not patently improper.' This standard is not satisfied by a return position which is merely arguable or that is merely a colorable claim."

–Conference report, H.R. 2264, August 4, 1993, page 205.

The disclosure aspect of penalty-proofing remains critical. None of what I outlined above has changed. Added is the requirement that your position have a *reasonable basis* in law and fact. I believe this standard requires one to exercise some due diligence prior to making any potentially troublesome claim. That is, you must make a reasonable effort to ascertain the correctness of your claim before asserting it. Provided you discovered sufficient evidence to persuade a reasonable person as to the correctness of the claim, the penalty is avoided if the claim is properly disclosed to the IRS and supported as shown above.

What is reprehensible about this tax law change is not so much that average citizens are now held to a higher standard when it comes to penalty avoidance. What is incredible is Congress opted to *leave in place* the not "frivolous" standard for penalties applicable to professional income tax preparers. See code section 6694 and page 205 of the Conference Committee report cited above.

This means that under Clinton's tax law changes, the average citizen, with no training or experience navigating the black, shark infested waters we call the tax code, is now held to a *higher standard* of knowledge and behavior than are trained professionals who make their living deciphering the nonsense!

This fact vividly illustrates how far out of focus our national tax policy has become. It makes it clear to even the most casual observer that Congress' intent is simply to get your money. Congress, it is now plain to see, has lost all regard for the burdens this system places upon the average citizen. Congress, assuming it *ever* considered the impact of tax administration on the public, cares only to get into your pocket on a broader scale. And this latest effort plainly shows Congress lacks the guts to just come out and declare the state of reality. Rather, it opts to use covert means to trap otherwise completely honest and unwitting citizens into making mistakes. Rest assured, mistakes are *guaranteed* each time it stirs the legislative pot.

The tax code did not become simpler with the new law. It became more complicated. How many average citizens, faced with the need to work long hours to feed their families, will spend equally long hours in the library reading, digesting and applying the *81 different tax law changes* discussed in the 304-page Conference Committee report? Will you? I don't even read them all! This proves radical changes must be made—and soon!

Now let me add insult to the injury Congress inflicted. A majority of the principal members of Congress' tax writing committees *do not* prepare their own tax returns. Those who created the burdens under which you must struggle every day, recognize the maze is now too hopeless, even for them. The April 1993, issue of *Money* Magazine indicated about 60 percent of the members of the House Ways and Means and Senate Finance Committees do not prepare their own returns. See April 1993, *Money*, page 96.

Clay Shaw, a Representative from Florida, is both a C.P.A. and attorney. He is quoted in the article as saying the U.S. tax code is "rat's next." Said an aid to Representative Mel Hancock, "The tax code is too complicated for a layman..." The current Chairman of the Finance Committee, Daniel Patrick Moynihan is reported to use a professional, as is Ways and Means Chairman Dan Rostenkowski. Even Treasury Secretary Lloyd Bentsen, long-time Chairman of the Finance Committee, appointed to the top Treasury post by Clinton, uses a tax pro. *Money* quotes him as saying the reason is because his return "is a complicated one." Ibid. page 97.

Unlike you, however, our fearless leaders do not have to go it alone. While the public pays $30 billion per year to employ return preparation professionals, Congress receives the service at *taxpayers' expense.* Those who prepare their own returns have the expert lawyers employed by the tax writing committees at their service.

Beyond that, the IRS funds and staffs two offices in Washington during tax preparation time. One is set within the Senate Office complex, the other in the House Office complex. They provide IRS advice, including outright preparation of the return, to members of Congress and their staffs. The cost to taxpayers, *Money* reports, is $100,000 annually. Each year, these IRS specialists provide advice to about "4,000 of the 20,000 people who work on Capital Hill." *Money*, page 99.

It is clear our nation's top tax authors cannot figure what they have done. Still, *you* are to be held to a higher standard of behavior than are tax professionals concerning a law the authors themselves do not understand. I declare to you, there is something seriously wrong with a law when reasonably intelligent people must hire a professional specialist to determine whether they have complied with its terms. This is precisely the level to which our federal tax laws have degenerated. It is not just "rich" people using paid preparers. During the years 1989, 1990 and 1991, slightly more than 80 percent of the returns filed with paid preparers were for citizens making less than $50,000 adjusted gross income. Make no mistake about it, friends. We must have change.

THE AFFIDAVIT:
AN AUDIT- AND PENALTY-PROOFING TOOL

I discussed affidavits in passing in Chapter One. Affidavits play an important role in the audit- and penalty-proofing scenario. There are cases in which the acceptability of a deduction depends on information which can't be provided through documentation obtained from a third party. Such information is just as essential to proving the deduction, but must be presented in another fashion.

For example, a home office claim is acceptable only after meeting all the elements of the deduction. One element is that the space in the home is used "regularly and exclusively for business purposes." No deduction is allowed when office space is used for personal, non-business purposes, such as an evening TV room. Thus, proof must be presented in the form of testimony to establish the "intangible" element of business use.

Achieve the task by using an affidavit. An affidavit is nothing more than a sworn statement presenting detailed facts. The statement becomes testimony when the affidavit is notarized. Testimony proves the truth of the matter asserted when it is plausible, believable and uncontroverted.

Of course, unless you are an outright tax criminal, the IRS does not attempt to offer evidence to refute your claims. In short, it simply does not have to. You must prove your return is correct and complete. If you are unable for any reason, you lose without the IRS lifting a finger. That is what makes an affidavit so effective. They are rarely, if ever, refuted with evidence to the contrary.

An affidavit under our example must declare, specifically and unequivocally, that office space is used regularly and exclusively for business purposes. It should state that no personal, non-business use occurs within the space. To be effective, one must also establish that he meets all other home office elements as well. We addressed those in Chapter One, in our discussion of the *Soliman* Supreme Court decision.

For further details on the use and preparation of affidavits, see my book *41 Ways to Lick the IRS With a Postage Stamp*, Chapters Three and Four.

AN INCREASED MEASURE OF FINANCIAL PRIVACY

With all its ability to demand the production of information, it is difficult to understand how anybody has any remaining degree of financial privacy. The truth is, measured against the yardstick of what may be considered Constitutional standards, we have little or no financial privacy. The IRS' ability to demand records, access your bank account and obtain data from other third-party recordkeepers makes true financial privacy a thing of the past.

But the procedures outlined in the first two chapters of this book restore some measure of privacy. It is ironic to believe by going the extra mile to create detailed records to fully disclose you in some capacity reclaim financial privacy. Nevertheless, my proposition is true.

Bear in mind your legal burden of proof with regard to claims made in your return. I regularly allude to that burden throughout this discourse. To review, you must prove the correctness of claims regarding income and expenses. If you claim to have earned $15,000 during the year, you must show the claim to be accurate. If you claim to have incurred $5,000 in charitable contribution deductions, you must prove the accuracy of that claim according to applicable rules.

It is important to understand the limits of the IRS' reach in this regard. The agency has the right under law to demand proof of any item claimed in the return. However, its power does not extend beyond that point. Stated another way, the IRS has no right or authority to delve into every aspect of your financial life if such ancillary issues have no bearing upon the correctness of your tax return.

For example, if you make no claim of any charitable deduction, the IRS has no right to question you or demand documentation regarding such a claim. Similarly, any demand for the production of records relative to medical expenses is entirely inappropriate if you claim no medical deductions on the tax return.

This distinction is important because during the course of a typical audit, agents routinely demand the production of a myriad of documents. They generally seek all canceled checks, all bank deposit slips, all monthly bank statements, documents concerning loans and repayments of such loans, and so on and on. But if these issues have no bearing upon the truthfulness of the claims in your return, they are entirely irrelevant. A more clear example arises with regard to the demand for "all canceled checks." If you were to you examine the checks written during the course of an average month, you would find payments for groceries, haircuts, green's fees, restaurants, dance lessons, car payments, gasoline, day care, theater tickets, maybe even a parking ticket, etc., etc., etc.

The point is, the vast majority of expenses incurred during the month are of an extremely personal nature and are entirely non-deductible. Moreover, unless you are a tax criminal, I suspect you made no effort to deduct such expenses.

Consequently, the nature, amount, or purpose of such expenses is simply of *no legitimate concern* to the IRS. In short, it is *none of their business* how you spend your money on non-deductible expenses. The agency therefore has no right to demand, and you are under no obligation to produce, records which have no bearing upon issues raised by the return.

This reality no doubt closes the door on much more than 50 percent of what the IRS has a right to see. By using the audit- and penalty-proof techniques outlined here, what they have a right to see is readily organized, easily understood, and probably already provided with the return. Under such circumstances, what further legitimate claim does the agency have to more information?

Using these techniques eliminates the need to sift through every document you own providing information in response to a steady stream of demands. In fact, it may entirely eliminate the need to deal with an auditor because all documentation necessary to prove the claims in the return was submitted with the return. Provided you did so, you enjoy the legitimate right and power to say "no" to further demands.

In essence, you have the right to terminate an audit when it exceeds the legal limits. You have the right to stop an agent from prying or attempting to pry into issues which have no bearing upon the correctness of the return. You have the right to assert your financial privacy and can make it stick when adequately prepared. Indeed, if you do not assert that right, you surely will enjoy no right of financial privacy. To be sure, the IRS portends no limits to its own power to know.

While this right certainly exists, few exercise it because they are afraid of the power of the tax auditor. The truth be told, tax auditors have no power. As I examine more closely in Chapter Five, auditors operate largely on tactics of bluff and intimidation. They employ misinformation and disinformation. Often, they overtly lie concerning audit issues, taxpayer obligations and potential consequences. When you understand these facts, you become more willing and able to exercise your rights. Your right of privacy naturally grows as a result.

CONCLUSION

Given Congress' overt and covert attempts to get deeper into *your pocket*, my audit- and penalty-proofing techniques are mandatory if you are to keep the IRS Out of Your Life. Do not delude yourself into believing they will not attack you because "I pay my taxes." In each of the case studies presented in the first two chapters of this book, the citizens attacked "paid their taxes." But the IRS was not satisfied with that. The IRS wanted more.

Given the financial condition of the United States, it is no longer sufficient for citizens to just "pay their taxes." This point is best illustrated by Clinton's attitude toward penalty administration. Paying your taxes is not enough to satisfy Congress' insatiable spending appetite. It requires you pay substantial amounts of penalties and interest as well. That is why it is mandatory that all honest citizens employ these audit- and penalty-proofing techniques.

3 SOCIAL SECURITY NUMBERS AND MINOR CHILDREN

SOLVING THE CHRISTIAN'S DILEMMA

The Tax Reform Act of 1986 was the most sweeping tax legislation in history. The act modified or added more than 2700 provisions of the code and created more than 2000 new forms and procedures. Among them was a requirement that minor children have an "identifying number" if they are to be claimed as exemptions on their parents' income tax return. The common belief is such identifying number must be a social security number.

When the law passed, the requirement for a number attached if the child reached the age of five years during the year he is claimed as an exemption. Subsequently, the threshold dropped. In 1988, it was reduced to two years. Current law demands a number if the child has reached "the age of 1 year before the close of (the) taxable year." See Code section 6109(e). This trend indicates the requirement may soon be mandated "at birth."

In the months and years following adoption of the requirement, I handled a rash of inquiries regarding the issue. Much concern involved the religious implications of branding a child with a social security number at such a tender age. Others raised a "right of privacy" concern. It is suggested a social security number facilitates invasions of one's personal privacy rights.

Congress first began the process of using social security numbers for tax administration purposes in 1963. It recognized the need to have an individual number assigned to each person if it were to harness the emerging computer technology to accurately track each person. Since then, the steady growth in information reporting laws has imposed a corresponding burden to provide social security numbers as the nexus between the data and the person to whom it applies. Without a peculiar number assigned to each citizen (who then uses it in all areas of his life), the government's ability to electronically spy on that person is virtually non-existent. An Orwellian-style government is upon us and the social security number is at the apex of that system.

SOCIAL SECURITY NUMBERS AND RELIGIOUS OBJECTORS

Objections to obtaining and using social security numbers, especially for minor children, go well beyond the issue of privacy. For many, the desire to *avoid* use of such a number is a matter of religious principle. For decades, numerous religious sects have objected to social security. Such groups are religiously opposed to the kind of insurance programs which social security represents. Groups such as the Amish are exempted from participation in the program based upon these beliefs. Content to trust the Lord and their church brethren for their daily bread as opposed to any "insurance" provider, they kindly and quietly stepped away from the system.

More recently, the trend in the growth of government and its use of the social security number has concerned many conservative Christian leaders and church members. The number is conspicuously tied to *all financial transactions*. Add to this the government's trend toward the elimination of cash and replacing it with a traceable money system. These facts bring many Christians to the conclusion that the social security number is somehow related to the "Mark of the Beast" spoken of the Biblical book of *Revelation*, Chapter 13, vs. 13-18.

As any literate person knows, there is no literature more hotly debated as to its literal and spiritual meaning than is the Bible. What is more, there is no book within the Bible itself whose meaning is more hotly debated than the Book of *Revelation*. For that reason, I do not intend fuel the debate by interjecting my personal opinions regarding the social security number or its spiritual ramifications. I do not attempt to either prove or disprove the number's relationship to scripture in general, or *Revelation* in particular. My personal opinions on the matter are irrelevant to this discussion.

The fact is, ten's of thousands of conservative Christians believe in their hearts the social security number poses a serious threat to their spiritual security. Based upon that reality, my purpose is solely to examine the legal authority of the government to require a number for minor children or adults. I wish further to explore viable options for those persuaded of the number's dubious spiritual implications.

Social Security Numbers and the Tax Law

Of course, the IRS' public declarations regarding the SSN leave most with the impression there is no alternative but to apply for one. Not surprisingly, IRS' statements make no mention of any right to avoid using or obtaining a number on religious grounds. True to form, misinformation and disinformation circulate regarding the matter. This was true at the time the 1986 act was passed, and it is true today. I shall set the record straight as to the legal requirements for a number.

I begin my analysis with a declaration likely to shock most Americans. While we have been taught to believe participation in the social security program of retirement benefits is mandatory, a study of the law indicates the contrary.

At the outset, to avoid confusion, I wish to distinguish between payment of the social security *tax* and participation in a retirement program which offers a *package of benefits*. When I say participation is not mandatory, I refer to the latter situation. That is to say, neither Congress nor any court has ever declared every citizen must apply for or receive any *benefits* under the social security program.

The Social Security Act, as presently in effect, is codified within Title 42 of the United States Code. A search of the law reveals no statute which can fairly be said to mandate participation in the *benefits* program. It is also true that no section of the act requires any citizen to obtain an SSN. However regulations under the act *do require* a person seeking *benefits* to apply for a social security number.

Regulations found at 20 C.F.R. (Code of Federal Regulations), section 422.103, hold that any person "needing a social security number" should apply for one on Form SS-5, *Application for Social Security Card*. The regulation goes on to state that a social security number will be issued by the administration only "if the applicant has completed Form SS-5" and the social security office determines that such applicant has not previously been assigned a number. 20 C.F.R. sec. 422.103(c)(1).

It is interesting to note this same section permits the Social Security Administration to establish a system under which *newborn children* are assigned numbers as "part of the official birth registration process." However, the regulation makes it plain that a number is to be assigned to a newborn *only* "where a parent has requested" such assignment. In that case, the State vital statistics office is instructed to "electronically transmit the request" to Social Security's central office. It then assigns a number to the newborn and mails the social security card to the "mother's address." 20 C.F.R. sec. 422.103(b)(2) and (c)(2).

There is no language in this regulation or any other I have read under the *Social Security Act* which *requires* application for or assignment of a number to any person in general, or newborn child in particular. This leads me to the very logical conclusion that participation in the *benefits* portion of the social security program is entirely voluntary. It naturally follows that having an SSN is likewise, entirely voluntary. In sum, you get a number only if *you* apply for one. You apply for one if you wish to participate in the social security benefits program.

This is not to say that paying *social security taxes* is likewise entirely voluntary. It is not. Whether you participate in the benefits program or not, social security taxes are levied upon your wages or self-employment income. Certain narrow exceptions apply as set forth in Code sections 1402(e) and (g). However, that topic is outside the scope of this treatise.

Proof which I believe makes this assertion irrefutable came to me in 1988. At that time, an associate began corresponding with Lloyd Bentsen, present Secretary of the Treasury. At the time, Bentsen was the Chairman of the Senate Finance Committee. That committee wrote the law which eventually became Internal Revenue Code section 6109(e).

The subject of the initial letter to then Senator Bentsen concerned the requirement of citizens to obtain an SSN. By letter dated May 24, 1988, Bentsen responded, saying, "There is no law requiring every citizen of the United States to obtain a Social Security number. There are a limited number of circumstances in which an individual would be able to meet his or her legal obligations without obtaining one." *(See Exhibit 3-1 on the following page.)*

You may be asking, if Senator Bentsen himself declared there is no requirement for all citizens to have an SSN, why on earth would *his committee* write a law requiring children to have an SSN? Please note the date of Bentsen's letter. It *follows* enactment of the Code section in question. The answer is quite simple. The law in question, Code section 6109(e), *does not* require SSN's for minor children, or anybody else. The common interpretation of the law is that an SSN is required, but that is certainly not what the law says. The applicable language of the statute is as follows:

> "If - (1) any taxpayer claims an exemption under section 151 (relating to dependent exemptions) for any dependent on a return for any taxable year, and (2) such dependent has attained the age of 1 year before the close of such taxable year, such taxpayer shall include on such return the *identifying number* (TIN) of such dependent."

Now I ask you, did you see the phrase "social security number" any place in that statute? The answer is clearly, no. What you read was a reference to an "identifying number," which, as we are about the learn, *can be much different* from a social security number. It is true that for *most* people, a TIN, or taxpayer identification number, is also his SSN. However, for those *religiously opposed* to the use of an SSN or participation in the social security retirement benefits program, *no SSN is required*.

While Lloyd Bentsen was chairman of the Senate Finance Committee, he and his Congressional colleagues produced a report describing the effect of section 6109(e). The Conference Committee report on Public Law 99-514, the *Tax Reform Act of 1986*, says this with regard to the question of SSN's and religious objectors:

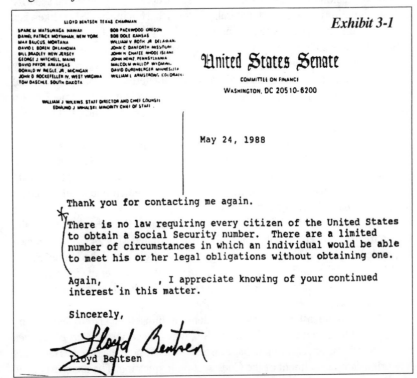

Exhibit 3-1

LLOYD BENTSEN TEXAS CHAIRMAN

SPARK M MATSUNAGA HAWAII
DANIEL PATRICK MOYNIHAN NEW YORK
MAX BAUCUS MONTANA
DAVID L BOREN OKLAHOMA
BILL BRADLEY NEW JERSEY
GEORGE J MITCHELL MAINE
DAVID PRYOR ARKANSAS
DONALD W RIEGLE JR MICHIGAN
JOHN D ROCKEFELLER IV WEST VIRGINIA
TOM DASCHLE SOUTH DAKOTA

BOB PACKWOOD OREGON
BOB DOLE KANSAS
WILLIAM V ROTH JR DELAWARE
JOHN C DANFORTH MISSOURI
JOHN H CHAFEE RHODE ISLAND
JOHN HEINZ PENNSYLVANIA
MALCOLM WALLOP WYOMING
DAVID DURENBERGER MINNESOTA
WILLIAM L ARMSTRONG COLORADO

United States Senate

COMMITTEE ON FINANCE
WASHINGTON, DC 20510-6200

WILLIAM J WILKINS STAFF DIRECTOR AND CHIEF COUNSEL
EDMUND J MIHALSKI MINORITY CHIEF OF STAFF

May 24, 1988

Thank you for contacting me again.

There is no law requiring every citizen of the United States to obtain a Social Security number. There are a limited number of circumstances in which an individual would be able to meet his or her legal obligations without obtaining one.

Again,   , I appreciate knowing of your continued interest in this matter.

Sincerely,

Lloyd Bentsen

"The conferees note that certain taxpayers, because of their religious beliefs, *are exempted* from social security self-employment taxes (sec. 1402(g)). The conferees intend that these taxpayers and their dependents who currently acquire their TINs from the IRS continue to be permitted to do so. It is the intent of the conferees that these taxpayers *continue to be exempted from the general requirement of obtaining a social security number from the Social Security Administration.* Others of these taxpayers obtain their TINs under special procedures with the Social Security Administration. *The conferees intend that these procedures continue to be available to these taxpayers.*" (Emphasis added.)

Do not let it be said that Code section 6109(e) mandates a *social security number* for minor children. As we see from the above data, it clearly does not. Specifically, Congress seemed sensitive to the religious beliefs of those opposed either to the social security benefits program or to a number. As we read in the text of the Conference Committee report on section 6109(e), Congress *never intended* the law to vitiate the rights of religious objectors.

The conclusion, therefore, is inescapable. Those religiously opposed to the use of SSN's for themselves or their minor children are under no legal compulsion to obtain or use one. As we examine later, there are alternatives to an SSN. In my opinion, they allow one to meet his tax obligations without infringing his religious liberty.

THE PENALTY FOR FAILURE TO PROVIDE A TIN

Despite the clear language of the law, the IRS continues to insist that all children must have a social security number if they are to be claimed as dependents on one's tax return. In fact, the IRS has been generous in administering the penalty for failure to supply a number.

Code section 6723 imposes a penalty of $50 for failure to supply the TIN of any dependent when claimed as an exemption on the return. Like all penalty sections, however, the IRS asserts the fine indiscriminately, without regard to circumstances of the case. The reason is the citizen bears the burden to prove the penalty is not applicable. When he does, the IRS must cancel it. For more information on penalty cancellation, please see Chapter Seven.

Each penalty provision of the code contains what is known as a "good faith," or "reasonable cause" provision. Section 6723 is no exception. When a citizen acts in good faith and based upon a reasonable cause for his actions, and not out of a deliberate attempt to deceive, mislead or cheat the IRS, the penalty simply does not apply.

A special reasonable cause provision is found within the text of Code section 6724. Section 6724(a) declares:

"*No penalty* shall be imposed under this part with respect to any failure (to provide a TIN) if it is shown that such failure is due to reasonable cause and not willful neglect." (Emphasis added.) See also section 6724(d)(3)(D).

Thus is it seen that in the absence of a TIN for minor children, the IRS is not at liberty to charge a penalty when there exists reasonable cause for the failure. As I explain in Chapter Seven, penalties are not to be used by the IRS merely as a means of raising revenue. Penalties must serve the purpose of encouraging compliance or they are improper. A person who otherwise complies with all the tax laws, but fails to obtain or use a social security number on religious grounds does not pose a threat to the tax system. Under such circumstances, no penalty is warranted.

In passing Code section 6724, Congress articulated what must be considered when determining if the penalty applies. In the Conference Report on Public Law 101-239, creating Code section 6724, the committee states:

> "* * *The bill provides that any of the information reporting penalties *may be waived* if it is shown that the failure to comply is due to reasonable cause and not willful neglect. The committee intends that for this purpose, reasonable cause exists if significant mitigating circumstances are present, such as the fact that a person has an established history of complying with the information reporting requirements.* * *" (Emphasis added.)

Revenue Regulations speak to the factors which establish reasonable cause. The regulation holds that one seeking cancellation of the penalty must establish he acted in a "responsible manner" regarding the TIN. See Revenue Regulation section 301.6724-1(d). This is a standard of care that a reasonably prudent person would use under the circumstances in the course of his business. One acts in a responsible manner if he undertakes to mitigate the failure; if he attempts to prevent the failure if foreseeable; if he improves the cause of the failure once it occurred; or if he rectified the failure once discovered. See Revenue Regulation section 301.6724-1(d)(1).

Based upon the above statements, it can be said there are two elements which must exist in order to cancel a penalty for failure to provide a TIN. First, the citizen must show the existence of "significant mitigating factors" which led to the failure. Next, he must show he acted in a "responsible manner" with regard to his legal obligation.

Surely a person's deep seated, sincerely held religious beliefs are a significant mitigating factor. This is particularly true when you consider Congress *expressly stated* it never intended to force those with religious objections to apply for a number or to use one. Moreover, an entire body of federal court rulings have supported the proposition that one religiously opposed to the use of a number cannot be forced by government to do so. We study some major cases below. The conclusion is, when you are a bona fide religious objector, that fact constitutes mitigating circumstances sufficient to eliminate the penalty.

Later in this chapter, I discuss alternatives to the SSN. I am well satisfied each of my proposed alternatives evidences an effort and desire to act in a responsible manner. They show the citizen has endeavored to meet his legal obligation while at the same time, preserving his religious objection. Given this level of reasonably prudent conduct, a person eliminates any potential penalty under Code section 6724.

Case Study No. One - *Stevens v. Berger,* 428 F.Supp. 896 (Federal District Court, New York) (1977).

David and Virginia Berger were raising four minor children in New York during the 1970s. Their income was below the subsistence level. As a result, they were drawing "home relief aid" - welfare benefits - from the State of New York.

In January of 1976, county officials notified Mr. Stevens he was to provide them with copies of the children's social security cards. The Stevens children did not have social security numbers. Furthermore, because of their religious opposition to the use of such numbers, the Stevens' refused to obtain them. They notified the county accordingly. Later, the county denied the Stevens' application for welfare benefits.

The Stevens sued the county in federal court. They claimed their First Amendment rights to religious liberty were infringed by the county's actions. Stevens marshalled several expert theologians who testified concerning the nature and meaning of the "mark of the beast" as spoken of in the Book of *Revelation*. The experts surmised that the social security number could indeed represent such a concept. Mr. and Mrs. Stevens themselves asserted in testimony they believed a link existed between the number and the mark.

Upon careful consideration of the facts and honestly weighing the testimony of all parties, including that of county officials, the court ruled in Stevens' favor. The court observed:

> "Since having a social security number has become a prerequisite for so many benefits (both from the public and private sectors), no great leap of imagination is necessary to travel from the exegesis of *Revelation* to the (Stevens') belief that such numbers could function, if the state were to become too powerful, like the mark of the Antichrist spoken of in the biblical text. With the history and literature marshalled by the (Stevens) to support their contentions, their belief must be characterized as religious for purposes of this case."

In conclusion, the court held that "benefits for which (the Stevens') otherwise qualify" *could not be denied* "solely because they refuse, for religious reasons, to obtain social security numbers for the children."

It is important to note that the court *did not* rule the SSN was in fact the mark of the Antichrist. Rather, it held that since the Stevens' *believed* it was, they could not be denied any rights or benefits to which they were otherwise entitled solely for refusing to obtain the number.

Case Study No. Two - *Callahan v. Woods,* 658 F.2d 679 (9th Circuit 1981) on rehearing, 736 F.2d 1269 (9th Circuit 1984).

Robert Callahan had precisely the same problem as Mr. and Mrs. Stevens. His daughter did not have an SSN due to Robert's religious opposition to its use. Robert was receiving AFDC payments from Sonoma County, California. When he refused to provide a number for his daughter, the county terminated her benefits. He sued in federal court on precisely the same grounds as expressed in the *Stevens* case.

The court ruled simply, "We conclude that the SSN requirement substantially interferes with the free exercise of Callahan's religious beliefs."

In both Case Studies, the courts found the citizens in question met the burden of proving their objections were religious in nature, subject to First Amendment protection. That burden is two-fold. First, the belief must be "sincerely held." The First Amendment does not extend to situations where the claims are patently devoid of "religious sincerity." Secondly, the claim must be rooted in religious belief, not in "purely secular" philosophical concerns.

In the scholarly discussion of the "mark of the beast" in the *Stevens* opinion, the court remarked the matter was one of deep religious concern. As such, it is fully entitled to First Amendment protection. For more discussion on religious liberty in general, see the Supreme Court decision of *Wisconsin v. Yoder*, 406 U.S. 205 (1972).

When this two-pronged test is met, the burden shifts to the government. It must carry the "heavy burden" of proving two points. First, when a government agency seeks to impose a burden which affects a constitutional right, it must prove the regulation severs a "compelling state interest." If it passes that test, the government must then prove its regulation is the "least restrictive" method of accomplishing its goal. When the compelling state interest can be accomplished despite the exemption of a particular individual, then any regulation which denies the exemption is "not the least restrictive means." See *Callahan*, 736 F.2d at 1272.

Given this fact, we explore alternatives to the SSN which allow the IRS to meet its needs, while at the same time, allow one the continued enjoyment of his sacred First Amendment rights.

ALTERNATIVES TO THE SSN

The compelling stated interest asserted by the IRS is the need to combat "exemption fraud." The IRS claims millions of dependent exemptions are falsified each year. Without a "universal identifier" assigned to each person, the IRS believes it lacks the capacity to abate the alleged fraud.

The idea of using SSN's to accomplish this is nothing new. State social welfare agencies have been doing it for decades, as seen in the two case studies cited above. It therefore should come as no surprise that the IRS adopted its use in the exemption fraud battle. Assuming the IRS has a legit-imate, compelling interest in adopting measures to accomplish its goal, the issue is whether the measures are "the least restrictive" means of doing so.

In the case of persons *with no* sincerely held objection rooted in religious belief, perhaps the use of an SSN is not restrictive in any means. However, for those with Christian beliefs rooted in the principles espoused by scripture, the requirement to obtain a number could very well fly in the face of such person's First Amendment rights. The above court decisions certainly confirm this point.

Consequently, those claims must be *accommodated* by the IRS. Interestingly, Congress declared its intention to do just that when it adopted the statute. The Conference Committee report cited earlier buttresses this assertion. In theory, therefore, no contest on this point should occur.

The question now is, how do we preserve religious objections while allowing the IRS to further its interest in combating exemption fraud? I believe there are two very specific methods of accomplishing this. Let's examine them.

1. THE INTERNAL REVENUE SERVICE NUMBER

Earlier we examined the Conference Committee report covering Public Law 99-514. The committee, you will recall, declared in passing Code section 6109(e), it *was not* Congress' intention to require those opposed on religious grounds to begin using an SSN. Congress expressly stated those opposed to the number on religious grounds could continue to use alternative means of providing a TIN to the IRS. Specifically, the committee explained the IRS is to continue its practice of assigning TIN's to SSN religious objectors.

For years, the IRS has been quietly assigning TIN's to those religiously opposed to SSN's. The TIN assigned by the IRS is not a social security number. It is referred to as an Internal Revenue Service Number, or IRSN. It is not and cannot be used by the Social Security Administration for benefits purposes. Remember, one can gain benefits under the social security system or obtain an SSN *only* by completing and signing Form SS-5.

On November 5, 1986, Sander Levin, Congressman from Michigan, wrote a constituent regarding the use of this alternative method of obtaining a TIN. Congressman Levin stated, "For most people, the TIN will be a social security number, but for those taxpayers who are exempted from social security due to their religious beliefs, the IRS will assign a TIN for the dependent just as for the principle." Congressman Levin is referring to the IRSN. A copy of his letter is reproduced as Exhibit 3-2 on the next page.

Beyond this, the IRS issued a Revenue Ruling which squarely addresses the issue. Revenue Ruling 85-61, 1985-1 C.B. 355, provides in part, that persons:

> ". . .who do not have social security numbers issued by the Social Security Administration, and who are not otherwise required to obtain them, may use identifying numbers issued by the Internal Revenue Service. The identifying numbers issued by the IRS are similar in appearance to social security numbers, but begin with the number 9 (9xx-xx-xxxx)."

The ruling concludes by saying such numbers may be used "for any federal tax related purpose for which an identification number is required."

You may be asking how the IRSN is, in practical effect, any different from the social security number. First, the IRSN does not operate to entitle one to benefits under the social security program. I already stated that entry into the benefits program is dependent upon signing an application, Form SS-5. No

Exhibit 3-2

SANDER M. LEVIN
17TH DISTRICT MICHIGAN

COMMITTEES
BANKING
GOVERNMENT
OPERATIONS
SELECT COMMITTEE
ON CHILDREN, YOUTH
AND FAMILIES

WASHINGTON OFFICE
323 CANNON HOUSE OFFICE BUILDING
WASHINGTON, D.C. 20515
(202) 225-4961

DISTRICT OFFICE
SUITE 1120
NORTH PARK PLAZA OFFICE BUILDING
17117 WEST NINE MILE ROAD
SOUTHFIELD, MICHIGAN 48075
(313) 559-4644

Congress of the United States
House of Representatives
Washington, D.C. 20515

November 5, 1986

Dear Mr.

Thank you for your thoughtful letter regarding tax reform. Your views are important to me as I consider legislation coming before the House.

I certainly understand your concern over the provision in the new tax reform law that will require a taxpayer claiming a dependent who is at least 5 years old to report the taxpayer identification number (TIN) on his or her tax return.

For most people, the TIN will be a social security number, but for those taxpayers who are exempted from social security due to their religious beliefs, the IRS will assign a TIN for the dependent just as for the principle. This change was made after studies indicated that in 1981 alone, $8.1 billion in overstated exemptions were claimed on individual tax returns, representing 5% of all misreporting of income and deductions.

The tax reform bill is the most sweeping overhaul of the tax code in over 40 years. In any such comprehensive legislation, there will be provisions, some of which will be favorable, and others which will be unfavorable to any individual taxpayer. Clearly, it's important to weigh the pluses and minuses. Due to the complexity of the tax reform package, the full ramifications of the new code are not clear. If inequities do arise, I hope Congress will act to correct these problems. I expect, however, that the broad outline of tax reform will remain largely intact for the near future.

Thank you again for sharing your views with me. I hope you will continue to do so on issues of concern.

Sincerely,

Sander Levin
Member of Congress

SML/sf

application, no number. No number, no benefits. It is that simple.

Furthermore, evidence accumulated over the years evidences the SSA cannot assimilate or utilize, for its own purposes, an IRSN. For example, those filing tax returns using IRSN's are often contacted by SSA regarding the number. The letter explains, "The name and 'Social Security number' reported to us does not agree with our records." They go on to ask one to verify his "social security number." The letter states that unless the discrepancy is "corrected," the SSA cannot "credit the earnings to the proper record."

Naturally, the number reported to SSA does not agree with their records. They never issued it! It was issued by the IRS. Further, their form letter suggests the number is an SSN. In fact, it is not. If the numbers were in practical effect the same, surely the SSA would be able to utilize an IRSN for its own purposes. Evidently, it cannot.

The relationship between the IRSN and the SSN seem much the same as that between a chicken and a duck. They are certainly both birds, but just as certainly, they are *not the same!* It is ridiculous to suggest that chickens and ducks share precisely the same characteristics because they are both birds. It is just as meritless to suggest a unity of purpose between the IRSN and the SSN, solely because they are both identifying numbers.

Perhaps the most significant distinction between the numbers has nothing whatsoever to do with any legal attributes. Rather, the distinction is found in the manner they are used by the citizen. There is a good reason it may be so easy for an SSN to become inextricably associated with your name. Most citizens generally spread their SSN around freely. They indiscriminately provide it to any person who asks, regardless of the fact there is no legal obligation for one to either have or use one. The SSN becomes inevitably associated with "buying and selling" when used on bank accounts, loan applications, credit cards, and other financial transactions.

By contrast, the IRS assigned TIN would *absolutely not* be used in any such fashion. Its sole and exclusive purpose is to comply with IRS regulations calling for an identification number in *tax filings* and related transactions. For purposes other than this narrow scope, the citizen would be rightfully entitled to claim he simply does not have such a number should anyone ask. This is of course the truth, since an IRSN is not, as proved earlier, an SSN. There is no obligation to dispense your IRSN to any person seeking a social security number.

Even more importantly, the IRS cannot release your tax return information, including any identifying number, to any person. For this reason, providing an IRSN to the IRS for tax purposes is not tantamount to providing it to other elements of society. Section 6103(b) of the Code prohibits the IRS from releasing any information without your consent if the information could be "associated with, or otherwise identify, either directly or indirectly, a particular taxpayer." Certainly an identifying number is within the range of this language.

In this way, a person legitimately and without risk of penalty or unfair scrutiny, disassociates himself from the SSN if, for religious purposes, he is hesitant to either obtain or use one.

The next question is how does one obtain an IRSN? The easiest way is at tax return filing time. On the tax return line seeking a social security number, enter the phrase:

"Religious objector - See attached." In attachments to the return per my suggestion in Chapter Two, explain you are religiously opposed to the use of social security numbers. Point out you are not required, by reason of your religious exemption, to obtain an SSN. State your desire for the IRS to issue an IRSN as contemplated under Revenue Ruling 85-61. The IRS should then issue the number.

In some cases, a TIN is needed prior to the time of filing a tax return. An example is where one submits a Form W-4 to his employer. The employer must have a number at the time of receiving the W-4 so wages and withholding can be accurately reported to the IRS. In this situation, one should apply for the IRSN in advance of filing the W-4.

Application is made by letter to the IRS Service Center in Philadelphia, PA. The address is 11601 Roosevelt Blvd, Philadelphia, PA., 19255. Mark your letter to the attention of the "Entity Section."

State in the letter of application you are a religious objector to the use of SSN's and are not, therefore, required to obtain one. Point out, however, you need a TIN for tax return filing and reporting purposes. Request the IRS issue an IRSN to you (or your dependents) to fulfill this need.

Often, this process leads to some frustrating correspondence with Service Center employees. Those in the Entity Section generally mail a form letter as their initial response to this inquiry. The form letter says, "IRS procedures allow for issuance of IRSN's only when tax returns are filed or estimated tax payments are made. After your return or payment is received by IRS, a number will be assigned to you and a letter will be sent informing you of this number."

This is well and good, but it does not satisfy the need for a number to allow third-party payors, such as a bank or employer, to record a number *prior to* making payments or submitting information returns. Without a number on file with the third-party payors, the law requires 31 percent of the payment to be withheld and sent to the IRS. This procedure is referred to as backup withholding. It is avoided when a TIN is on file with the payor.

If you push Entity Control with explanations of the immediate need for a number to accommodate third-party payors, it will issue the number. It may take a couple letters, however, to make them understand the situation.

Upon receipt of an IRSN, you would do well to refrain from using it in situations other than where a TIN is lawfully demanded for tax purposes.

2. AFFIDAVIT PROVING THE DEPENDENT EXEMPTION

The IRSN serves well for those adults required to file an annual tax return, but who oppose the use of an SSN. The question remains, however, why brand a young child with a number, regardless of its nature or origin, if that child earns no income or otherwise, has no independent obligation to file returns? That answer for some may be that *no* number of any kind is appropriate. The next question is whether minor children can be claimed on an income tax return, even without an IRSN. I believe the answer to be yes.

Please recall the purpose, according to Congress, of requiring TIN's for minor children in the first place. Congress claimed in 1986 the level of exemption fraud required TIN's to enable the IRS to ensure both that the claimed children actually exist, and that they are not claimed on any other tax return. The issue then, is not one of a number *per se*. The issue is whether you can prove the children exist and are not claimed on any other tax return.

Code sections 151 and 152 prescribe the right to claim dependents as exemptions and the conditions under which they might be claimed. Under Code section 151, an exemption is allowed for the citizen himself, his spouse, and his children, provided they meet certain requirements. The general requirements for children are that they must be fewer than 19 years of age at the close of the year claimed. If the child is a student, he must be fewer than 24 years of age at the close of the year claimed. Under Code section 151(d), no exemption can be claimed for any dependent, if that dependent is claimed on some other tax return.

Code section 152 defines a dependent broadly as any person related by blood or marriage to the principle citizen. This includes, of course, a son or daughter, or stepson or stepdaughter. Section 152 also mandates allowance of the exemption when "over half" of the annual support of the dependent is paid by the principle citizen.

Interestingly, neither section 151 nor 152 make any mention of the need for an SSN, or any TIN for that matter, in order to claim the exemption. The key to winning a dependent exemption, therefore, has little to do with a TIN. Rather, it has to do with proving the elements of the exemption as outlined above. And this stands to reason. The mere presence of a TIN of any kind does not prove a blood or marriage relationship between the dependent and the principle citizen. Nor does it prove "over half" the support of the dependent was provided by the principle citizen.

In fact, the presentation of a TIN of any kind does not even prove the TIN was legitimately assigned by either the IRS or the SSA. Many studies have proven social security fraud is rampant. It takes nothing to obtain such a number, other than a simple application on Form SS-5. The SSA issues the number under any name appearing on the SS-5. This accounts for the fact that there may be as many as 4 million bogus social security numbers in circulation. Then what good is *any TIN* in the battle against exemption fraud?

Therefore, the best solution to the problem addresses both the needs of the IRS, *and*, those of the citizen opposed to the use of identifying numbers for minor children. The best solution is the use of an affidavit establishing facts which independently prove the elements of Code sections 151 and 152. As we learned in Chapter Two, an affidavit is a sworn statement providing testimony as to the matter asserted. When the testimony is plausible, believable and *uncontradicted*, it must be accepted as legitimate proof of a deduction, or in this case, an exemption.

To independently prove the existence of dependent exemptions lacking a TIN, use an affidavit to establish the elements of the statute mentioned. Your affidavit should declare that you are religiously opposed to the use of social security numbers for minor children. Therefore, you are exempt from the requirement to use such numbers for your exemptions. State the names, dates of birth and ages of your children. State that each of the claimed dependents is related to you by blood or marriage, and state the nature of the relationship. State that you provided more than 51 percent of the support for the children during the year in question.

I provide a pattern affidavit as an example of how to accomplish drafting the claim. See Exhibit 3-3, reproduced on the following page. In addition to the affidavit, it may be desirable to provide further proof of the existence of the children. This is easily accomplished by attaching a copy of the child's birth certificate to the affidavit.

In addition to using the affidavit to verify the legal elements of the exemptions, use Form 8275 to audit- and penalty-proof the claim. (See Chapter Two for details.) While the law is clear no SSN is required for religious objectors, we can't be sure the IRS won't react in a negative fashion. Therefore, support the claim with the necessary disclosures at the time you file the return. When completing Form 1040, simply enter: *"Religious objector—see attached"* on the line calling for dependents' social security numbers. The attachments are those documents I just described.

As I said earlier, there is no language in either Code section 151 or 152 that requires a number in order to enjoy the exemption. However, the IRS has been known to disallow exemptions claimed without an SSN, if they *are not* otherwise adequately proven with an affidavit. Should the IRS issue a challenge, take comfort in knowing you have the right to appeal its decision. No decision is final unless and until you have an opportunity to appeal it. (See Chapter Five for more details on this important right.)

RECOVERING LOST EXEMPTIONS

Some time after Congress enacted Code section 6109(e), the IRS issued a report entitled, *Where Have All the Dependents Gone?* In it, the agency bragged that millions fewer exemptions were claimed on tax returns as a result of the new law. The agency was quick to conclude the missing exemptions must have been fraudulent. Otherwise, parents surely would have obtained social security numbers in order to continue claiming them. The thought that countless Christians *gave up* their right to claim legitimate exemptions because of the law's conflict with their religious principles never occurred to them.

I know for a fact that untold numbers of Christian parents simply surrendered the issue when faced with what seemed to be no alternative. Rather than compromise their sincere religious convictions, they chose instead to pay more taxes than lawfully required. I know this happened because I have spoken with dozens of people who did this very thing. As a result of the IRS' campaign

Exhibit 3-3

EXHIBIT 3-3 -- AFFIDAVIT VERIFYING DEPENDENT EXEMPTIONS

AFFIDAVIT OF _____(Your full Name)_____

STATE OF _____)
) ss
COUNTY OF _____)

    I, _____(Your full Name)_____, being first duly sworn on oath, depose and state as follows:

    1. I am the principle citizen named in the attached Form 1040, Individual Income Tax return for the year _____.

    2. I am religiously opposed to the use of social security numbers. As a result of my deep-seated, sincerely held religious opposition to the use of a social security number, I have not obtained such numbers for my minor child (children).

    3. I am claiming _____ dependent exemption(s) on the attached income tax return. The exemption(s) is/are for the minor child (children) who lived with me during the year _____.

    4. The name(s), age(s), date(s) of birth and relationship of the child (children) is/are as follows:

        a. (Separately list names, ages, birth dates, and relationship of children, i.e., son, daughter, stepdaughter, etc.)

    5. Attached to this affidavit and made a part hereof please find a true and correct copy (copies) of the birth certificate(s) for the child (children) named in paragraph 4.

    6. I provided at least 51 percent of the support of each of the children named above during the year in question.

    7. None of these children are claimed as exemptions on any other income tax return for the year _____. (Note: The year entered here must match that mentioned in paragraphs 1 and 3.)

    Date: _____

_____
Your Signature

Subscribed and sworn to before me
this _____ day of _____, 19_____.

_____
Signature and Seal of Notary Public

NOTE: This affidavit must be signed in the presence of a notary public. Attach the original affidavit to your return with Form 8275 and keep a copy with your tax records. Include copies of birth certificates, not originals. Keep the originals in your personal files.

insisting all must have a number, these Christians felt trapped. They were literally bluffed into paying more taxes than they owed.

Any person who fell victim to the disinformation disseminated by the IRS on this topic has a remedy. Code section 6402 permits a citizen to recover any tax, penalty or interest erroneously paid or collected. The process of obtaining a refund is done through the administrative vehicle of a Claim for Refund. Code section 6511(a) provides the Claim for Refund must be made "within 3 years from the time the return was filed or 2 years from the time the tax was paid, whichever of such periods expires the latter. . ."

In the case of a tax return which abandoned dependent exemptions, the right to file a claim for refund expires three years after filing the return. For example, suppose you timely filed a 1991 return without claiming dependent exemptions because of intimidation. The filing date of the 1991 return is April 15, 1992. The three-year period for filing a Claim for Refund expires on April 15, 1995.

The Claim for Refund on this issue is made by filing Form 1040X, *Amended Individual Income Tax Return*. The form and instructions are available from the IRS. Reproduced here is the 1992 version of the 1040X for review purposes. *(See Exhibit 3-4 on the following two pages.)*

Note the top of page 2 of the form. The remarks plainly indicate this form is available to claim exemptions not claimed on the original return. (See line 30.)

Of course you may also note that line 30 seeks the dependent's SSN. In the space provided for the number, enter the phrase *"Religious objector - see attached."* Attach to the 1040X documentation necessary to prove the independent existence of the children as outlined in the previous section. This includes the affidavit, Form 8275 and copies of the childrens' birth certificates.

As I have already proven, the IRS cannot deny an exemption simply due to lack of a TIN when you prove the elements of sections 151 and 152 through independent means.

Don is a Christian father who used these very techniques to recapture his lost dependent exemptions. When Don first saw IRS announcements concerning the need for a social security number, he did not take them seriously. He filed his 1987 return claiming his children as exemptions without numbers and without stating any objection to the number. He received a "stern" letter from the IRS explaining that if he persisted with this practice, he would be "penalized."

As a result of the threat and Don's religious objections, he simply gave up on the exemptions. He filed both state and federal income tax returns for the years 1988, 1989 and 1990, without claiming his lawful exemptions. He believed he was simply "dutifully bound" to suffer the financial loss to stand up for his religious liberty.

Then Don happened upon my newsletter articles addressing this issue. He followed the Claim for Refund procedures I outline in this chapter. On August 19, 1991, Don happily reported that he received a refund of all excess taxes paid for 1988 and 1989. Don recovered a total of $2,184 dollars, money which had been given up for lost. Exhibit 3-5 is a copy of Don's letter.

Exhibit 3-4 (page one)

Form 1040X
(Rev. October 1992)

Department of the Treasury—Internal Revenue Service
Amended U.S. Individual Income Tax Return
▶ See separate instructions.

OMB No. 1545-0091
Expires 10-31-94

This return is for calendar year ▶ 19____ , OR fiscal year ended ▶. ____ , 19____ .

Please print or type

Your first name and initial Last name	Your social security number
If a joint return, spouse's first name and initial Last name	Spouse's social security number
Home address (number and street). If you have a P.O. box, see instructions. Apt. no.	Telephone number (optional) ( )
City, town or post office, state, and ZIP code. If you have a foreign address, see instructions.	For Paperwork Reduction Act Notice, see page 1 of separate instructions.

Enter name and address as shown on original return. If same as above, write "Same." If changing from separate to joint return, enter names and addresses from original returns.

A Service center where original return was filed

B Has original return been changed or audited by the IRS? ☐ Yes ☐ No
If "No," have you been notified that it will be? . . . . ☐ Yes ☐ No
If "Yes," identify the IRS office ▶

C Are you amending your return to include any item (loss, credit, deduction, other tax benefit, or income) relating to a tax shelter required to be registered? . . . . ☐ Yes ☐ No
If "Yes," you must attach **Form 8271**, Investor Reporting of Tax Shelter Registration Number.

D Filing status claimed. Note: You cannot change from joint to separate returns after the due date has passed.

On original return ▶ ☐ Single ☐ Married filing joint return ☐ Married filing separate return ☐ Head of household ☐ Qualifying widow(er)
On this return ▶ ☐ Single ☐ Married filing joint return ☐ Married filing separate return ☐ Head of household ☐ Qualifying widow(er)

Income and Deductions (see instructions) Caution: Be sure to complete Part II on page 2.		A. As originally reported or as adjusted (see instructions)	B. Net change—Increase or (Decrease)—explain on page 2	C. Correct amount
1 Total income	1			
2 Adjustments to income	2			
3 Adjusted gross income. Subtract line 2 from line 1 . . .	3			
4 Itemized deductions or standard deduction	4			
5 Subtract line 4 from line 3	5			
6 Exemptions. If changing, fill in Parts I and II on page 2 . .	6			
7 Taxable income. Subtract line 6 from line 5	7			
Tax Liability 8 Tax (see instructions). Method used in col. C	8			
9 Credits (see instructions)	9			
10 Subtract line 9 from line 8. Enter the result but not less than zero .	10			
11 Other taxes (such as self-employment tax, alternative minimum tax, etc.)	11			
12 Total tax. Add lines 10 and 11	12			
Payments 13 Federal income tax withheld and excess social security, Medicare, and RRTA taxes withheld. If changing, see instructions	13			
14 Estimated tax payments	14			
15 Earned income credit	15			
16 Credits for Federal tax paid on fuels, regulated investment company, etc.	16			
17 Amount paid with Form 4868, Form 2688, or Form 2350 (application for extension of time to file) .			17	
18 Amount paid with original return plus additional tax paid after it was filed			18	
19 Add lines 13 through 18 in column C			19	

Refund or Amount You Owe

20 Overpayment, if any, as shown on original return or as previously adjusted by the IRS . . .	20	
21 Subtract line 20 from line 19 (see instructions)	21	
22 **AMOUNT YOU OWE.** If line 12, column C, is more than line 21, enter the difference and see instructions .	22	
23 **REFUND** to be received. If line 12, column C, is less than line 21, enter the difference . . .	23	

Sign Here
Keep a copy of this return for your records.

Under penalties of perjury, I declare that I have filed an original return and that I have examined this amended return, including accompanying schedules and statements, and to the best of my knowledge and belief, this amended return is true, correct, and complete. Declaration of preparer (other than taxpayer) is based on all information of which the preparer has any knowledge.

▶ Your signature   Date   ▶ Spouse's signature. If a joint return, BOTH must sign.   Date

Paid Preparer's Use Only

Preparer's signature ▶	Date	Check if self-employed ☐	Preparer's social security no.
Firm's name (or yours if self-employed) and address ▶		E.I. No.	
		ZIP code	

Cat. No. 11360L

Form **1040X** (Rev. 10-92)

5

Exhibit 3-4 (page two)

Form 1040X (Rev. 10-92)   Page **2**

Part I	Exemptions. See Form 1040 or Form 1040A instructions.		A. Number originally reported	B. Net change	C. Correct number
	If you are not changing your exemptions, do not complete this part. If claiming more exemptions, complete lines 24–30 and, if applicable, line 31. If claiming fewer exemptions, complete lines 24–29.				

			A. Number originally reported	B. Net change	C. Correct number
24	Yourself and spouse	24			
	Caution: *If your parents (or someone else) can claim you as a dependent (even if they chose not to), you cannot claim an exemption for yourself.*				
25	Your dependent children who lived with you	25			
26	Your dependent children who did not live with you due to divorce or separation . . . . .¹.	26			
27	Other dependents	27			
28	Total number of exemptions. Add lines 24 through 27	28			
29	**For tax year 1992,** if the amount on page 1, line 3, is more than $78,950, see the instructions. Otherwise, multiply $2,300 by the number of exemptions claimed on line 28. **For tax year 1991,** if the amount on page 1, line 3, is more than $75,000, see the instructions. Otherwise, multiply $2,150 by the number of exemptions claimed on line 28. **For tax year 1990,** use $2,050; **for tax year 1989,** use $2,000. Enter the result here and on page 1, line 6	29			

30   Dependents (children and other) not claimed on original return:

(a) Dependent's name (first, initial, and last name)	(b) Check if under age 1 (under age 2 if a 1989 or 1990 return)	(c) If age 1 or older (age 2 or older if a 1989 or 1990 return), enter dependent's social security number	(d) Dependent's relationship to you	(e) No. of months lived in your home	
					No. of your children on line 30 who lived with you . . ▶ ☐
_____					No. of your children on line 30 who didn't live with you due to divorce or separation (see instructions) ▶ ☐
_____					
_____					No. of other dependents listed on line 30 . . . ▶ ☐
_____					

31   If your child listed on line 30 didn't live with you but is claimed as your dependent under a pre-1985 agreement, check here   .   .   .   . ▶ ☐

Part II	Explanation of Changes to Income, Deductions, and Credits

Enter the line number from page 1 for each item you are changing and give the reason for each change. Attach all supporting forms and schedules for items changed. If you don't, your Form 1040X may be returned. Be sure to include your name and social security number on any attachments.

If the change pertains to a net operating loss carryback or a general business credit carryback, attach the schedule or form that shows the year in which the loss or credit occurred. See instructions. Also, check here .   .   .   . ▶ ☐

_____

_____

_____

_____

_____

_____

_____

_____

_____

_____

Part III	Presidential Election Campaign Fund

Checking below will not increase your tax or reduce your refund.

If you did not previously want to have $1 go to the fund but now want to, check here .   .   .   . ▶ ☐
If a joint return and your spouse did not previously want to have $1 go to the fund but now wants to, check here .   .   . ▶ ☐

Exhibit 3-5

DON

IL 61761 (309)

August 19, 1991

Mr. Daniel J. Pilla
c/o WINNING Publications
506 Kenny Rd., Suite 120
St. Paul, MN 55101

Dear Dan:

Here's the letter I promised you.

In 1986 when the IRS stated that I could no longer claim my children as dependents on future federal tax returns unless I "numbered" them, I did not take them seriously. With my '87 return, I claimed my children as usual without SSN's and promptly received a refund for overpayment of taxes along with a *stern* letter from the IRS demanding that "numbers" be submitted on future returns or I would be *penalized*. I took it to heart and did not claim my children on my '88 and '89 returns.

It must be understood that I truly have a religious conviction regarding the "numbering of my children", and was therefore dutifully bound to suffer the financial loss every April. *Until I found out the TRUTH — thanks to you.*

Using information from your books, "Pilla Talks TAXES" newsletter, and our phone conversations, I filed my '90 return claiming my children without SSN's. I simply wrote *religious objection* where the SSN's were to go and provided the IRS with certified copies of my children's birth certificates. Additionally, I filed '88 and '89 amended 1040X returns doing the same. I am delighted to inform you that I received all money due me from my federal '88, '89, and '90 1040 returns — $1405 plus interest for '88 and '89 and an additional $779 for '90. I am still waiting for my refunds from my '88 and '89 amended state returns.

My sincere thanks!

P.S. The info I purchased from you has provided the best rate of return for any financial investment I have ever made.

For more information on the Claim for Refund process and applicable law, please see Chapter Five, *Taxpayers' Ultimate Defense Manual.*

Conclusion

While the growth of the IRS certainly poses a direct threat to our constitutional system, Congress has yet to muster the courage to toss our national heritage into the legal trash bin. As seen from the analysis presented here, both Congress and the courts acknowledge a great many citizens are affronted by the claimed need to number each child, practically at birth. As long as government adheres to the principle of religious liberty expressed in the plain language of the First Amendment, no Christian can be required to surrender his beliefs regarding social security numbers.

4

THE UNTAX PROMISE

Taxes produce more than revenue for government. They often produce economic calamity, political oppression and ultimately, *Tax Protesters*.

Tax protesters can operate legally or illegally. The best example of a *legal* tax protester is Howard Jarvis. He used the political process, backed by the power of public opinion, to radically alter California's real estate tax system. His efforts over a decade ago produced change which positively affected and continues to benefit every California home owner.

On the other hand, IRS defines an *illegal* tax protester as one who attempts to reduce or eliminate his tax burden through methods which are *not legal*. See Internal Revenue Manual, section 4293.11. History provides a plethora of examples of how tax protesters attempted to eliminate their tax burden in a fashion considered *illegal* by the IRS and the federal courts. Such efforts usually involve the non-filing of tax returns and non-payment of taxes based upon the claim the nation's tax laws or the manner in which they are implemented are unconstitutional.

The arguments suggest the filing of income tax returns and payment of taxes is voluntary, not mandatory. They suggest numerous other reasons why one need not comply with the tax laws.

The arguments are not new. What changes from time to time are the people who make them or the number of people willing to listen. It seems that as our national tax burdens increase, so do the number of citizens willing to take a chance on the correctness of the arguments espoused.

What does not change is the IRS' reaction to the arguments. As I reveal in this chapter, the IRS and federal courts neither agree with nor tolerate the claims. Even before Bill Clinton took the oath of office, there were as many as 25 million citizens facing tax debts they cannot pay. With Clinton's tax increase and enforcement agenda, that number is sure to escalate. As it does so will the number of people willing to risk their future by gambling on the success of one or more programs designed to eliminate taxes.

The discussion of these issues is critical for the simple reason that arguments against filing returns and paying taxes just do not work. In virtually every case, utilizing these methods of "solving" IRS problems has only made them worse. History has proven therefore, that staying away from these arguments is an effective method of keeping the IRS out of your Life.

The Latest Wave of Protester Activity

In recent years, much noise has been made by various groups which purport to be able to *"untax"* a citizen. The groups go by various names and hail from various locals. They conduct seminars throughout the country extolling the merits of their particular "untax" program. Each claim their program will eliminate a person's obligation to file income tax returns or pay taxes, forever! Each group asserts their program is the best for any number of reasons.

To claim the benefits of being "untaxed," one is charged a substantial fee. In speaking with people who have paid or have been asked to, I find fees ranging from $500 to over $5,000. In exchange, documents are drafted, mailed to the IRS and other government agencies. They purport to accomplish the "untax" feat. The promise is made that, in the "unlikely event" the IRS challenges one's untax position, the organization will come to his defense.

As you might imagine, a person in trouble with the IRS could easily be lured with the promise of a fast and painless solution to his problem. Similarly, those pressured each year to pay taxes they cannot afford find themselves reasoning that while $5,000 is a lot of money, if successful, they will save many times that amount in years to come.

I have no way of knowing exactly how many people have been induced into the "untax" program. I do know some "untax" advocates claim tens of thousands have joined their ranks. I also know that while appearing on talk shows this past tax season, I was questioned on numerous occasions by those touched with the "untax" message. Either the caller wanted my view on the legitimacy of the program, or lambasted me for my opposition to it. In any event, the matter is of great interest.

The Untaxers' Claims

Several legal arguments are advanced to substantiate the claim that one can "untax" himself. Here I will identify the major arguments, and present a response to each.

1. "The tax laws are voluntary. No law requires one to file a return or pay taxes."

Often, promotional literature claims there is no law requiring the filing of income tax returns, or payment of federal income taxes. The argument contends that filing income tax returns and paying taxes is entirely voluntary.

To support the claim, they point to selected statements of former IRS Commissioners. The statements are usually found in the *Introduction* portion of tax return instruction packages. Such statements declare that our tax system is "based upon voluntary compliance."

For example, at page three of the 1992 instruction booklet for Form 1040, IRS Commissioner Shirley Peterson states:

"You are among the millions of Americans who comply with the tax law *voluntarily.* * * *"

Do you believe IRS' use of the term "voluntary," in this context, means you have the option of either paying or not paying your taxes? What do you think the IRS would say if asked this question? The answer lies in IRS Publication 7285, *Income Tax Compliance Research*, at page 1. There we see an IRS definition of "voluntary compliance." It is said to be the payment of taxes "without actual enforcement action, such as examination, collection or criminal investigation."

When you file your return and pay your taxes, it is done voluntarily only in the sense that nobody is holding a gun to your head at that moment. However, make no mistake about it, the law provides serious civil and criminal penalties should you fail in your legal duty regarding return filing and tax payment.

In Commissioner Peterson's opening statement referred to above, she is discussing the IRS' "new attitude." The attitude change is the subject of my book, *How to Get Tax Amnesty*. She points out the IRS is making an effort to bring non-filers back into the system and make life easier on those who cannot pay. But she tempers those words with this threat:

> "* * *At the same time, *we will direct our enforcement efforts* toward those who willfully fail to report [i.e. file returns] and pay the proper amount of tax. All must pay their fair share, just as you are doing."

Tax enforcement implies the power to lien, levy and seize property for the payment of taxes. It also implies the power to audit returns and assess additional taxes when appropriate. Finally, it implies the power to criminally prosecute and imprison those who willfully fail to comply with the law.

The claim that tax return filing is voluntary is not new. It was not conceived by any of the latest wave of untaxers. The argument is at least *eleven years old*. (Please bear in mind that I have been a tax consultant for seventeen years and have seen each of these arguments come and go.)

The first time I saw the argument presented as a legal defense to paying income taxes was in a book by Irwin A. Schiff. That book is entitled, *How Anyone Can Stop Paying Income Taxes*. Schiff's book was published in 1982. Schiff was the only protest promoter ever to achieve national prominence of any kind. He appeared on radio talk shows around the nation and made two appearances on the old NBC *Tomorrow Show*, with Tom Synder.

Schiff's position was very straigh forward. He contended filing an income tax return was a violation of one's Fifth Amendment right. He contended because the IRS can and often did use one's tax return information against him for either civil or criminal purposes, filing a return could not legally be compelled. Schiff contended that because you could not be compelled in any other legal circumstance to waive your Fifth Amendment right against self-incrimination, you cannot therefore be compelled to do so where tax collection is concerned.

Schiff concluded that filing a return must therefore be entirely *voluntary*. He went on in his work to claim the IRS used a vast system of bluff and intimidation to make Americans believe they were required to file, when in fact they were not. Schiff also opined if one elected not to file a return, the IRS was entirely powerless to do anything about it.

Schiff presented carefully excised portions of the tax code to support his proposition. Using carefully crafted sections of the code and equally selective passages from various court decisions, the case was made that Schiff's position was entirely correct. To the legally untrained or inexperienced, Schiff's position seemed not only sound, but incontrovertible.

So convinced he was correct, Schiff offered a $100,000 reward to anyone who could show him any law that required the filing of a tax return. His challenge was publicized on radio in every city.

I took him up on it. In a letter to Schiff in about 1984, I detailed the statutory scheme which, based upon judicial declarations, requires the filing of a return and payment of taxes. My letter explained the tax code is an intentionally complex compilation of statutes which must be *read together, not individually*. Only in rare instances can a particular code section stand alone. When considering whether one must file a return and pay taxes, a series of code sections must be read together. Let me illustrate.

Code sections 6011 and 6012 establish the requirement to file a return on the part of any person who receives income in excess of the threshold amounts shown in the statutes. The term "income" as used in the tax code is defined in Code sections 61, 62 and 63. The tax liability itself is imposed under Code section 1. That section specifies the amount of tax based upon one's filing status and income brackets. The tax liability is "imposed upon the taxable income" of each person within the specified categories. See Code section 1.

Having established the requirement to file and pay, let us now address more clearly the "voluntary" nature of the matter. Code section 6651 establishes a civil penalty of up to 75 percent of the tax due, for failure to file a required return in a timely manner. In addition, Code sections 6653 and 6661 (other sections may apply depending upon the time period involve) impose civil penalties for failure to pay on time and failure to pay the correct amount of tax. The penalties are based upon a percentage of the tax due. They increase as the underpayment increases.

Criminal sanctions for failure to file a return or pay the tax are found in Code section 7203. That provision makes it a misdemeanor offense for any person to willfully fail to file any return required by law, or fail to pay any tax due. Upon conviction, a person may be fined up to $25,000 or imprisoned for up to one year. Section 7201 is the felony "tax evasion" statute. It provides a penalty of up to five years in prison and a $100,000 fine for willfully attempting to evade or defeat payment of the tax.

Without going into greater detail, the code provides over *150 different civil and criminal penalties* addressing all imaginable actions and failures to act. The IRS issues some 30 million civil penalties each year, and prosecutes about 2,500 citizens for various crimes, including failure to file returns and tax evasion.

In June of 1992, Commissioner Peterson testified before Congress concerning the IRS' non-filer program. The program was offered to allow non-filers to obtain forgiveness. After explaining the positive aspects of the program, Commissioner Peterson stated:

"* * *But, for those taxpayers who don't accept our encouragement, we will use a more direct approach. For example, during 1993, over 1200 examiners will audit the books and records of non-filers, including high income non-filers. Through coordination between IRS and the Department of Justice, we are also employing criminal sanctions in appropriate cases. About 300 criminal cases involving failure to file tax returns have been brought within the past few months. We expect that this number will increase as we identify more taxpayers who persist in willfully failing to comply with the law."

I submit to you it would be a legal impossibility for any person to be prosecuted, never mind convicted, of failure to file a tax return, if the matter were purely voluntary. The reality is, there is nothing voluntary about the filing requirement. As I point out above, specific statutes mandate the filing of returns when income exceeds specified levels. When one fails to do so, the IRS is adequately equipped with over 150 civil and criminal penalty provisions to enforce the law.

Not the least of these tools is the ability, under Code section 6621(c), to charge interest at the rate of 120 percent the usual applicable rate, when the underpayment is considered "tax motivated." That is to say, when one fails to properly report or pay his taxes on grounds purely associated with an effort to improperly reduce his tax burden

Whatever Happened to Irwin Schiff? The father of the theory that paying federal income taxes is purely voluntary was convicted of tax evasion and spent time in federal prison on three separate occasions. All Schiff's arguments were considered and rejected by the courts. Anyone interested in pursuing the "untax" theories must first read the history of Schiff's litigation with the IRS. The following cases provide much insight to the effectiveness of the "voluntary" argument: *United States v. Schiff*, 780 F. 2d 210 (2nd Cir. 1986); *United States v. Schiff*, 801 F.2d 108 (2nd Cir. 1986); *United States v. Schiff*, 876 F.2d 272 (2nd Cir. 1989); *United States v. Schiff*, 919 F.2d 830 (2nd Cir. 1990); *Schiff v. Commissioner*, 751 F.2d 115 (2nd Cir. 1985); and *Schiff v. Commissioner*, 47 TCM 1706 (U.S. Tax Court 1984) (the last two decision address the pure income tax aspects of Schiff's arguments).

I also insist one read the case of *Ficalora v. Commissioner*, 751 F.2d 85 (2nd Cir. 1984). That case answers the question once and for all whether the filing of income tax returns is voluntary. Using precisely the argument I outline above as to the Code's construction, the Second Circuit Court of Appeals held that section 1 of the Code "provides in plain, clear, and precise language that a tax is imposed on the taxable income of every individual." *Ficalora* takes the guesswork out of the voluntary argument.

If you still doubt it, read *United States v. Stafford*, 93-1 U.S.T.C. 50,235 (5th Cir. 1993). Stafford failed to file returns and was convicted in a criminal prosecution of three counts of tax evasion, a felony under code section 7201. He was sentenced to three years' probation with six months served in a half-way house. Stafford's claim that filing a return was purely voluntary got him nothing more than a felony conviction.

Modern untaxers have done nothing more than resurrect and face-lift an old Irwin Schiff argument. The Tax Court has ruled literally hundreds of times against this and similar arguments. The court, frankly, is losing its patience with those making these arguments. Under the authority of Code section 6673, the Court is fining citizens up to $10,000, for wasting the Court's time raising arguments which have failed time and again. In various cases, the Court has referred to the "voluntary" argument as frivolous, meritless, groundless and patently ridiculous.

2. "The IRS is not a government agency. It is a private corporation incorporated in Delaware, July 11, 1933."

Unlike others claims, this one relies upon no legal theory. It makes no challenge, however far-reaching or unsound, of the legal principles behind the government's right to collect taxes. Rather, it asserts the somewhat incredible theory that IRS is not part of the federal government. This theory claims the IRS is a private corporation and our taxes do not fund the federal government.

To determine the legitimacy of this contention I did some research. On July 12, 1933, a company was granted a corporate charter under the laws of the State of Delaware. The corporation was entitled, *Internal Revenue Tax and Audit Service, Inc.* Within the corporate charter is a description of the purpose of the *Internal Revenue Tax and Audit Service, Inc.* In part, the document reads:

> "* * *Generally to conduct an Income Tax Accounting and Auditing business, and to act as Income Tax Accountants and Auditors for persons, firms, corporations, syndicates and others, and to make charges for the sale of (our) Income Tax Accounting Book of Forms, and for such other services as may be appropriate."

The three founders of the *Internal Revenue Tax and Audit Service, Inc.*, were accountants. They compiled a book of tax preparation forms and instructions. They incorporated their business to sell the book and prepare income tax returns. That company was nothing more than an old-time equivalent of H & R Block. That company did not, in its day, collect income taxes due the government any more than H & R Block does today.

As one reads the corporate charter of *Internal Revenue Tax and Audit Service, Inc.*, he finds no authority whatsoever to collect taxes. The company does not purport to be a tax collector, nor could it. What we have is nothing more than a similarity in name, but absolutely no relationship in legal standing or authority.

All taxes in this country are collected by the Internal Revenue Service, an agency under the direct authority of the Department of Treasury. All IRS employees are federal government employees. The Commissioner of IRS and Secretary of Treasury, the two top tax officials in the nation, are both Presidential appointees. Each must be confirmed by the United States Senate prior to taking office.

It is also interesting to note the date on which the Internal *Revenue Tax and Audit Service, Inc.*, came into existence. That alone should prove the assertion is meritless. Please note that the corporation was created in July of *1933*. However, the income tax came into being in *1913*. What happened to income tax revenues for the first 20 years if they are not collected by the government?

Another small fact untaxers overlook is that the *Internal Revenue Tax and Audit Service, Inc.*, no longer exists! The corporation was *involuntarily dissolved* by the State of Delaware in April of 1936, not three years after it was created. Can you guess why the company was dissolved? *Because it failed to pay its corporate income taxes for two consecutive years!* I find it hysterically ironic that the company alleged to collect all U.S. taxes was dissolved against its will for failure to pay taxes!

The above information can be verified with the Office of Secretary of State, State of Delaware. The applicable corporate file number is 0325720. Check it out for yourself and do not be misled. The cost is too high.

3. "Secret IRS memo proves the Sixteenth Amendment was never ratified."

To explain this argument, I must provide some history. In 1984, Bill Benson, a former investigator for the Illinois Department of Revenue, began a sweeping research project. Bill went state by state, reviewing the historical documents surrounding the ratification of the 16th Amendment. That amendment, you should know, established the federal income tax in 1913.

Bill conducted a very costly, time consuming project. It took him deep into the archives of every state capital in the nation. When completed, Bill possessed documentary evidence certified by the Secretaries of State of each state. The evidence revealed first hand information on how the various legislatures voted regarding ratification.

Bill's irrefutable research proved the 16th Amendment *was not* ratified by the requisite three-fourths of the states. However, when the states' ratification resolutions were presented to U.S. Secretary of State Knox, he incorrectly deemed them to have ratified the amendment. He then falsely reported ratification to Congress. Consequently, Congress improperly declared the amendment ratified and enacted it into law. Bill's research is compiled in two lengthy volumes, entitled *The Law that Never Was*, Volumes I and II.

After Bill completed his initial research, but prior to writing his first volume, he contacted Attorney Lowell (Larry) Becraft of Huntsville, Alabama. Larry is a consummate trial attorney. He has been working tirelessly in the courts for taxpayers' rights for years. I have worked with Larry many times over the years. I have the utmost respect for his skill and judgment. Because of his encyclopedic approach to legal issues, he was the best–the only–attorney to present Bill's research in a court of law.

At that time, Larry was defending Janie Ferguson of Indiana. She was charged with tax evasion under Code section 7201. Her case was set for trial in Indianapolis on January 15, 1985. It was decided the ratification issue would be presented as a defense.

On January 15, 1985, Larry presented evidence to the court through testimony of Bill. The prosecutor, Assistant U. S. Attorney Roger Duncan, admitted Bill's documents were unimpeachable and authentic. According to Larry, Duncan had no real idea as to how to reply. However, the next day, the trial judge ruled the matter to be a "political issue." As such, it could not be addressed by any court. The Ferguson case went to trial and Janie was eventually found guilty of failure to file and sentenced to prison on April 15, 1985. Larry immediately appealed the case to the Seventh Circuit Court of Appeals.

In the meantime, two fellows by the name of Thomas and Foster from the Chicago area got wind of the ratification issue. They were charged with tax crimes but had no idea how to defend the charges. Rather than seek Larry's assistance in their own case, they filed mere pro forma motions based upon Larry's argument in the Ferguson case. They never went to the trouble of obtaining any proof to support their contention. Naturally, they lost. They were convicted and appealed their case, also to the Seventh Circuit Court of Appeals.

On Appeal, Thomas and Foster again raised the ratification issue. Again, however, they failed to present any evidence or argument in support. Instead, they simply made reference to Larry's substantial work in the Ferguson case. This practice is strictly forbidden by the Rules of Procedure for Appeals Courts.

Faced with three cases raising the ratification issue as a defense, the court decided to rule on the Thomas and Foster cases first. Because the arguments were entirely unsupported in those cases, it was not surprising the court ruled against the issue. The Seventh Circuit agreed with the lower court, declaring the matter a "political issue." See *United States v. Thomas*, 788 F.2d 1250 (7th Cir. 1986) and *United States v. Foster*, 789 F.2d 457 (7th Cir. 1986).

Those two decisions established a precedent — a bad precedent. That bad precedent was then used to kill Larry's well-documented argument in the Ferguson case. See *United States v. Ferguson*, 793 F.2d 828 (7th Cir. 1986). That bad precedent then quickly spread throughout the court system. Each time the issue was presented, by Larry or anybody else, the *Thomas, Foster and Ferguson* decisions of the Seventh Circuit were used to kill them. See, for example, *United States v. Stahl*, 792 F.2d 1438 (9th Cir. 1986) and *United States v. Sitka*, 845 F.2d 43 (2nd Cir. 1988).

Larry's reaction to this gross injustice is explained by him in this fashion:

> ". . .[T]he lesson to be learned about this issue is that we simply cannot permit parties who are not prepared to brief and argue a major tax issue on appeal to carry the issue up. We were denied a major battle and possible victory on the question of the non-ratification issue because of what Thomas and Foster did." –Letter of Larry Becraft, 8/21/91.

The bottom line is this: The 16th Amendment ratification issue has not prevailed in the courts because of what Thomas and Foster did. As a result, Larry has ceased using it as a legal defense. However, he and Bill continue to press the matter in the legislative arena, both with the states and with Congress.

Copies of Bill's books have been distributed to every Representative and Senator, as well as U.S. Attorneys, federal judges, governors and state attorneys general. Bill and Larry travel extensively and present the issue on both radio and television. However, both are quick to point out the issue does not constitute any defense against the income tax in general, or a tax crime in particular.

So what about the secret memorandum? Against this factual backdrop, let us now turn to the secret memorandum circulated by some untaxers and their spin-off groups and disciples. The memo first appeared in April of 1985. We do not know who was responsible for initially creating it. The memo purports to be a statement from IRS Commissioner Roscoe Egger, Jr. It purports to be directed to "All District Directors." It purports to be an IRS response to the ratification issue and the Ferguson case. The memo reads as follows:

> "On March 5, 1985, a charge of tax evasion was filed in U.S. District Court in Indianapolis, Ind. by U. S. Attorney Geo. Duncan. The charges were dismissed! The defense atty., Lowell Becraft of Huntsville Alabama presented irrefutable evidence that the 16th Amendment to the U.S. Constitution was never properly ratified. This amendment which established the 'income tax', was signed into law despite serious defects. In reality, only two States ratified the amendment and ratification requires 36 states to be valid. The effect of this is such that every tax paid into the Treasury since 1913, is due and refundable to every citizen and business.

> "The official position of the service is, as it has always been to aid and assist the citizens of the United States. We will not publish or advertise this finding as a total immediate refund would cause a serious drain on the resources of the Treasury. For those citizens who become aware of this finding and apply for a total refund, expedite their refund documents as quickly and quietly as possible. A simple 1040X form will suffice until a new form is designed and printed. Advise each of your managers that they are not to discuss this situation with anyone. There will be no written communication and you are to destroy this memorandum.

> "The Secretary of the Treasury assures me that there will be no reduction in the workforce (sic) as this refunding activity will take a minimum of 5 years to complete. Further direction will be forwarded as the need arises."

This letter, purporting to be an official notice from the IRS, is a forgery. It was not issued by the IRS. I knew it when I first saw it in about 1986, and of course Larry and Bill knew it the first time they laid eyes on it. Apart from the fact it is written on IRS letterhead and not its internal memo document, and apart from the fact it in no way even resembles the style, format or pattern of any internal IRS memo I have ever seen (and I've seen hundreds of them), it is laden with factual errors and typos.

For example, the prosecutor in the Ferguson case was *Roger* Duncan, not George Duncan. Next, Larry's argument was presented on *January 15*, 1985, not March 5, 1985. Most importantly, the charges against Ferguson *were not dismissed.* She was convicted after the court expressly rejected the ratification issue as a defense. In sum, the memo is a complete fraud!

When it first appeared, Larry, Bill and others of us who knew it was a fraud did our best to communicate that fact to the public. Bill even went so far as to run newspaper ads in selected papers explaining the facts. Eventually, the memo disappeared. However, it has now resurfaced.

While in Dallas early in 1993, I appeared on numerous radio talk shows. Without exception, a caller explained to me the 16th Amendment was not properly ratified. His proof? The IRS' "secret memorandum." The callers also announced they learned this by attending an "untax" seminar.

Larry has also been inundated with calls from those attending "untax" seminars. Since his name appears in the memo, anybody seeking more information naturally phones him. In January of 1993, Larry told me personally he was sick and tired of the "untax" crowd circulating this bogus memo and causing his phone to ring off the hook with curious taxpayers sucked into the "untax" scam. Larry asked me to do all I could to put an end to the fraud once and for all. Naturally, I agreed.

Reproduced below, as Exhibit 4-1, is Larry's personal letter to me addressing the bogus memo. Please read it carefully. As you do, bear in mind there is no more reliable source on this subject than Larry Becraft. In this regard, *he is* the horse's mouth.

Exhibit 4-1   LOWELL H. BECRAFT, JR.
                                     ATTORNEY AT LAW
                                    209 LINCOLN STREET
                                HUNTSVILLE, ALABAMA 35801

Mr. Danny Pilla   January 19, 1993
Suite 107-C
450 Oak Grove Parkway
Vadnais Heights, Minn. 55127

Re: I.R.S. Letter to District Directors

Dear Danny:
    In about May of 1985, Bill Benson and I became aware of a letter floating around within certain circles of the tax freedom movement which appeared to be authored by former Commissioner of the Internal Revenue, Roscoe Egger. That letter explained that in the Janie Ferguson case which I tried in Indianapolis in January, 1985, I had raised the issue of the non-ratification of the Sixteenth Amendment to the U.S. Constitution and had prevailed upon it. The letter stated that refunds for income taxes were due to be made to all Americans. Needless to say, both Bill and I knew from the gross factual errors within the letter that it was a forgery. And we thereafter made every effort to inform all parties possessing copies of

that letter that it was a forgery.

Everywhere we went, this letter became a subject of discussion and we informed the parties asking questions about the letter that it was a forgery. After becoming extremely tired of answering endless questions about the letter, Bill finally published an advertisement in the *Justice Times* which explained the fraudulent nature of the letter. Apparently, this message was received by the various members of the tax freedom movement and the issue involving the letter died down.

Within the last two years, the same worn out argument based on this phony letter has resurfaced, and it appears to me to be distributed by folks within the "untax" camp. Enclosed, please find a copy of a letter I have been sending to parties making inquiries of me regarding this letter. Frankly, I am tired of answering such questions con-cerning this letter and I no longer return phone calls coming from people obviously wanting some response to the letter from me. These people chase me down at home, bother me at the office, and will even call me when I am out of town. If I ever get my hands on the party responsible for the renewed distribution of this letter, I will give him more than just a piece of my mind.

As I promised, I also enclose herewith a brief I wrote many years ago regarding the issue of whether the "non-positive" law titles within the U.S. Code are valid law. Back in 1982 or sometime thereafter, this issue obtained some notoriety within the free-dom movement and I wrote this brief in answer to that argument. Peggy Christensen at Golden Mean even published this brief in her newsletter. Now after having stopped that stupid issue some years ago, it has resurfaced again within the "untax" camp.

These "flaky" arguments based upon the April 4, 1985 Egger letter, as well as arguments such as Title 26, U.S.C., is not "positive" law, serve no purpose and only harm too many gullible people. I will appreciate any effort you can make to stop these arguments from gaining any acceptance by the overtaxed American people.

Sincerely,
Larry
Lowell H. Becraft, Jr.

P.S. Hope to hear you soon on Marlin.

The IRS issued an official response concerning the bogus memo. It came from the Director of the Ogden, Utah, Service Center on December 2, 1992. It reads in part, as follows:

> "The copy of the letter you sent to us dated April 5, 1985, is fictitious. There are certain letterheads and formats used by each department of the Internal Revenue Service. It is interesting to note that several different styles have been incorporated into this one letter, and not one of them is a letterhead that would have been used by the Commissioner. It is quite obvious that several letters have been blended to come up with the finished product. This is a felony."

To the extent that any untax group circulates the bogus memo and claims it is genuine, it is knowingly and intentionally defrauding the public.

4. "The Internal Revenue Code is not law, never has been 'positive law,' and is not passed by Congress."

This argument suggests the tax code was never passed by Congress and hence, is not valid law. This issue is a dusty claim which failed many years ago.

The claim is based upon an obscure statement contained in the introductory portion of the United States Code. That is a compilation of all the laws currently in effect at the federal level. The code is broken down into fifty titles, each addressing a specific subject matter. Title 26, for example, is known as the Internal Revenue Code. It contains all the nation's tax laws.

The obscure statement found in the introduction to the code reads, "The following titles have been passed into positive law." Following is a list of several, but not all the fifty titles. Title 26, the Internal Revenue Code, is not among those which have been passed into "positive law." Based upon this statement, the claim was made a decade ago that the Internal Revenue Code was "not law." Therefore, it could not impose any obligation on the citizen to file tax returns or pay taxes. It was a variation of the "voluntary" argument we addressed above.

In approximately 1983, under pressure from various groups and individuals to "press the issue," Attorney Larry Becraft once again shined the light of truth, reason and common sense upon the "positive law" argument. Larry did extensive legal research into the system of statutory codification used by the United States Government. His research dates all the way back to March 4, 1789, when the first Congress convened in New York City.

Like all of Larry's work, his research was detailed, thorough and irrefutable. The research paper he produced is 17 pages in length. It should have put the matter to rest. It was published sometime in 1983. Without going into great detail on the intricate workings of the federal statutory reporting mechanism, Larry's findings can be summarized as follows:

All the acts of Congress, as they are passed into law and signed by the President, are published in law books known as the Statutes at Large. They appear in the Statutes at Large in the order passed. Some laws are short, with as many as four or five appearing on a given page. Others, like the tax code, go on page after endless page.

When the United States was young and few laws were passed, this system was fine. However, as Congress became more prolific in the creation of laws, it became apparent a more effective codification system would be necessary. Over the years, individuals both in and out of government combined to create the United States Code.

The code is organized topically. Each of the fifty topics is given a number, known as a title. Each title is broken down into sections. Each section constitutes a specific law. Hence, when you see the citation "26 USC 7203," that is a reference to Title 26 of the United States Code, (the Internal Revenue Code), at section 7203. That section is the criminal statute covering failure to file a tax return. In addition to the logical organization of topics, the United States Code is extensively indexed, allowing a researcher easy access to acts of Congress.

This system presently operates *along side* the Statutes at Large. It remains the practice of Congress to codify all its acts into the Statutes at Large. However, after they are passed, such acts are also codified into the United States Code for ease of research.

Any act of Congress which is codified in the Statutes at Large is considered "positive law." Its presence in the Statutes at Large constitutes irrefutable proof such law exists, was passed by Congress and was signed by the President. Acts which appear in the United States Code are not necessarily positive law. Still, the United State Code is considered "prima facie proof" of the existence of the law. Its use is suitable in court, but can be contradicted by showing what the underlying statutes are and that the code sections are different from the Statutes at Large. In such event, the statutes control. Hence, the statutes are considered "positive law." This system was established by operation of H.R. 10000, passed by Congress on June 30, 1926. It is in effect today.

In 1947, Congress began enacting entire titles of the Code into "positive law." By doing so, it eliminated the necessity to trace a law back to the Statutes at Large into order to verify its existence and status. However, not all titles have been enacted into positive law. As of the date of Larry's memo, 22 titles were enacted into positive law. Title 26, the Internal Revenue Code, is not among them.

This does not mean Title 26 is not valid law enacted by Congress. Quite the contrary. As Larry observes on page 15 of his memo, "a 'non-positive law' title is *prima facie evidence of the law*, or a reflection of the law as exemplified by the underlying statutes. . ." (Emphasis added.)

Anyone who has ever done any legal research whatsoever knows that within the Internal Revenue Code, the "Legislative History" of each individual statute is shown immediately following the text of the statute. For example, Code section 7203, according to the legislative history, was last amended by Public Law 101-647, section 3033(a), 101st Congress, Second Session, November 29, 1990.

By referencing a publication within every law library known as the *U.S. Code Congressional and Administrative News*, for the 101st Congress, I would instantly learn where within the Statutes at Large to locate the text of Public Law

101-647, section 3033(a). After locating, I would know section 7203, as it appears in Title 26, is a law indeed passed by Congress.

The entirety of the Internal Revenue Code is passed by Congress and signed into law by the President. If one wished to go to the time and trouble to trace each section back to the Statutes at Large, it is entirely possible to do so. You can bet the untaxers have not done so. Without an understanding of how the Congressional process operates, it is *grossly irresponsible*, at best, and criminal fraud, at worst, for any person to claim the Internal Revenue Code is not binding law in the United States.

Please review the final paragraph of Larry's January 19, 1993, letter to me. There he classifies this argument as "flaky." He points out the arguments "serve no purpose and only harm too many gullible people."

5. *"The Federal Reserve is receiving and keeping all the tax money you pay. None of it goes to the U.S. Treasury."*

This argument has various facets. The primary contention grows out of the mechanical process in which your tax payment is negotiated by the IRS. Untaxers contend that because your tax check is endorsed by the IRS and paid into a Federal Reserve Bank (the FED), "to the credit of the U.S. Treasury," such endorsement constitutes proof the FED got the money, and the U.S. Government did not.

This argument, like the others, is based upon a fundamental misunderstanding. In this case, the misunderstanding is as to the manner in which the banking system operates. It is true the FED is a private corporation, not a part of the U.S. Government. It is not true, however, it retains all the tax dollars deposited to FED banks throughout the nation.

The FED lends money to the United States Government to allow it to pay its obligations. The difference between what is collected in taxes and what is spent constitutes the national debt. That amount is about $4.145 trillion and rising. Between the FED and other lenders, such as purchasers of U.S. Treasury obligations, money is lent to the government at interest. Interest is paid to both the FED and other private lenders. To the extent the FED receives any payments from the U.S. Government, those payments represent interest (and perhaps principle) on the loans made to the government.

In addition to lending money to the federal government, the FED operates as a clearing house for all checks written in the United States. Have you ever considered the mechanics involved in clearing the checks you write? Consider this: you live in Orlando, Florida and bank nearby. You write a check for a magazine subscription and mail it to a company in San Francisco. The company deposits the check to its account, and within a matter of a few days, it is presented to your bank for payment. This process is known as check truncation.

The ink used to print the impression on your check blanks is magnetic. It allows the banks' processing equipment to route the checks electronically. That way, individuals do not have to hand sort millions of checks criss-crossing the nation each day. As checks are deposited to the recipients' accounts and those banks begin clearing them, a series of stamps and codes are placed on each check.

In combination, the stamps and codes indicate the bank which processed the check, the account to which the money was credited, a routing code and a sequence code.

The latter codes allow one to trace a microfilm copy of the check to the bank which processed it. Using these codes, you can verify your check was deposited to a given bank on a particular day, processed through a FED bank as a central clearing house, then presented to your own bank for payment.

The stamps and codes which appear on the back of your tax check indicate only the check was deposited to a FED bank, cleared through the FED, presented to your bank for payment, and the amount of the check was credited to the U.S. Treasury. They mean nothing more. It is as simple as that.

How do I know this? In late 1988, I was involved in a civil tax fraud trial which took place in Birmingham, Alabama. My friend and long time associate, Attorney Mike Parham, tried the case. The IRS claimed our client, Don, underreported his income by $10,700. Don used two bank accounts during the year in question. He wrote 54 checks from one account and deposited them to the other. The checks were not cashed, so all the income appeared in the bank statements, and hence, on his tax returns. The IRS attorney simply refused to accept the data in the bank statements as proof of this fact. We were forced to prove it in some other way.

We enlisted the aid of Don's banker who explained in sparkling detail how the code systems work. Without going to great length here, we were able to prove in court each check was not only redeposited to Don's second account, but we proved the precise dates the check was deposited and credited. In the January, 1989, issue of *Pilla Talks Taxes*, I report the entire story and demonstrate the manner in which the credit and sequence codes operate.

The bottom line is simple. The stamps and codes on the back of your canceled tax check prove your taxes were paid to the U.S. Government. It is ludicrous to suggest because the check was deposited to or cleared through a FED bank, the FED and not the U.S. Treasury received the money.

This argument cannot operate to eliminate any obligation to file tax returns or pay taxes.

A BRIEF HISTORY OF THE TAX MOVEMENT

As I stated earlier, tax protesters have been around since as long as taxes. In the United States, a visible and somewhat forceful tax protester movement has operated since the early 1970's. Many of these tax protesters, sometimes referred to by their peers as tax patriots, are motivated by a sincere, deep seated belief that the tax system is improper and must be changed. They make every effort to change the system in whatever way possible, including in some cases, civil disobedience.

Some tax protesters however, are motivated by greed. They see what appears to be an opportunity to keep all they earn and they take a chance. When called to account for their actions, they grasp desperately at any straw hopes of saving themselves from the consequences of their actions. In doing so, these legally uneducated and ill-prepared individuals virtually eliminate any opportunity for the well intentioned to redress their legitimate grievances. There is no better example of this than Larry's 16th Amendment case. His opportunity to correct a grave injustice was completely destroyed by Thomas and Foster.

Interestingly, the seminal issues in the infant stages of the tax protest movement were the Federal Reserve and the Fifth Amendment. As early as *1950*, Art Porth, considered the grandfather of the tax movement, challenged the FED and government's fiscal policies through tax protest. Porth sincerely believed that because U.S. currency was not backed by gold or silver, the government had no right to collect taxes on the money. However, Porth was jailed for acting on his beliefs and refusing to pay taxes. See *United States v. Porth*, 426 F.2d 519 (10th Cir. 1970) and *Porth v. Broderick*, 214 F.2d 925 (10th Cir. 1954).

Later, a former Minnesota attorney named Jerome Daly put legal polish on Porth's constitutional arguments. Daly developed the so-called Fifth Amendment tax return. Using Daly's technique, a person asserted his Fifth Amendment right against self-incrimination as a defense to completing a tax return or paying taxes. Daly was disbarred by the Minnesota Supreme Court and eventually prosecuted, convicted and served time for filing Fifth Amendment income tax returns. The IRS now refers to such returns as *Porth/Daly protest returns*. See *United States v. Daly*, 481 F.2d 28 (8th Cir. 1973).

Daly's teachings on the Fifth Amendment caught fire in the 1970's, despite his failure to file conviction. By the mid-1970's Marvin Cooley, of Phoenix, conducted seminars around the nation on the Fifth Amendment and income taxes. He sold a package known as the *Fifth Amendment Guide*. Cooley sold thousands of packages and led thousands in a claim against the government that income tax return filing violated one's constitutional rights. Cooley's claims were rejected by the courts and he too served time for failure to file tax returns. See *United States v. Cooley*, 501 F.2d 1241 (9th Cir. 1974).

In the late 1970's, along came Irwin Schiff, a man whose legal position we already examined. It is interesting to note that Schiff was the first to conduct "untax" seminars throughout the United States. He adapted the Porth/Daly/Cooley constitutional arguments into the claim that income taxes were voluntary. We already know what the courts said about those claims and what happened to Schiff.

By 1979, the IRS developed and implemented a comprehensive plan to deal administratively and judicially with tax protesters. In September of 1979, IRS issued Manual Supplement 9G-93. It was a supplement to the Criminal Investigation Handbook for Special Agents. It promulgated a system-wide procedure for identifying and dealing quickly with tax protester claims. Those policies remain in effect today.

In 1982, with the passage of the Tax Equity and Fiscal Responsibility Act (TEFRA), Congress made sweeping changes to the tax penalty and enforcement system. The changes were implemented based upon a GAO report entitled,

Illegal Tax Protesters Threaten Tax System. July 8, 1981. Under the laws, broad regulations were put into effect to deal with Forms W-4, Withholding Certificates, used by some to stop income tax withholding at the source of payment. Under these regulations, employers are mandated to send questionable Forms W-4 directly to the IRS for its review. If instructed, the employer must disregard the W-4 and withhold at the most expensive rates. See Code section 3402 and regulations thereunder. The IRS was also empowered to penalize those who file inappropriate Forms W-4. See Code section 6682 and regulations thereunder.

The penalty for filing a frivolous legal claim with the Tax Court was increased to $10,000 by TEFRA. See Code section 6673. The Tax Court, overwhelmed with what it called "frivolous claims," began handing out such penalties much like traffic tickets. It greatly reduced the number of such claims filed in the court.

Substantial changes were made to Code sections 7602 and 7609, allowing the IRS greater access to bank records for criminal prosecution purposes. The changes were made specifically because tax protesters loaded the courts with "frivolous challenges" to the IRS' summons power, hindering investigations.

Both civil and criminal penalties for failure to file and failure to pay taxes increased substantially. Among the tools now used by the IRS is the so-called interest penalty under Code section 6621(c). That law allows the IRS to charge interest on unpaid taxes at the rate of 120 percent the usual interest rate. This penalty is regularly used against tax protesters said to have engaged in a transaction solely for the purposes of improperly reducing or eliminating their tax liability. With normal interest rates and penalties already crushing, this penalty represents a policy of annihilation with respect to tax protesters.

By the mid-1980's, the IRS really began playing hardball with tax protesters. Prior to that time, the government prosecuted the vast majority of protester cases under the misdemeanor failure to file statute. Conviction under Code section 7203 carried the penalty of up to one year in prison and a $25,000 fine.

Beginning in about 1985, the IRS instituted a policy of prosecuting tax protesters under the *felony tax evasion statute,* Code section 7201. Conviction under that statute carries a penalty of up to *five years* in prison and a fine of up to $100,000. At the same time, judges began to whack tax protesters with serious sentences and fines to set an example. Now, a person faces substantial risk for following the tax protest trail.

Untaxers are either horribly ignorant and naive of the long history of tax protest litigation, or they are outright criminals, leading people down a sure path of destruction for their own personal profit. In either case, the policies they advocate failed in the past and cannot be expected to prevail in the future. As Larry pointed out in his letter (Exhibit 4-1), this stuff is the same "flaky" arguments we have seen fail for years.

Art Porth and Jerome Daly could not untax themselves 30 years ago. Marvin Cooley could not do it 20 years ago. Irwin Schiff could not do it 10 years ago. Do you believe contemporary untaxers can do it today using the same worn out, beaten-to-death arguments?

At the same time, there are those who recognize the IRS is an unjust agency which regularly violates its own laws, never mind the constitution. Those citizens, honestly persuaded that something must be done to stop this growing tyranny, insist they must take a stand against such injustice. The real crime of untaxers is they play upon these legitimate, patriotic concerns. They lead such citizens down a path perceived to be beneficial to the nation as a whole on the promise the IRS can do nothing about their "legal" protest. They are wrong.

To those citizens determined to "take a stand," I offer this grave caution: Count the cost, my friend. I am afraid you will find such a stand likely to cost your fortune, your liberty and perhaps your family. Again I say, do not undertake to build the tower until you have thoroughly *COUNTED THE COST!*

THE GOVERNMENT'S RESPONSE TO UNTAXERS

What can we expect will be government's reaction to these claims? I wish to answer this question from two perspectives. First, is from the viewpoint of the individual citizen following untax advice. Second, is from the viewpoint of the untaxers themselves.

1. What Untax Followers Can Expect. As I state earlier, the IRS developed a comprehensive manual directing agents' actions in tax protester cases. The manual describes specific types of protest documents and actions. It also addresses the manner in which the IRS is to respond to them. Consider this language from the *Introduction* to IRS Manual Part 4231, *Tax Audit Guidelines for Internal Revenue Examiners*, section (11)31 (February 23, 1982):

"(1) Some tax protesters are making speeches and offering seminars around the country at which serious misrepresentations about the tax laws are being presented to the public as fact. Generally, these protesters are counseling taxpayers not to comply with the Federal income tax return filing statutes on the ground that they violate a person's constitutional rights.

"(2) Those who use constitutional arguments have often been encouraged by promoters to use the same tactics used by other tax protesters to frustrate, intimidate, or confuse examiners in conducting their examination. Documents filed using these arguments are not generally considered valid returns, and thus do not normally satisfy the taxpayers' filing requirements."

The manual goes on to describe, in detail, the nature of the specific arguments, including those outlined above. Instructions are given on the manner of dealing with the argument and the appropriate penalties and other sanctions to employ in such cases.

Untaxers claim the IRS either does not or cannot do anything to enforce the tax code in the face of their claims. As shown above, this claim is pure nonsense. Let me give you a specific case history to prove my point. Elmer was involved in a tax audit for the year 1989. He filed a proper income tax return which came under examination in 1991. In September of 1991, during the course of the examination, Elmer became "untaxed" by one prominent untax group. Instead of handling the audit in the proper fashion, he showered the auditor with "untax" arguments and claims.

In response, the auditor disallowed all Elmer's deductions for failure to prove their correctness. The IRS issued a notice of deficiency claiming he owed $96,000 in taxes, interest and of course a full complement of penalties. Elmer turned to the untaxer for further help. After all, they claimed the IRS could do nothing once he was "untaxed." They also claimed to be able to help in the "unlikely" event of IRS attack.

The group failed to advise Elmer of the proper method of dealing with the notice of deficiency. He should have petitioned the Tax Court and undertaken to prove the correctness of his return. However, under untax guidance and using their standard "form letter," Elmer handed the IRS a pile of legal garbage which the untaxer ensured would solve the problem.

On September 14, 1992, the IRS responded to Elmer's challenge. This is a portion of what the letter said:

> "This is in response to your August 25 and 26 letters stating your position of not being a person with any tax liability.
>
> "It is Internal Revenue Service (IRS) policy not to respond to letters the type you have written on a point-by-point basis. This type of response only precipitates further endless questions. The courts have repeatedly upheld the constitutionality of income tax laws, and the subject does not warrant further debate or justification.
>
> * * *
>
> "We will be happy to assist you if you have legitimate questions or problems with your tax return. However, we continue to encourage you to voluntarily comply with the law. If you fail to discharge your legal responsibility, we will have to enforce the law to the full extent of our authority."

Assured the IRS could "do nothing," Elmer allowed the 90-day grace period on the notice of deficiency to expire. As a result, $96,000 was assessed and became collectible. By December of 1992, just a few short months later, the IRS made good on its promise to "enforce the law to the full extent" of its authority.

On December 3, 1992, the agency filed a federal tax lien against Elmer. The lien was in the amount of $120,166.18. Shortly thereafter, the IRS began issuing wage and bank levies. By the time Elmer contacted me in late January of 1993, he faced four such levies and the tax lien. The real tragedy of this story is that Elmer owed the IRS nothing. If he had done no more than follow the appropriate audit defense procedures, he could have left the tax audit without owing the IRS a dime.

Instead, Elmer sums up his situation in a letter to me saying, "My wife and I are retired, and are very much concerned of the possibility of losing everything we have worked so hard for. Mr. Pilla, can you help us?" Signed: Elmer S. - Minerva, Ohio.

A similar letter was received in April, 1993, from William F., of West Los Angeles, California. His story is somewhat different in that he failed to file returns for 1991 and 1992. William now owes about $10,000 to the IRS and is looking for "education" on how to solve his problem. He stated to me, "I got into this situation because I thought I could 'Untax' myself."

These are just two examples of the plight suffered by citizens all across the nation who follow untax advice. The fact is, these methods do not work and will only lead to very serious trouble.

In a recent conversation with Larry Becraft, I asked to him render a legal opinion of untax claims based upon his training and more than 10-years experience in the courts. This was Larry's response, with the express admonition that I recite it *word for word*:

> "The 'untax' material is legal swill lacking substance entirely and will not prevail in any court."
> –Attorney Larry Becraft - June 6, 1993.

I also queried Mac MacPherson, a seasoned criminal tax attorney, for his opinion on the issue. Those familiar with my newsletter *Pilla Talks Taxes*, know my association with Mac goes back well over 10 years. He is without a doubt among the most experienced and successful criminal tax attorneys in the nation. He has vast experience in tax protester claims of all kinds, including the latest wave of untaxer claims. This is Mac's opinion:

> "The untax material is worse than 'legal swill' because it's misleading. Unfortunately, it's leading honest people into serious civil and criminal problems with the IRS."
> –Attorney Mac MacPherson - June 9, 1993.

What about Untaxers' Claimed Success Stories? I have a very simple question when confronted with claims of repeated successes using untax material. I merely ask the claimant to show me a *court decision* which expressly holds in favor the specific issues presented. The answer is, and always has been, there are *no such court cases*! What's more, each of the hundreds of tax cases on these issues which *I have personally examined*, expressly reject the arguments.

The only evidence of success ever presented is merely anecdotal. By that I mean, a proponent will offer second hand information of what so-and-so accomplished by using the material. The "success story" follows a common pattern. It goes something like this: "So-and-so was contacted by the IRS after 'untaxing' himself. He responded using such-and-such a letter. The IRS 'went away' and he hasn't heard from them for x period of time."

To the inexperienced, this may sound like a victory. The citizen fired off an "untax" letter. The IRS went away and has not been heard from since. The longer the period of time without contact, the more impressive the claim appears. However, there are two very important reasons, unknown or overlooked by untax promoters, why such "success stories" do not even begin to approach the level of true success.

The first I already gave you. There is no *court opinion* to support the story. Secondly, and more compelling, is the operation of the statute of limitations to cases such as untax claims. Because untaxers have such a fundamental misunderstanding of the operation of tax law, it is not surprising they overlook this critical issue. You see, when one fails to file an income tax return, as counselled by untaxers, there is *no statute of limitations on the IRS' power to assess a tax against you.* See Code section 6501(c)(3). Under that provision of law, the IRS may assess a tax or "begin a proceeding in court for the collection of such tax" *at any time.*

The mere fact that one may not be contacted by the IRS for one month, five months, or even five years after writing an "untax" letter is absolutely no proof the IRS has given up. In my seventeen years experience dealing with that agency, I have seen case after case where the IRS waits five, six, even seven *or more* years before forcefully challenging a non-filer.

Not only does section 6501(c)(3) make this waiting game entirely possible, but such a tactic is *much to the benefit* of the IRS because of the operation of Code sections 6601, 6621, and 6622. These sections provide for the assessment of interest on unpaid tax bills. Section 6601 holds that interest on a tax debt is computed beginning with the "due date" of the tax, up to the "date the tax is paid." Therefore, if the IRS waits 10 years to make its claim against a non-filer, the bill will include 10 years' worth of interest!

Section 6621 provides the rate of interest shall be recomputed twice each year, based upon prevailing market rates. Section 6622 commands the interest shall be "compounded daily." Throw in a few penalties and it is not uncommon to see the principle amount owed increase by seven to ten times!

The IRS' policy of annihilation of tax protesters is well-served by the agency biding its time. It has everything to gain, and you have everything to lose as a result. It is interesting to note that untaxers generally *do not mention* the interest assessment statutes in their promotional literature.

Do not be duped by the claims suggesting "the IRS went away." Rest assured, my friend, *they will be back.*

2. Legal Attacks on the Untaxers. Since the untax movement regained popularity in the past few years, the IRS went on the offense. It raided the offices of a group once located in California. That particular group has gotten much attention in Texas and other western states.

The purpose of the raid was to serve a search warrant. No arrests were made, but according to reports, IRS agents seized office equipment, *files and records*, several computers and the fax machine. (Hum. . .the IRS seized files and records. What do you suppose they will do with those?) Other headquarters of untax groups have also been raided by the IRS.

In addition, several untaxers have been sued by government authorities. On January 28, 1993, the Texas Attorney General filed a consumer fraud complaint in District Court for Dallas County, at Dallas, Texas. The complaint charges a group operating in Texas Summers with fraud and conspiracy. Specifically, the complaint contends the following:

"Defendants' tax avoidance program supplies consumers with factually incorrect information contrived to convince them that by exercising a few supposed rights they can persuade the Internal Revenue Service to cancel their federal income tax liability. Defendants fail to disclose to consumers that their program has not been upheld in the courts and that use of its remedies could in all likelihood lead to civil or criminal penalties or prosecution or imprisonment." State of Texas Complaint, para. 11, Civil Action No. 93-00931, Filed January 28, 1993, Dallas County District Court, Dallas, Texas.

The complaint seeks a court order preventing the group from selling or advertising the "Untax program, or any other tax avoidance program based upon any theory that no law has been enacted ordering citizens of the United States to pay income tax." Complaint, para. 16(c).

In the meantime, the IRS has taken specific action with regard to the "untax" program. Please recall earlier I said the IRS obtained files and records of untaxers in its raids. What do you suppose the agency learned from those files? Obviously, they learned the *names and addresses* of group members and those who attended seminars. And what do you suppose the IRS will do with those names and addresses? Let me give you a hint. On April 21, 1993, the IRS mailed a letter to all citizens known to have at least attended an untax seminar. After the letter hit the streets in late April, my phone rang off the hook with people who received it. Some bought into the system; others merely attended a seminar. All were greatly concerned. Exhibit 4-2, at right, is a copy of that letter.

As you carefully read the entire letter, pay particular attention to the final paragraph. There we read the following:

"The Internal Revenue Service will review taxpayer individual accounts after April 15, 1993, to ensure that federal income tax returns are filed with us. We thank you for your continued compliance."

After reading this letter, do you believe filing income tax returns and paying taxes is voluntary? Do you believe the IRS will look the other way if you fail to file a return using any untax program? Do you believe this letter "gives credence" to the claims that taxes are entirely voluntary? Do you believe this letter constitutes a "license" from the IRS for untaxers to continue in business? By now, the answers to all these questions should be painfully obvious.

This letter was mailed in accordance with IRS Revenue Procedure 83-78, 1983-2 C.B. 595, modified by Rev. Proc. 84-84, 1984-2 C.B. 782. That procedure was designed in 1983 as a means of heading tax litigation off at the pass. Prior to adopting this procedure, the IRS would wait until returns were filed. It would then grapple with citizens over the correctness of the returns. Under this procedure, the warning letter is mailed first, putting citizens on notice of likely IRS retaliation should they take the action in question.

The warning letter serves a dual purpose. First, it acts to deter those on the fence, persuading them that following a particular course would be unwise.

Exhibit 4-2

Internal Revenue Service

Department of the Treasury

District
Director

316 N. Robert St., St Paul, Minn 55101

Kenneth ████
Route 1, Box 141
████████ MN ████

Refer to:
    P.O. Box 64556
    Stop 4117
    St. Paul, MN 55101

Telephone Number:
    (612) 222-8755

Date: APR 2 1 1993

Dear Mr. ████

It has come to the attention of the Internal Revenue Service that you may have
been supplied with information provided by The Pilot Connection Society which
is informing people that federal income tax need not be paid for a number of
reasons. We have addressed some of these arguments briefly below.

Internal Revenue Laws are mandatory. Failure to comply with these laws may
make you liable for civil and criminal penalties including prosecution. While
the mission of the Internal Revenue Service is to encourage voluntary
compliance with Federal Internal Revenue Laws and Regulations, the Service is
mandated to enforce compliance whenever necessary. Contrary to instructions
by some of these groups promising to "untax" you, a person cannot revoke a
filed tax return. An attempted revocation of a filed federal tax return does
not prohibit criminal prosecution for violation of Internal Revenue laws.

It also came to the attention of the Internal Revenue Service that on
January 28, 1992, the Texas Attorney General's office filed suit against
Certified Untax Consultants/The Pilot Connection for selling false and
misleading information and advising consumers that they do not have to pay
federal income taxes.

The Internal Revenue Service is now and always has been an agency of the
United States Department of Treasury. The Internal Revenue Service is not,
nor has it ever been, a private corporation. The United States Congress has
enacted various Internal Revenue statutes, including Title 26 of the United
States Code, authorizing the Internal Revenue Service through the Secretary of
the Treasury to administer and enforce the Internal Revenue Laws and related
rules and regulations.

If you have any questions regarding the Internal Revenue Service and your
obligations under the Internal Revenue Laws, or if you need assistance in
preparing current or past federal tax returns, please contact the Internal
Revenue Service at (612) 644-7515 or 1-800-829-1040, or contact a tax return
preparer, advisor, lawyer, or accountant in your area. Should you have any
questions concerning this letter, you may either write me or call me at the
above address and telephone number.

The Internal Revenue Service will review taxpayer individual accounts after
April 15, 1993, to ensure that federal income tax returns are filed with us.
We thank you for your continued compliance.

Sincerely,

Inar Morics
District Director

Second, as to those who insist on following the course, it operates to remove any defense they may have later. By reason of having been warned ahead of time, such persons cannot later contend they were misled, misunderstood the law; or acted in good faith based upon the "promoter's advice." The IRS' specific warning virtually eliminates any defense one might otherwise present.

CONCLUSION

In summary, if you decide to follow one or more of the untax programs, you are a) on your own, b) in very deep and very dangerous waters, and c) creating a problem which may follow you for a long, long time. Before you build, count the cost.

My goal with this chapter is simply to light a lamp and place it on top of a bushel for all to see the hazards in the road. As you consider this topic, please recognize the wise man builds his house upon a rock, that it may withstand the assault of winds and rain. But the foolish man builds his house upon sand. And when the winds and rain come, it will fall with a great crash.

The fact that so many are willing to risk their jobs, families and financial security on schemes such as these is testimony to how desperate our citizens have become. Most who follow the untax programs already have IRS problems. Many are convinced they can end the horror by employing the scheme. Sadly, they soon realize their nightmare has only deepened.

Others follow the program seeking relief from confiscatory levels of taxation, the annual drudgery of recordkeeping and the responsibility to keep up with tax law changes that pop up like dandelions. Relief from the constant fear of a tax audit, which if it occurs has been deemed a fate worse than death. And relief from what seems to be confiscatory levels of taxation. Not only is the financial life-blood drained from so many citizens, but they must tolerate the annual drudgery of recordkeeping. They must learn about the tax law changes that pop up each year like dandelions. They must prepare and file their returns, which itself is a nightmare. Then, after enduring all that, they wait and wonder whether they will be audited. If they are, it begins a completely different odyssey.

The fact that so many people are duped into following such a program speaks loudly of the need for sweeping changes in the way we administer our tax laws. No citizen should be forced by reason of desperation to reach out for solutions so flimsy as those presented by untaxers. For that solution is nothing more than a larger problem in disguise. The true solution is to adopt the changes I call for in Part III of this book.

2

GET THE IRS
OUT OF YOUR LIFE

Solving
Tax Collection Problems

Over the years, I wrote thousands of pages concerning the rights of citizens and limitations of the IRS. Most people do not realize there are specific limitations on IRS' power. One man I spoke with concerning his problem said, "I'm tired of hearing what *they* can do. I want to know what I can do!"

His frustration sums up the general attitude of the nation. "The IRS has all the power and we have none." My message over the years has been simple. This proposition is not accurate. True, the IRS will have you believe its authority is autonomous and unlimited, but that just is not the case.

Earlier in this book, I spoke of the concept of stopping a runaway train. Every sensible person knows you do not stop such a train by standing on the track with a rake, hoping to de-rail it as it speeds by. To be successful, you must take an approach which is more surely to succeed, to say nothing of being safer.

In every way, the IRS is like a runaway train. The agency itself believes its powers are unlimited, and most of its observers believe the same. Therefore, to stop the train, you must stay off the track and approach it from a different angle. You do not, for example, stop the IRS by taking the "untax" approach exposed in Chapter Four. That technique amounts to little more than standing on the track with hands extended forward. You will surely be squashed as the train passes.

However, you certainly may stop the IRS by learning, then applying, your rights. When you learn and apply them, you reduce the number of potential victims capable of being abused by the IRS.

Never lose sight of the fact the IRS is a hungry collection machine which must, by its nature, collect as much money as quickly and easily as possible. When faced with informed resistance based upon *clearly defined and established legal authority*, it must move on to the next, hopefully ignorant, prospect. As more and more citizens become educated, the pool of available victims is reduced. IRS abuse must eventually end merely because there are no more citizens available to abuse.

This process is surely slow, but necessary. The alternatives are both illegal and unmanageable. For example, open resistance to the tax laws, ala "untax" programs, serve only to add to the IRS' powers. The agency, citing such violations, retreats to Congress seeking yet more power, ostensibly to battle the illegal actions of a few. This is one reason the IRS has so much power today. Congress is too willing to accommodate IRS demands, considering its own insatiable appetite for your money. Therefore, our tactics of firing the IRS must be based squarely upon settled principles of law.

In Part II, I discuss what is distilled into the most important rights a citizen must know to *solve* IRS problems.

5 RIGHT NUMBER ONE: SAY "NO"
USE YOUR RIGHT OF APPEAL

Experience tells me people are terrified of a tax audit and general dealings with the IRS because they believe the IRS has the final word. We repeatedly hear stories of how friends and associates are raked over the coals by IRS tax examiners. The stories have a similar theme. They tell of auditors who disallow deductions without considering all the facts. They tell of auditors who ignore plain evidence or otherwise make life miserable for the taxpayers they face.

What these and others do not realize is the tax auditor has no authority to make any final decision in your case. That's right! The tax auditor does not have the power to disallow your deductions, disregard plain evidence or, as is sometimes threatened, put you in jail. The auditor does not even have the power to change your return, without your consent! If you understand the role of the auditor and your right to challenge his decision, the auditor's professed power evaporates faster than a puddle in the Sahara.

THE ROLE OF THE AUDITOR

The *purported* role of the tax auditor, also known as a revenue agent, is to determine the correctness of your tax return. Auditors review all documentation and evidence in your possession to support the claims in the return. We know from our earlier conversation, however, the true role of the auditor is to get more money. That is why IRS abuse at the audit level is so great.

Recent IRS statistics concerning tax audits are quite revealing. For example, the IRS assesses, on the average, *$5,814 per face-to-face tax audit* conducted by a revenue agent. The statistics indicate, of the 1.039 million returns examined in this fashion during 1992, just 11 percent were found to be correct. In the remaining *89 percent* of cases, the citizen was assessed with some additional tax. See *Internal Revenue Annual Report*, 1992, pages 34-35.

On the other hand, the same statistics reveal that of the citizens who appeal the decision of the revenue agent, 69 percent win all or part of their case. In the office of Appeals, the division of IRS established to hear and resolve disputed examination cases, 88 percent of the cases reach an amicable settlement. Thus, we can conclude the tax auditor does not place accuracy on a high priority when conducting audits. The fact is, he need not. The reason is, most people have no clue they may appeal the auditor's decision. If they are aware of the right, they have no clue the probability of success on appeal is so great.

Add to this the fact that tax auditors attempt to discourage an appeal. They do so either by claiming the citizen cannot win the case, or by threatening the citizen with continued heavy interest and penalty accumulations while the appeal is pending. Faced with such obstacles, the average citizen, alone and mostly ignorant, simply pays the tax. This explains why in 1991 just 10 percent of audit decisions were appealed by the public. See 1991 Annual Report, pg. 32, Table 16.

THE RIGHT TO CHALLENGE THE AUDITOR

IRS Publication One, *Your Rights as a Taxpayer*, discusses in very general terms, your right of appeal. At page two of the document, we find the following:

An Appeal of the Examination Findings

"If you don't agree with the examiner's findings, you have the right to appeal them. During the examination process, you will be given information about your appeal rights. Publication 5, *Appeal Rights and Preparation of Protests for Unagreed Cases*, explains your appeal rights in detail and tells you exactly what to do if you want to appeal."
–Publication One, page 2.

A copy of the full text of Publication One is included on the following four pages. *(Please see Exhibit 5-1.)*

Most people are terrified of tax auditors. They are afraid because of what they perceive are very powerful people with direct control over their financial affairs. The truth is, tax auditors have absolutely no power whatsoever to lien, levy or seize your assets. They cannot take your automobile, your bank account or anything else necessary to the preservation of your family's security.

In a very real way, tax auditors are the quintessential example of a paper lion. They have all the roar but no teeth. Not only may you challenge the final decision of the audit, but you may challenge the various demands made along the audit route. For example, it is common for tax auditors to make demands for details and information which have absolutely no bearing on the tax return.

I have witnessed tax auditors ask a citizen how much money he has in his pocket during the audit! I have witnessed tax auditors ask citizens how much money they spend on haircuts and who they make gifts to during the year. I ask you, how can this information have any bearing on the correctness of a tax return filed many years before the audit?

I steadfastly maintain such questioning is entirely irrelevant. It serves a psychological function but has no valid legal basis. The psychological function is to break you down; make you feel invaded; persuade you to do anything (such as pay more money) to end the terrible ordeal. Sadly, that is exactly what most people do.

Exhibit 5-1 (page one)

Your Rights

AS A TAXPAYER

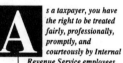

As a taxpayer, you have the right to be treated fairly, professionally, promptly, and courteously by Internal Revenue Service employees. Our goal at the IRS is to protect your rights so that you will have the highest confidence in the integrity, efficiency, and fairness of our tax system. To ensure that you always receive such treatment, you should know about the many rights you have at each step of the tax process.

Free Information and Help in Preparing Returns

You have the right to information and help in complying with the tax laws. In addition to the basic instructions we provide with the tax forms, we make available a great deal of other information.

Taxpayer publications. We publish over 100 free taxpayer information publications on various subjects. One of these, Publication 910, *Guide to Free Tax Services*, is a catalog of the free services and publications we offer. You can order all publications and any tax forms or instructions you need by calling us toll-free at 1-800-TAX-FORM (829-3676).

Other assistance. We provide walk-in tax help at many IRS offices and recorded telephone information on many topics through our *Tele-Tax* system. The telephone numbers for *Tele-Tax*, and the topics covered, are in certain tax forms' instructions and publications. Many of our materials are available in Braille (at regional libraries for the handicapped) and in Spanish. We provide help for the hearing-impaired via special telephone equipment.

We have informational videotapes that you can borrow. In addition, you may want to attend our education programs for specific groups of taxpayers, such as farmers and those with small businesses.

In cooperation with local volunteers, we offer free help in preparing tax returns for low-income and elderly taxpayers through the Volunteer Income Tax Assistance (VITA) and Tax Counseling for the Elderly (TCE) Programs. You can get information on these programs by calling the toll-free telephone number for your area.

Copies of tax returns. If you need a copy of your tax return for an earlier year, you can get one by filling out Form 4506, *Request for Copy of Tax Form*, and paying a small fee. However, you often only need certain information, such as the amount of your reported income, the number of your exemptions, and the tax shown on the return. You can get this information free if you write or visit an IRS office or call the toll-free number for your area.

Privacy and Confidentiality

You have the right to have your personal and financial information kept confidential. People who prepare your return or represent you *must* keep your information confidential.

You also have the right to know why we are asking you for information, exactly how we will use any information you give, and what might happen if you do not give the information.

Information sharing. Under the law, we can share your tax information with State tax agencies and, under strict legal guidelines, the Department of Justice and other federal agencies. We can also share it with certain foreign governments under tax treaty provisions.

Courtesy and Consideration

You are always entitled to courteous and considerate treatment from IRS employees. If you ever feel that you are not being treated with fairness, courtesy, and consideration by an IRS employee, you should tell the employee's supervisor.

Protection of Your Rights

The employees of the Internal Revenue Service will explain and protect your rights as a taxpayer at all times. If you feel that this is not the case, you should discuss the problem with the employee's supervisor.

Complaints

If for any reason you have a complaint about the IRS, you may write to the District Director or Service Center Director for your area. We will give you the name and address if you call our toll-free phone number listed later.

Representation and Recordings

Throughout your dealings with us, you can represent yourself, or, generally with proper written authorization, have someone represent you in your absence. During an interview, you can have someone accompany you.

Department of the Treasury
Internal Revenue Service
Publication 1 (Rev. 10-90)

Cat. No. 64731W

Exhibit 5-1 (page two)

If you want to consult an attorney, a certified public accountant, an enrolled agent, or any other person permitted to represent a taxpayer during an interview for examining a tax return or collecting tax, we will stop and reschedule the interview. We cannot suspend the interview if you are there because of an administrative summons.

You can generally make an audio recording of an interview with an IRS Collection or Examination officer. Your request to record the interview should be made in writing, and must be received 10 days before the interview. You must bring your own recording equipment. We also can record an interview. If we do so, we will notify you 10 days before the meeting and you can get a copy of the recording at your expense.

Payment of Only the Required Tax

You have the right to plan your business and personal finances so that you will pay the least tax that is due under the law. You are liable only for the correct amount of tax. Our purpose is to apply the law consistently and fairly to all taxpayers.

If Your Return is Questioned

We accept most taxpayers' returns as filed. If we inquire about your return or select it for examination, it does not suggest that you are dishonest. The inquiry or examination may or may not result in more tax. We may close your case without change. Or, you may receive a refund.

Examination and inquiries by mail. We handle many examinations and inquiries entirely by mail. We will send you a letter with either a request for more information

or a reason why we believe a change needs to be made to your return. If you give us the requested information or provide an explanation, we may or may not agree with you and we will explain the reasons for any changes. You should not hesitate to write to us about anything you do not understand. If you cannot resolve any questions through the mail, you can request a personal interview. You can appeal through the IRS and the courts. You will find instructions with each inquiry or in Publication 1383, *Correspondence Process.*

Examination by interview. If we notify you that we will conduct your examination through a personal interview, or you request such an interview, you have the right to ask that the examination take place at a reasonable time and place that is convenient for both you and the IRS. If the time or place we suggest is not convenient, the examiner will try to work out something more suitable. However, the IRS makes the final determination of how, when, and where the examination will take place. You will receive an explanation of your rights and of the examination process either before or at the interview.

If you do not agree with the examiner's report, you may meet with the examiner's supervisor to discuss your case further.

Repeat examinations. We try to avoid repeat examinations of the same items, but this sometimes happens. If we examined your tax return for the same items in either of the 2 previous years and proposed no change to your tax liability, please contact us as soon as possible so we can see if we should discontinue the repeat examination.

Explanation of changes. If we propose any changes to your return, we will explain the reasons for the changes. It is

important that you understand these reasons. You should not hesitate to ask about anything that is unclear to you.

Interest. You must pay interest on additional tax that you owe. The interest is generally figured from the due date of the return. But if our error caused a delay in your case, and this was grossly unfair, we may reduce the interest. Only delays caused by procedural or mechanical acts not involving the exercise of judgment or discretion qualify. If you think we caused such a delay, please discuss it with the examiner and file a claim for refund.

Business taxpayers. If you are in an individual business, the rights covered in this publication generally apply to you. If you are a member of a partnership or a shareholder in a small business corporation, special rules may apply to the examination of your partnership or corporation items. The examination of partnership items is discussed in Publication 556, *Examination of Returns, Appeal Rights, and Claims for Refund.* The rights covered in this publication generally apply to exempt organizations and sponsors of employee plans.

An Appeal of the Examination Findings

If you don't agree with the examiner's findings, you have the right to appeal them. During the examination process, you will be given information about your appeal rights. Publication 5, *Appeal Rights and Preparation of Protests for Unagreed Cases,* explains your appeal rights in detail and tells you exactly what to do if you want to appeal.

Appeals Office. You can appeal the findings of an examination within the IRS through our Appeals Office. Most

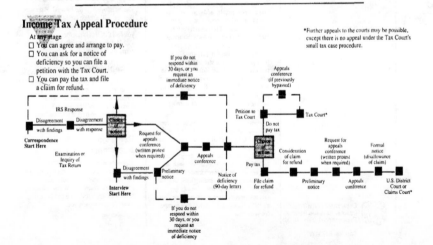

Income Tax Appeal Procedure

At any stage
☐ You can agree and arrange to pay.
☐ You can ask for a notice of deficiency so you can file a petition with the Tax Court.
☐ You can pay the tax and file a claim for refund.

*Further appeals to the courts may be possible, except there is no appeal under the Tax Court's small tax case procedure.

Exhibit 5-1 (page three)

differences can be settled through this appeals system without expensive and time-consuming court trials. If the matter cannot be settled to your satisfaction in Appeals, you can take your case to court.

Appeals to the courts. Depending on whether you first pay the disputed tax, you can take your case to the U.S. Tax Court, the U.S. Claims Court, or your U.S. District Court. These courts are entirely independent of the IRS. As always, you can represent yourself or have someone admitted to practice before the court represent you.

If you disagree about whether you owe additional tax, you generally have the right to take your case to the U.S. Tax Court if you have not yet paid the tax. Ordinarily, you have 90 days from the time we mail you a formal notice (called a "notice of deficiency") telling you that you owe additional tax, to file a petition with the U.S. Tax Court. You can request simplified small tax case procedures if your case is $10,000 or less for any period or year. A case settled under these procedures cannot be appealed.

If you have already paid the disputed tax in full, you may file a claim for refund. If we disallow the claim, you can appeal the findings through our Appeals Office. If you do not accept their decision or we have not acted on your claim within 6 months, then you may take your case to the U.S. Claims Court or your U.S. District Court.

Recovering litigation expenses. If the court agrees with you on most issues in your case, and finds that our position was largely unjustified, you may be able to recover some of your administrative and litigation costs. To do this, you must have used all the administrative remedies available to you within the IRS. This includes going through our Appeals system and giving us all the information necessary to resolve the case.

Publication 556, *Examination of Returns, Appeal Rights, and Claims for Refund*, will help you more fully understand your appeal rights.

Fair Collection of Tax

Whenever you owe tax, we will send you a bill describing the tax and stating the amounts you owe in tax, interest, and penalties. Be sure to check any bill you receive to make sure it is correct. You have the right to have your bill adjusted if it is incorrect, so you should let us know about an incorrect bill right away.

If we tell you that you owe tax because of a math or clerical error on your return, you have the right to ask us to send you a formal notice (a "notice of deficiency") so that you can dispute the tax, as discussed earlier. You do not have to pay the additional tax at the same time that you ask us for the formal notice, if you ask for it within 60 days of the time we tell you of the error.

If the tax is correct, we will give you a specific period of time to pay the bill in full. If you pay the bill within the time allowed, we will not have to take any further action.

We may request that you attend an interview for the collection of tax. You will receive an explanation of your rights and of the collection process either before or at the interview.

Your rights are further protected because we are not allowed to use tax enforcement results to evaluate our employees.

Payment arrangements. You should make every effort to pay your bill in full. If you can't, you should pay as much as you can and contact us right away. We may ask you for a complete financial statement to determine how you can pay the amount due. Based on your financial condition, you may qualify for an installment agreement. We can arrange for these payments to be made through payroll deduction. We will give you copies of all agreements you make with us.

If we approve a payment agreement, the agreement will stay in effect only if:

You give correct and complete financial information,

You pay each installment on time,

You satisfy other tax liabilities on time,

You provide current financial information when asked, and

We determine that collecting the tax is not at risk.

Following a review of your current finances, we may change your payment agreement. We will notify you 30 days before any change to your payment agreement and tell you why we are making the change.

We will not take any enforcement action (such as recording a tax lien or levying on or seizing property), until after we have tried to contact you and given you the chance to voluntarily pay any tax due. Therefore, it is very important for you to respond right away to our attempts to contact you (by mail, telephone, or personal visit). If you do not respond, we may have no choice but to begin enforcement action.

Release of liens. If we have to place a lien on your property (to secure the amount of tax due), we must release the lien no later than 30 days after finding that you have paid the entire tax and certain charges, the assessment has become legally unenforceable, or we have accepted a bond to cover the tax and certain charges.

Recovery of damages. If we knowingly or negligently fail to release a lien under the circumstances described above, and you suffer economic damages because of our failure to release a lien, you can recover your actual economic damages and certain costs.

If we recklessly or intentionally fail to follow the laws and regulations

for the collection of tax, you can recover actual economic damages and certain costs.

In each of the two situations above, damages and costs will be allowed within the following limits. You must exhaust all administrative remedies available to you. The damages will be reduced by the amount which you could have reasonably prevented. You must bring suit within 2 years of the action.

Incorrect lien. You have the right to appeal our filing of a Notice of Federal Tax Lien if you believe we filed the lien in error. If we agree, we will issue a certificate of release, including a statement that we filed the lien in error.

A lien is incorrect if:

You paid the entire amount due before we filed the lien,

The time to collect the tax expired before we filed the lien,

We made a procedural error in a deficiency assessment, or

We assessed a tax in violation of the automatic stay provisions in a bankruptcy case.

Levy. We will generally give you 30 days notice before we levy on any property. The notice may be given to you in person, mailed to you, or left at your home or workplace. On the day you attend a collection interview because of a summons, we cannot levy your property unless the collection of tax is in jeopardy.

Property that is exempt from levy. If we must seize your property, you have the legal right to keep:

Necessary clothing and schoolbooks,

A limited amount of personal belongings, furniture, and business or professional books and tools,

Unemployment and job training benefits, workers' compensation, welfare, certain disability payments, and certain pension benefits,

The income you need to pay court-ordered child support,

Mail,

An amount of weekly income equal to your standard deduction and allowable personal exemptions, divided by 52, and

Your main home, unless collection of tax is in jeopardy or the district director (or assistant) approves the levy in writing.

If your bank account is levied after June 30, 1989, the bank will hold your account up to the amount of the levy for 21 days. This gives you time to settle any disputes concerning ownership of the funds in the account.

We generally must release a levy issued after June 30, 1989, if:

You pay the tax, penalty, and interest for which the levy was made,

The IRS determines the release will help collect the tax,

Exhibit 5-1 (page four)

You have an approved installment agreement for the tax on the levy,

The IRS determines the levy is creating an economic hardship, or

The fair market value of the property exceeds the amount of the levy and release would not hinder the collection of tax.

If at any time during the collection process you do not agree with the collection officer, you can discuss your case with his or her supervisor.

If we seize your property, you have the right to request that it be sold within 60 days after your request. You can request a time period greater than 60 days. We will comply with your request unless it is not in the best interest of the government.

Access to your private premises. A court order is not generally needed for a collection officer to seize your property. However, you don't have to allow the employee access to your private premises, such as your home or the non-public areas of your business, if the employee does not have court authorization to be there.

Withheld taxes. If we believe that you were responsible for seeing that a corporation pay us income and social security taxes withheld from its employees, and the taxes were not paid, we may look to you to pay an amount based on the unpaid taxes. If you feel that you don't owe this, you have the right to discuss the case with the collection officer's supervisor. You may also request an appeals hearing within 30 days of our proposed assessment of employment taxes. You generally have the same IRS appeal rights as other taxpayers. Because the U.S. Tax Court has no jurisdiction in this situation, you must pay at least part of the withheld taxes and file a claim for refund in order to take the matter to the U.S. District Court or U.S. Claims Court.

The amount of tax withheld from your wages is determined by the W-4, *Employees Withholding Allowance Certificate,* you give your employer. If your certificate is incorrect, the IRS may instruct your employer to increase the amount. We may also assess a penalty. You have the right to appeal the decision. Or, you can file a claim for refund and go to the U.S. Claims Court or U.S. District Court.

Publications 586A, *The Collection Process (Income Tax Accounts),* and 594, *The Collection Process (Employment Tax Accounts),* will help you understand your rights during the collection process.

The Collection Process

To stop the process at any stage, you should pay the tax in full. If you cannot pay the tax in full, contact us right away to discuss possible ways to pay the tax.

Start here

First notice and demand for unpaid tax

10 days later

Enforcement authority arises (a notice of a lien may be filed)

Up to 3 more notices sent over a period of time asking for payment

Notice of intent to levy is sent by certified mail (final notice)

30 days later

Enforcement action to collect the tax begins (levy, seizure, etc.)

Refund of Overpaid Tax

Once you have paid all your tax, you have the right to file a claim for a refund if you think the tax is incorrect. Generally, you have 3 years from the date you filed the return or 2 years from the date you paid the tax (whichever is later) to file a claim. If we examine your claim for any reason, you have the same rights that you would have during an examination of your return.

Interest on refunds. You will receive interest on any income tax refund delayed more than 45 days after the *later* of either the date you filed your return or the date your return was due.

Checking on your refund. Normally, you will receive your refund about 6 weeks after you file your return. If you have not received your refund within 8 weeks after mailing your return, you may check on it by calling the toll-free Tele-Tax number in the tax forms' instructions.

If we reduce your refund because you owe a debt to another Federal agency or because you owe child support, we must notify you of this action. However, if you have a question about the debt that caused the reduction, you should contact the other agency.

Cancellation of Penalties

You have the right to ask that certain penalties (but not interest) be cancelled (abated) if you can show reasonable cause for the failure that led to the penalty (or can show that you exercised due diligence, if that is the applicable standard for that penalty).

If you relied on wrong advice you received from IRS employees on the toll-free telephone system, we will cancel certain penalties that may result. But you have to show that your reliance on the advice was reasonable.

If you relied on incorrect written advice from the IRS in response to a written request you made after January 1,

1989, we will cancel any penalties that may result. You must show that you gave sufficient and correct information and filed your return after you received the advice.

Special Help to Resolve Your Problems

We have a Problem Resolution Program for taxpayers who have been unable to resolve their problems with the IRS. If you have a tax problem that you cannot clear up through normal channels, write to the Problem Resolution Office in the district or Service Center with which you have the problem. You may also reach the Problem Resolution Office by calling the IRS taxpayer assistance number for your area. If you are hearing-impaired with TV/Telephone (TTY) access, you may call 1-800-829-4059.

If your tax problem causes (or will cause) you to suffer a significant hardship, additional assistance is available. A significant hardship may occur if you cannot maintain necessities such as food, clothing, shelter, transportation, and medical treatment.

There are two ways you can apply for relief. You can submit Form 911, *Application for Taxpayer Assistance Order to Relieve Hardship,* which you can order by calling 1-800-TAX-FORM (829-3676). You can choose instead to call 1-800-829-1040, to request relief from hardship. The Taxpayer Ombudsman, Problem Resolution Officer, or other official will then review your case and may issue a Taxpayer Assistance Order (TAO), to suspend IRS action.

Taxpayer Assistance Numbers

You should use the telephone number shown in the white pages of your local telephone directory under U.S. Government, Internal Revenue Service, Federal Tax Assistance. If there is not a specific number listed, call toll-free 1-800-829-1040.

You can also find these phone numbers in the instructions for Form 1040. You may also use these numbers to reach the Problem Resolution Office. Ask for the Problem Resolution Office when you call.

U.S. taxpayers abroad may write for information to:

Internal Revenue Service
Attn: IN:C:TPS
950 L'Enfant Plaza South, S.W.
Washington, D.C. 20024

You can also contact your nearest U.S. Embassy for information about what services and forms are available in your location.

To tell the truth, you do not have to tolerate such an inquisition. The right to challenge the tax auditor goes far beyond merely appealing his final decision. You have the right to say "no" to these types of questions, and you can make it stick. The rule is very simple. You have an obligation to verify the correctness of your return. Any records you have which will shed light upon the correctness of the return must be presented to the IRS upon demand. However, the obligation ends there.

You need not comply with unreasonable demands for information which sheds no light upon the correctness of the tax return. You have the right to say "no" when the agent crosses the bounds I just defined. What is more important, if you do say "no," there is nothing the agent can do to retaliate. The most common objection I hear after making this statement is the idea that the agent will become angry and somehow "make me pay."

The one and only thing the agent can do is recommend the disallowance of one or more deductions. "Wait a minute," you say. "If he disallows deductions, it means I pay more taxes."

I said, "He can *recommend* the disallowance of one or more deductions." But, he has no authority to make a *final decision*. You always have the right of appeal and when you appeal, you will win 69 percent of the time.

The moral, therefore, is take back the power! The IRS auditors terrorizing this nation have absolutely no power. Therefore, do not be afraid. Use your right of appeal. Say no and make it stick!

WHEN AND HOW TO MAKE AN APPEAL

An appeal is made after the tax auditor makes his recommendations in writing. His recommendations arrive in the form of a written report known as an Examination Report, sometimes referred to as a Revenue Agent's Report (RAR). The report contains an itemization of all changes to your tax return as *recommended* by the agent. It also contains an outline of what to do next.

The statement explains you should sign the waiver provided as part of the report *if you agree* with the changes. The waiver referred to is IRS Form 870. By signing that form, you waive your right of appeal and agree the IRS may assess and collect the tax, penalty and interest shown in the report. You are not required to sign the waiver. Furthermore, nothing "bad" will happen if you refuse. In fact, if you disagree with the report, it is mandatory that you not sign.

The report goes on to explain your options if you disagree. Generally, you have three routes available. First, is the right to submit more information to the auditor. Or, you may call for an appointment with the auditor's supervisor. Last, you may exercise your right to appeal the matter. By appealing the case, all authority to make any proposals or decisions is removed from the Examination Division. You no longer deal with a tax auditor or his supervisor. You at that point deal strictly with the Appeals Division.

The case is appealed by submitting a written protest letter to the Appeals Division. The letter must be submitted within 30 days of the date stamped on the face of the examination report. The protest letter must set out the following information:

1. A plain statement that you wish to appeal the auditor's recommendations;
2. Your name and address;
3. The date and symbols from the revenue agent's letter transmitting his proposed changes;
4. The tax years involved;
5. An itemized schedule of the adjustments with which you disagree;
6. A statement of facts and all reasons supporting your position on the issues with which you do not agree.

IRS Publication 5, *Appeal Rights and Preparation of Protests for Unagreed Cases*, explains the appeal procedures and the manner in which a protest letter is to be written and submitted. The two-page publication is reproduced on the following page. *(Please see Exhibit 5-2.)*

THE ROLE OF THE APPEALS OFFICER

I am fond of describing the difference between the tax auditor and the appeals officer as follows: The role of the tax auditor is to cause problems, while the role of the appeals officer is to solve problems. Truthfully, which would you rather deal with?

The role of the IRS' Appeals Office is to resolve every case without the need of litigation. If you cannot agree with the Appeals Division, the IRS is obligated to issue a notice of deficiency. The notice of deficiency is a formal statement setting forth the agency's proposed changes to your tax liability. The notice gives you the right to file an appeal with the United States Tax Court. That involves litigation, but the IRS' desire is to stay away from that whenever possible. In fact, the Appeals Division does resolve about 88 percent of its cases without the need of further effort.

Therefore, you can expect the Appeals Officer to be much more professional, courteous and willing to be reasonable than was the auditor. The written job description of the Appeals Officer is to negotiate a settlement with the citizen. Consequently, you will find yourself in an atmosphere of negotiation, or give-and-take, on the issues.

Ultimately, if you provide reasonable proof and reasonable arguments on the issues, you will prevail. Exactly what constitutes such proof is the subject of Chapter One. Naturally, you cannot expect to run a scam or con on any Appeals Officer. In my experience, Appeals personnel are much more knowledgeable than are auditors. That works to your advantage if you are fair and honest, but cuts strongly against you if you cheated.

My prior books discuss in greater detail the concepts outlined here. *How Anyone Can Negotiate with the IRS - And Win!*, shows you step-by-step how to deal with tax auditors and appeals officers. The *Taxpayers' Ultimate Defense Manual* illustrates how to write protest letters and draft Tax Court petitions. It explains how to deal with IRS lawyers at the Appeals level and in Tax Court .

Exhibit 5-2

Appeal Rights and Preparation of Protests for Unagreed Cases

Department of the Treasury
Internal Revenue Service

Publication 5 (Rev. 11/90)
Catalog Number 46074I

If You Agree

If you agree with the examiner's findings in the enclosed examination report, please sign the agreement form and return it with our transmittal letter. By signing, you are agreeing to the amounts shown on the form.

If the agreement shows you owe additional tax you may pay it without waiting for a bill. Include interest on the additional tax and on any penalties at the applicable rate from the due date of the return to the date of payment. Figure the interest as shown in the enclosed Notice 433, Yearly Interest and Certain Penalty Rates.

If you do not pay the additional tax when you sign the agreement, you will receive a bill for the additional tax. Interest is charged on the additional tax from the due date of your return to the billing date. However, you will not be billed for more than 30 days interest from the date we receive your signed agreement. No further interest or penalties will be charged if you pay the amount you owe within 10 days after the billing date.

Please make your check or money order payable to the Internal Revenue Service and include on the check or money order your social security number (individual tax) or employee identification number (business tax), the tax form number, and the tax period for which payment is being made. Do not send cash through the mail.

If the examination report shows a refund is due you, you should sign and return the agreement form promptly so the Service can send your refund sooner. You will receive interest on the refund.

If You Don't Agree

If you decide not to agree with the examiner's findings, you have the option of requesting a meeting with the examiner's supervisor to discuss the findings. If you still do not agree, we urge you to appeal your case with the Service. Most differences can be settled in these appeals without expensive and time-consuming court trials. (Appeals conferences are not available to taxpayers whose reasons for disagreement do not come within the scope of the internal revenue laws. For example, disagreement based solely on moral, religious, political, constitutional, conscientious, or similar grounds.)

The following general rules tell you how to appeal your case.

Appeals Within the IRS

You may appeal an IRS decision to a regional Appeals Office, which is independent of your local District Director or Service Center Director. The regional Appeals Office is the only level of appeal within the IRS. Appeals conferences are conducted in an informal manner.

If you want an appeals conference, write to your District Director or Service Center Director according to the instructions in our letter to you. Your director will give your request to the Appeals Office to arrange a conference at a convenient time and place. You and/or your representative should be prepared to discuss all disputed issues at the conference. Most differences are settled at this level.

Special appeals procedures, including a consolidated appeals conference, may be held for all producers in certain windfall profit tax cases. See the heading Procedures for Crude Oil Windfall Profit Tax Cases for procedures on these cases if you are appealing a windfall profit tax issue.

If an agreement is not reached at your appeals conference, or if you do not want to appeal your case to the IRS, you may, at any stage of the proceedings, take your case to court. See **Appeals to the Courts,** later.

Written Protests

When you request a conference, you may also need to file a written protest or a brief statement of disputed issues with your District Director or Service Center Director.

You do not have to file anything in writing if:

The proposed increase (including penalties) or decrease in tax, or refund, determined by the examination is not more than $2,500 for any of the tax periods involved, or

Your examination was handled by mail or in an IRS office by a tax auditor.

A brief written statement of the disputed issues is required if:

The proposed increase (including penalties) or decrease in tax, or claimed refund, determined by the examination is more than $2,500 but not more than $10,000 and

Your examination was a field examination by a revenue agent or a revenue officer.

Written protests are required:

If as a result of a field examination by a revenue agent or a revenue officer, the proposed increase (including penalties) or decrease in tax, or claimed refund, is more than $10,000 for any tax period; or

In all employee plan and exempt organization cases; or

In all partnership and S corporation cases.

If a written protest is required, you should send it within the time limit specified in the letter you received with the examination report. Your protest should contain:

1) Your name and address,

2) A statement that you want to appeal the examination findings to the Appeals Office,

3) The date and symbols from the letter showing the proposed changes and findings you disagree with,

4) The tax periods or years involved,

5) An itemized schedule of the changes with which you disagree,

6) A statement of facts supporting your position on any issue with which you disagree, and

7) A statement stating the law or other authority on which you rely.

You must declare that the statement of facts under (6) is true under penalties of perjury. Do this by adding the following signed declaration:

"Under the penalties of perjury, I declare that I have examined the statement of facts presented in this protest and in any accompanying schedules and, to the best of my knowledge and belief, it is true, correct, and complete."

If your representative submits the protest for you, he or she may substitute a declaration stating:

1) That he or she prepared the protest and accompanying documents and

2) Whether he or she knows personally that the statement of facts in the protest and accompanying documents are true and correct.

Representation

You may represent yourself at your appeals conference, or you may be represented by an attorney, certified public accountant, or an individual enrolled to practice before the Internal Revenue Service. Your representative must be qualified to practice before the Internal Revenue Service. If your representative appears without you, he or she must file a power of attorney before receiving or inspecting confidential information. Form 2848, Power of Attorney and Declaration of Representative, or any other properly written power of attorney or authorization may be used for this purpose. You can get copies of Form 2848 from an Internal Revenue Service office.

You may also bring witnesses to support your position.

Procedures for Crude Oil Windfall Profit Tax Cases

The Statement of Procedural Rules allows the Service to provide a single consolidated appeals conference to address all oil items arising in connection with a property *or lease whenever the Service determines* that a consolidated procedure is necessary for effective administration of the windfall profit tax law. Generally, oil items are items taken into account in computing the windfall profit tax that can be more readily determined at the property or lease level such as:

- The tier or tiers of the crude oil;
- The quantity of crude oil in each tier;
- The adjusted base price and removal price; and
- The severance tax.

All producers having an interest in the property or lease will be permitted to participate in this conference if a written request to attend is made within 60 days of the mailing of the letter proposing the adjustment. If a written protest is required, it should also be sent within the 60-day period. If you do not agree with the adjustments but decide not to attend the conference, and the issue is appealed by the other owners, your case will be held in suspense until the final administrative determination is made.

The determination by the Appeals Office is the final administrative determination with respect to oil items arising in connection with the property or lease for the period under examination.

These procedures do not affect the producers' administrative appeal rights with respect to producer items, that is, items more readily determined at the producer level such as exemptions and independent producer status. All unagreed producers are still entitled to a separate Appeals conference to resolve producer item issues. A separate notification of appeal rights relating to producer items will generally be issued following the final administrative determination of the oil items.

See Publication 556, Examination of Returns, Appeal Rights, and Claims for Refund for additional information if you are not the producer of the oil as shown in the 60 day letter you received.

Appeals To The Courts

If you and the Service disagree after your conference or if you skipped our appeals system, you may take your case to the United States Tax Court, the United States Claims Court, or your United States District Court. (However, if you are a nonresident alien taxpayer, you cannot take your case to a United States District Court.) These courts are independent judicial bodies and have no connection with the Internal Revenue Service.

Tax Court

If your case involves a disagreement over whether you owe additional income tax, estate or gift tax, or certain excise taxes, you may go to the United States Tax Court. To do this, ask the Service to issue a formal letter, called a notice of deficiency. You have 90 days from the date this notice is mailed to you to file a petition with the Tax Court (150 days if addressed to you outside the United States). *If you do not file the petition within* the 90-day period (or 150 days as the case may be), the law requires that we assess and bill you for the deficiency.

If you discuss your case with the Internal Revenue Service during the 90-day period (150-day period), the discussion will not extend the period in which you may file a petition with the Tax Court.

The Court will schedule your case for trial at a location convenient to you. You may represent yourself before the Tax Court, or you may be represented by anyone permitted to practice before that Court.

NOTE: If you do not exhaust your administrative remedies, including Appeals consideration, the Court will normally request that you attempt settlement with Appeals prior to the court date.

If you dispute not more than $10,000 for any one tax year, there are simplified procedures. You can get information about these procedures and other matters relating to the Court from the Clerk of the Tax Court, 400 Second St. N.W., Washington, DC 20217.

District Court and Claims Court

You may take your case to your United States District Court or to the United States *Claims Court. Certain types of cases,* such as those involving manufacturers' excise taxes and employment taxes can be heard only by these courts. Generally, your District Court and the Claims Court hear tax cases only after you have paid the tax and have filed a claim for refund. You can get information about procedures for filing suit in either court by contacting the Clerk of your District Court; or the Clerk of the Claims Court. If we haven't acted on your claim within 6 months from the date you filed it, you can then file suit for refund. If we have disallowed your claim, you may request Appeals reconsideration of the disallowance, or a suit for refund must be filed no later than 2 years from the date of our disallowance. Please note that appeals reconsideration does not extend the two year period for filing suit.

Recovering Administrative and Litigation Costs

You may be able to recover your litigation and administrative costs if you are the prevailing party and if:

You exhaust all administrative remedies with the IRS, which are described in **Appeals Within the IRS** and **Written Protests.**

Your net worth is below a certain limit (see **Net worth requirements,** later), and

You provide all requested documentation and you do not otherwise unreasonably delay the administrative and court proceedings.

Prevailing party. You are the prevailing party if you meet all the following requirements:

You can show that the IRS's position in the civil proceeding was not substantially justified.

You substantially prevailed with respect to the amount in controversy, or on the most significant tax issue or set of issues in question.

You meet the net worth requirement, discussed later.

Although the court will generally decide who is the prevailing party, a final determination of liability at the administrative level is decided by the IRS. Thus, administrative costs may be received from the IRS without a taxpayer going to court.

Reasonable litigation costs generally include:

Reasonable amounts for court costs,

Expenses of expert witnesses,

The costs of studies, analyses, engineering reports, tests, or projects which the court agreed were necessary for the preparation of your case, and

Attorney fees that generally may not exceed $75 per hour.

Reasonable administrative costs generally include:

All of the costs listed under litigation costs, except court costs, and any administrative fees or similar charges made by the IRS. Administrative costs (described above) include costs incurred on or after the earlier of the date the taxpayer receives the appeals decision letter or the date of the notice of deficiency.

Net worth requirements. An individual taxpayer may be able to recover litigation and administrative costs if his or her net worth was not more than $2,000,000 when the litigation began and/or when administrative costs become recoverable. To qualify, the net worth of the owner of an unincorporated business, or a partnership, corporation, association, *unit of local* government, or organization cannot be more than $7,000,000 and cannot have more than 500 employees when the litigation began.

Penalty

Whenever the Tax Court determines that proceedings before it have been instituted or maintained by you primarily for delay or that your position in such proceedings is *frivolous or groundless, a penalty not in* excess of $25,000 shall be awarded to the United States by the Tax Court in its decision.

Publication 5 (Rev. 11-90)
*U.S. GPO:1991-817-016/49028

Conclusion

The right to appeal an audit decision is a vitally important tool in Firing the IRS. Surely, the threat of an audit will lose its sting, as will the intended results of the audit process, when citizens use this critical right. The IRS is successful in audits 88 percent of the time, not because 88 percent of citizens make mistakes. The success rate is high because tax auditors regularly use the tactics of bluff and intimidation to squeeze money from people which is not owed.

It is time to *Fire* IRS agents who employ such tactics against honest citizens. You do this by exercising your right of appeal. When you assert this right, you literally strip the revenue agent of any and all authority, limited as it is, from the case. You take the matter from his hands entirely and place the decision making authority into the hands of one more capable *and willing* to make a fair and reasonable decision on the issues. Under these circumstances, why would anybody ever again allow a revenue agent to run roughshod over his rights?

6

RIGHT NUMBER TWO: HOW TO SHUT DOWN THE IRS

UNDERSTANDING THE STATUTES OF LIMITATIONS

The concept of "Keeping the IRS out of your Life" involves techniques to chase the agency away - period. You would be shocked to learn how often the IRS makes an effort to audit a citizen or collect a tax which it legally has no right to attempt. Contrary to popular belief, the IRS may not chase you the rest of your life or audit every return you have ever filed. The law greatly limits these abilities. At some point, you are set free of the audit and collection threat.

The most commonly asked question about tax collection concerns statutes of limitations. I never do a radio show without somebody asking, "How far can the IRS go back to audit my return?" Or, "Can they chase me forever on taxes I owe?" My answers bring smiles to the faces of citizens expecting the worst.

In fact, let me share an example with you. It involves a citizen who, upon reading my first book, *The Naked Truth*, had his life changed when learning the IRS was limited in the time it had to collect taxes. Jon writes of his friend Gene:

"In 1970 I met Gene, a person who taught me a lot of the art of selling. We were working for a company as direct, self-employed, commissioned salesmen. Gene had just gone broke. As an officer of a corporation he had been assessed for employment taxes, etc. The amount was staggering. All his 'advisors' (book-keepers, lawyers, etc.) told him that he couldn't bankrupt, couldn't own property and he would owe these taxes for the rest of his life if he didn't pay them. I heard him lament for years, 'I'll take it to my grave!'

"* * * Gene kept working. And *Hiding*. Selling carpet in rented garages in back alleys. Forced into hiding because of a debt that he'll 'take to my grave.' He would buy a house and put it in his child's name. Hiding. Hide the carpet. Hide the car.

"But all this stopped. It changed in 1986.

"I don't remember where I ordered *The Naked Truth* but it came in the mail. In it, Dan Pilla told me about the statute of limitations on collections. I couldn't believe it!! I called Gene. 'I'll be right there.'

"At this point I cannot find adequate words. Excited? Relieved? It was like serving many years of a life sentence and having a guard open the cell door and say, 'You have been pardoned. You are free to go.'

"Gene immediately went from a 'shady black marketeer' to now one of the largest carpet warehouses in our city. From hiding to high profile. Rags to riches. Failure to success. The credit must go to Daniel Pilla and Publisher David Engstrom. The IRS didn't give Gene his rights. . .Dan and Dave did."

Whether the details of the statutes of limitations will mean as much to you as it did to Jon and his friend Gene, I don't know. I do know countless citizens face grim prospects for their financial future due to unpaid tax bills. The assessments mount year after endless year as penalties and interest are heaped on an already out-of-reach bill. Others, not facing such a bleak future, struggle with the question of when the garage can be cleared of boxes of antique records. Those questions and others are addressed here.

Limiting the Audit – The General Rule

Section 6501 of the Code provides the rules that limit the IRS' ability to assess taxes. Generally, the statute reads:

"Except as otherwise provided in this section, the amount of any tax imposed by this title shall be assessed within 3 years after the return was filed (whether or not such return was filed on or after the date prescribed). . ."

Very simply, the IRS must make assessments of tax within three years of the date the return is filed. From then on, the agency's ability to assess taxes evaporates. It is therefore precluded from examining a tax return *after* three years from the date of filing. An assessment is the process by which the IRS records a debt on its books, making it an official liability.

For example, suppose your 1992 tax return was filed on time on April 15, 1993. The IRS has until April 15, 1996, in which to make an examination and assessment of taxes with respect to that return. After April 15, 1996, the return is considered a "closed year." It can be examined only under especially extenuating circumstances. We consider some exceptions later.

Before we examine some of the special exceptions, we must address certain rules which apply when determining the *starting point* of the three-year period of limitations.

1. Return must be complete. To commence the running of the statute of limitations, the return must be complete. It must disclose gross income, deductions and taxable income in such a manner as to enable the IRS to determine the correctness of the return. A return that does not disclose sufficient information from which a tax liability can be computed on its face is not a return within the meaning of the law. It is not required, however, that such return be "perfect" (as if that's possible). The return need only evidence an honest and genuine attempt to comply with the law. Inadvertent omissions or inaccuracies do not suspend the statute of limitations.

2. Returns filed early. Returns filed before the April 15 filing deadline do not trigger the running of the three-year period on the date filed. Rather, section 6501(b)(1) of the Code provides the period of limitations begins to run on the *due date* of the return if filed early. Therefore, even though you may have filed your 1990 return on January 31, 1991, the statute of limitations did not begin to tick until April 15 of 1991.

3. Returns filed late. Returns filed *after* the due date trigger the running of the statute of limitations as of the date of filing. This is true even if you were under a valid extension of time to file. Thus, if your 1990 return was filed on July 15, 1991, the statute of limitations expires on July 15, 1994.

EXCEPTIONS TO THE GENERAL RULE:
When is the Three-Year Period Extended?

There are several circumstances under which the normal three-year rule is trashed. In some circumstances, the period is merely *extended*. In other situations, the period of limitations is entirely *suspended*. The following circumstances discuss the conditions.

1. Certain amended returns. Section 6501(c)(7) extends the statute of limitations when certain amended returns are filed. An amended return filed during the 60-day period immediately before the expiration of the statute of limitations extends the statute for 60 days from the date the amended return is received.

For example, suppose the statute covering your 1987 tax return was set to expire on April 15, 1991, (three years from the due date of the return). Suppose further that on March 15, 1991, (during the 60-day period immediately before the expiration of the statute) you file an amended return showing additional taxes due. Under these circumstances, the statute of limitations is extended to May 15, 1991, 60 days from the date of filing the amended return.

2. Substantial omission of income. Section 6501(e) provides conditions under which the assessment statute of limitations is extended to six years from the filing date. The rule is simple. When the citizen omits "in excess of 25% of the amount of gross income stated in the return" the period in which the tax may be assessed extends to six years.

There is an important restriction on this rule. As you now know from reading Chapter One, the citizen generally bears the burden of proof with respect to all items claimed in the return if questioned in a civil audit. When the IRS asserts the 25% omission rule, however, *the agency* bears a two-pronged burden. It must prove both that the citizen had more income than shown on the return, and the amounts omitted should have been included in gross income.

For purposes of determining whether 25% of gross income is omitted, the calculation is made without respect to any deductions or credits which may be taken against such income.

3. Loss and credit carry backs. Under certain circumstances, operating losses incurred in connection with a business, capital losses incurred in connection with investments, and unused credits may be carried back to previous years. This operates to reduce taxes for the previous years, usually resulting in a refund. This technique was one upon which the two foundational premises of every tax shelter program was built. We do not address here the circumstances under which either operating or capital losses may be carried back. We merely address the impact such a carry back has on the statute of limitations.

Sections 6501(i) and (j) provide when a loss or credit is carried back to a prior year, the statute of limitations on that year is held open as long as the year in which loss or credit was generated is open.

To illustrate, suppose you incur a capital loss in 1990. Suppose further you carry back a portion of that loss to tax year 1989, resulting in a refund of taxes paid in 1989. The normal statute of limitation for 1989 expires on April 15 (assuming you filed timely), 1993. The loss was incurred in 1990, and the statute of limitation on 1990 expires April 15, 1994. Therefore, tax year 1989 (the year to which the loss was carried) remains open until April 15, 1994.

4. False or fraudulent return. Code sections 6501(c)(1) and (2) wholly suspend the assessment statute of limitations in either of two circumstances. The first is when a return is filed which is false or fraudulent "with the intent to evade the tax." The second is where the citizen attempts "in any manner to defeat or evade tax." These are the so-called fraud exceptions to the statute of limitations. When invoked by the IRS, it may assess taxes for any year whatsoever, without respect to any limitation. It should be noted, though, the fraud exception carries the same burden for the government as the 25% understatement rule.

The IRS shoulders the burden to prove with clear and convincing evidence, one of two facts. Either, the citizen filed a false or fraudulent return with the intent to evade taxes, or, he committed an affirmative act calculated to deceive or mislead the IRS, all in an effort to evade or defeat payment of the tax. Unless the IRS can prove fraud with clear and convincing evidence, it cannot assess taxes beyond the normal three-year statute unless some other exception applies.

We must point out here that the "no statute" rule for fraud applies only in civil cases. Criminal prosecutions for fraud are governed by a separate rule.

5. No Return filed. The normal rules governing the assessment of taxes *do not apply* when no return is filed. Thus, if you failed to file a tax return for 1985, the IRS may move to assess and collect taxes despite the passage of time.

As with the fraud rule, the "no statute" rule for failing to file applies only in civil cases. Separate rules govern criminal prosecutions for failure to file tax returns.

6. Commissioner filed returns. When the IRS believes a false return was filed, or a citizen failed to file, the agency may take remedial action. It asks the citizen to correct the return or to file the required return. If the citizen does not, the IRS is authorized by Code section 6020(b) to make a return for the citizen based upon available information. The Courts consider Commissioner-filed returns, or substitute for returns, to be entirely legal and proper. The burden is upon the citizen to prove the return is erroneous.

The normal statute of limitations on assessment does not apply to Commissioner filed returns. Because the returns are made only in cases where the citizen filed a false return or failed to file entirely, the statute of limitations on assessment is entirely suspended.

7. Judicial actions. Under some circumstances, judicial actions undertaken by a citizen can toll the assessment statute of limitations. Two examples are:

a. Tax Court. A citizen may petition the Tax Court within 90 days of receiving a notice of deficiency. The IRS may not assess the tax while the 90-day grace period is pending. From then on, it may not assess the tax if the citizen files a timely petition with the Tax Court. The tax may be assessed after the grace period expires when no petition is filed. It may also be assessed after the Tax Court rules in favor of the IRS. In the later case, the tax assessment must be consistent with the Tax Court's determination. See Code section 6215.

At the time of mailing the notice of deficiency, the statute of limitations on assessment is tolled. The statute remains tolled until the earlier of, the expiration of the 90-day grace period, or, a ruling from the Tax Court. In either case, the statute begins running 60 days after the occurrence of one of the above events. See Code section 6503(a)(1).

b. Summons enforcement. During a criminal investigation or civil examination, the IRS, under Code sections 7601 and 7602, may issue summonses to third parties, such as banks, etc. The summons requires a party to produce records relating to the citizen in question. Section 7609 of the Code affords the citizen the right to invoke the power of the federal courts to "quash," or prevent the summons from being enforced. When the citizen moves under section 7609 to judicially quash a summons, all applicable statutes of limitation are suspended during the time in which the proceeding is pending. See Code section 7609(e)(1).

Additionally, if the summoned party does not release the records sought within six months of service with the summons, all applicable statutes of limitations are suspended. The suspension begins with the date six months after service with the summons. It ends on the date of compliance or resolution of the summoned party's response. See Code section 7609(e)(2).

8. Voluntary Extensions. The statute of limitations on assessment may be suspended if both parties agree in writing to a suspension. The agreement is formalized on Form 872. Once executed, the agreement extends the period of limitation on the power of assessment.

The agency uses two general versions of Form 872. The first, Form 872, *Consent to Extend Time to Assess Tax,* is the so-called fixed date extension. It extends the statute of limitations to a specific date. This form is generally used when the Examination Division needs more time to fully consider all the issues involved in an audit. In such case, the agent sends Form 872 to the citizen with a request for his signature.

The second consent, Form 872-A, *Special Consent to Extend Time to Assess Tax,* is the so-called open-ended extension. This form is typically used when the citizen wishes to have the case reviewed by the Appeals Office before the expiration of the statute. The Form 872-A is open-ended because it is operative for 90 days after, 1) the IRS notifies the citizen the case will no longer be considered, 2) the IRS issues a notice of deficiency, or 3) the citizen files IRS Form 872-T.

Form 872-T, *Notice of Termination of Special Consent to Extend Time to Assess Tax*, is executed by the citizen when he wishes to *withdraw* his consent to extend the statute of limitations.

LIMITING THE COLLECTION OF TAXES – THE GENERAL RULE

As is true with the IRS' ability to *assess* taxes, it is limited in its ability to *collect* taxes once assessed. The general rule is set forth in Code section 6502. Section 6502 reads in pertinent part as follows:

"Where the assessment of any tax imposed by this title has been made within the period of limitation properly applicable thereto, such tax may be collected by levy or by a proceeding in court, but only if the levy is made or the proceeding in court begun --

"1) within 10 years after the assessment of the tax, or

"2) prior to the expiration of any period for collection agreed upon in writing by the Secretary and the taxpayer before the expiration of such 10-year period. . ."

You will note the IRS has at least 10 years to collect taxes once assessed. The 10-year rule is relatively new. It became law in November of 1990, when former President Bush signed the *Omnibus Budget Reconciliation Act of 1990*. Before passage of that act, the IRS had just six years from the date of assessment in which to collect.

I wrote of this amendment in the January 1991, issue of my newsletter, *Pilla Talks Taxes*. I pointed out that we were hoodwinked with this provision of law because it did not appear in any of the committee reports prior to passage. Only after the Act was signed into law did the language appear. The provision was added as a last minute amendment by Senators John Glenn (D. Ohio) and Joseph Liebermann (D Conn.).

The 10-year rule operates this way. Concerning assessments of taxes made after November 5, 1990, (the date the act was passed), the IRS has 10 years to collect the tax or commence a proceeding in court. Concerning assessments made on or before November 5, 1990, the rule extends collection from six to 10 years *only if* the tax was collectible as of November 5, 1990.

To illustrate, suppose a tax is assessed against you on November 1, 1984. Assuming you did nothing to extend the statute of limitations, collection rights expire on November 1, 1990. On the day the act was passed (November 5, 1990), your collection case was closed because the six-year period expired. Therefore, the new law has no no effect on you.

On the other hand, suppose a tax is assessed against you on November 6, 1984. The six-year statute was originally set to expire on November 6, 1990.

However, at the time the new law passed (November 5, 1990) your collection case was open. Therefore, in this situation, the statute adds *four more years* to the time in which the IRS may collect.

If you face a current collection problem, the first order of business is to determine when the statute of limitations on collection expires. This is done by referencing your Individual Master File (IMF). My *Defense Manual* illustrates how to read the IMF. The IMF shows a transaction code (TC) indicating the date of the assessment. Taxes assessed by filing a return are shown with a TC 150. The date adjacent to the TC is the date of the assessment.

Taxes assessed pursuant to an examination of your return are shown with a TC 300. Again, the date adjacent to the TC is the date of the assessment. Also, IRS tax liens state on their face the date of the assessment. I like to cross-check this with the master file.

The next step is to count forward six years. If the count ends on or before November 5, 1990, and you did *nothing* to extend the limitation period (discussed below), the statute is expired. The IRS is not at liberty to collect further. However, if by counting forward six years you are taken beyond November 5, 1990, your collection statute does not expire until 10 years from the date of assessment. It may even be longer if it was extended by other factors.

It is important to know when the statute of limitations expires in your case. If for no other reason, you know the date on which you become free of IRS pursuit. By knowing the expiration date, you can save yourself untold amounts of hassle and hardship.

This is best illustrated with the case of a citizen with whom I talked some time ago. She explained that a revenue officer demanded she sign IRS Form 900, *Tax Collection Waiver*, (the waiver is discussed below). She wondered whether she was obligated to sign.

I asked, "What is the expiration date of the collection statute?"

She did not know off hand, so I asked her to read from the tax lien that was in front of her. From the lien, we learned the assessment date was sometime in mid-1983.

I then asked whether she previously signed a waiver or did anything else to extend the statute of limitations (see list below). She assured me she did nothing. I therefore concluded the statute expired as of mid-1989. I explained she was under no obligation to sign Form 900 since the IRS' power to collect already expired. Upon further questioning, she explained that out of the blue, a revenue officer appeared on the scene demanding she sign the Form 900. He issued threats if she refused. It was plain the revenue officer was clearly attempting to coerce her into signing a Form 900 in a pathetic attempt to breathe life into an already dead collection case.

Of course, the revenue officer did not explain the case was already dead. Nor did it matter that the law plainly declares a Form 900 is *only valid* if signed *prior* to the statute's expiration! He merely huffed and puffed, issuing demands with accompanying threats.

Obviously, somebody in the Collection Division, perhaps that very revenue officer, fell asleep at the switch, allowing the statute to expire. To rectify his own non-feasance, he attempted to browbeat a citizen into signing a waiver after the fact. Had the woman not known the case was closed, signing Form 900 would no doubt have been a perceived license to the revenue officer to begin enforced collection.

EXCEPTIONS TO THE GENERAL RULE:
When is the 10-Year Period Extended?

There are a number of conditions which extend the statute of limitations on collection. We already discussed the Congressional extension from six to 10 years. Let us now examine other means by which the collection statute is extended.

1. The voluntary extension. A voluntary waiver is the most common way the collection statute is extended. As mentioned above, Form 900, *Tax Collection Waiver,* is used by revenue officers to extend the statute. Form 900 is presented to the citizen when the circumstances make it plain the IRS cannot collect the amount due within the statutory collection period. An example is where the citizen negotiates a long-term installment agreement. As I discuss at length in Chapter Eight, a signed Form 900 is always a prerequisite to a long-term installment agreement.

The first question one asks when presented with a Form 900 is, "Should I sign?" That question is sometimes difficult to answer. However, the revenue officer usually makes the decision somewhat simple. If you refuse to sign, he explains, the agency has no choice but to enforce collection. It must, they say, in order to maximize collection before the statute expires. In other words, if you do not sign, liens, levies and seizures are sure to follow.

Still, one should never sign a Form 900 purely on the basis of the statements and demands of a revenue officer. As we saw from the above case study, their representations are not always factually pure. Consider all the facts and circumstances of your case. Most importantly, ascertain when the statute is to expire. If the statute will not expire for several years, signing the Form 900 may not be too prejudicial.

However, if the statute is to expire shortly, it may be financially better to endure enforced collection for a short time rather than extend collection for several years.

Forms 900 are written as either open-ended extensions, with no set date for expiration, or as fixed date extensions, set to expire on a specific date in the future. Under no circumstances I can imagine, would an open-ended extension benefit the citizen.

2. The offer in compromise. The offer in compromise is the means by which the citizen offers the IRS a lesser sum of money than is due in satisfaction of an outstanding liability. This procedure constitutes the heart and sole of the IRS' amnesty program, discussed in my book, *How to Get Tax Amnesty.* Since the IRS revised the procedure in February of 1992, we have been wildly successly in resolving cases in which outstanding tax debts could not be paid.

However, by making the offer, you waive the statute of limitations on collection. The statute is tolled for the time the offer is pending, plus one year. Therefore, by submitting an offer, you automatically extend the statute from at least 10, to at least 11 years. While this is a negative aspect of the offer, it should not, by itself, dissuade your filing an offer. Consider all the facts before making your decision. For more information on the offer process, please see Chapter Eight of *How to Get Tax Amnesty*.

3. Citizen outside the United States. When a citizen is outside the United State for a continuous period of at least six months, the collection statute is tolled during his absence. See Code section 6503(c).

4. Judicial actions. Under some circumstances, judicial actions commenced by a citizen *or the government* toll the collection statute of limitations. Three situations come to mind.

a. Bankruptcy. Section 6503 of the Code provides that the period of limitations on collection is suspended during the time in which the IRS is precluded by law from making an assessment or collecting taxes, plus 60 days. Code section 6503(b) specifically states when the assets of the citizen are in the custody or under the control of a court, such as occurs when one files bankruptcy, the statute is tolled during such period of time, and for 60 days thereafter.

Generally, taxes that are not discharged in bankruptcy are therefore collectible after the bankruptcy case is closed. The collection statute extends for a period equal to the time in which your case was pending in bankruptcy, plus 60 days after termination. Naturally, those taxes that are discharged by the bankruptcy are no longer subject to collection regardless of the statute of limitations.

Yes, federal income taxes *are dischargeable in bankruptcy!* If you have been told the opposite, *forget it!* See Chapters Nine and 10 of *How to Get Tax Amnesty!*

b. Civil actions by the United States. Code section 6502 expressly provides that the normal 10-year period of limitation is extended if, before the expiration of that time, the government commences a suit in court to collect. Such a suit is contemplated under Code section 7403. That section permits the government to sue the citizen to reduce its tax lien to a judgment. It also permits the IRS to seek judicial approval to execute its judgment against property owned by the citizen.

By so doing, the IRS obtains possession of the property through the judicial process. In turn, it extinguishes, or in some other way, provides for the interests of non-debtor third parties claiming ownership to the property. A classic example of this is where a husband owes taxes but his wife does not. At the same time, the couple owns their home jointly. Because the wife has no tax debt, the property cannot legally be seized without the IRS making some provision for her interests. A section 7403 suit is the usual way the IRS obtains permission to sell the property free of the wife's claim. Filing such a suit within the 10-year period extends the statute of limitations on collection.

5. The wrongful levy. A wrongful levy exists when the IRS takes the property of one citizen to satisfy the tax liability of another. We all heard of cases where the IRS seizes junior's bank account because daddy owes taxes. This is the typical wrongful levy case.

Code section 6503(f) provides the collection statute is tolled from the period beginning when the IRS receives the wrongfully levied property (including money) until the agency either returns the property or the victim obtains a judgment against the IRS under Code section 7426. However, the extension under this provision of law applies only to an amount of the assessment *equal to* the amount of money or value of property returned by the IRS.

LIMITING THE CRIMINAL PROSECUTION – THE GENERAL RULE

At last count, the Internal Revenue Code contains approximately 17 provisions which define and set penalties for criminal conduct. Be warned, however, the number of penalties in the code increase with the passage of every new tax law. Among these are the more famous crimes of tax evasion, failure to file tax returns and submitting false documents. Among the less famous are the crimes of failure to collect taxes and making fraudulent statements to employees.

Code section 6531 establishes the limitation period in which a person may be charged with a criminal offense. The statute reads in part as follows:

"No person shall be prosecuted, tried or punished for any of the various offenses arising under the internal revenue laws unless the indictment is found or the information instituted within three years next after the commission of the offense. . ."

Consistent with the power to assess taxes, generally speaking, there is a three-year limitation on the power of the IRS to prosecute one for a criminal offense. This three-year rule applies to approximately one-half of the criminal provisions of the code. There are exceptions to the three-year rule built into Code section 6531.

EXCEPTIONS TO THE GENERAL RULE:
When is the Three-Year Period Extended?

Section 6531 of the Code sets forth eight exceptions to the general three-year period of limitation. In any one of those eight circumstances, the citizen may be charged with a criminal offense within *six years* after the commission of the offense. These are the exceptions:

1. Fraud. Offenses involving fraud or an attempt to defraud the United States in any manner, see 18 USC (US Criminal Code) section 1001;

2. Evasion. Offenses involving attempting in any manner to evade or defeat any tax or payment of any tax, see Code section 7201;

3. Aiding and Assisting. Offenses involving aiding and assisting in, or counseling, or advising in the preparation or presentation to the IRS of a false or fraudulent return, statement or other document, see Code section 7206(2);

4. Failure to file. Offenses involving the failure to file required returns or pay any tax at the time required by law, see Code section 7203;

5. False Return. Offenses involving the preparation and presentation to the IRS of a false or fraudulent return, statement or other document, see Code sections 7206(1) and 7207;

6. Intimidation. Offenses relating to making threats against or intimidating IRS agents while in the act of performing their duties, see Code section 7212(a);

7. Unlawful acts of agents. Any unlawful act committed by an IRS agent, officer or employee in connection with the performance of his duties, such as extortion, accepting bribes, etc., see Code section 7214; and

8. Conspiracy. Offenses involving a conspiracy, the object of which is to attempt in any manner to evade or defeat the payment of any tax, or to defraud the United States by impeding and impairing the lawful functions of the Internal Revenue Service, see 18 USC section 371.

The IRS often uses bogus jail threats to extract cooperation from citizens who otherwise, may have no obligation to give the agency what it seeks. Such threats quickly lose their sting when measured against the yardstick of the criminal statute of limitations. I believe it important to know and use this information when dealing with potentially oppressive agents. Simply by informing them that you understand the statute of limitations placed upon their authority by the plain language of the law, you make great strides toward eliminating IRS abuse.

CONCLUSION

The statutes of limitations are designed expressly for the purpose of protecting the citizen from stale claims. Their presence requires the government to act promptly in the administration of tax laws relating to the assessment and collection of taxes and prosecution of criminal acts. You should know these limitations because the IRS routinely ignores them. Using these tools is a sure way to Fire the IRS when faced with illegal demands.

CHAPTER 7

RIGHT NUMBER THREE: THE RIGHT TO CANCEL PENALTIES

Penalties are big business for the IRS. Every year, the IRS assesses millions of penalties against individuals and businesses. Through those assessments, the IRS collects billions in additional revenue. For example, during 1992 alone, the IRS handed out a total of 33.7 million penalties, for assessments totalling $8.875 billion. 1992 IRS Annual Report, Table 15. This is a 27 percent increase in penalty revenue compared to 1991.

The IRS Code provides an awesome arsenal of penalties available to the agency. At last count, there are approximately 150 different civil and criminal penalties. Even penalty reform legislation passed in 1989 did not substantially reduce the number of penalty provisions within the Code. Nor did it reduce penalty assessments. For example, since 1989, penalty assessments have increased from 29.6 million to the current level of 33.7 million.

The sheer number and variety of penalty sections ensures nearly all of us will be blind-sided by a penalty assessment at some time. The IRS is trigger happy when it comes to penalties. Without inquiring into the facts and circumstances of the case, the agency automatically issues a penalty assessment when "it appears" the penalty may apply.

The reason the action is taken, with no investigation whatsoever, is simple. The IRS does not have any burden of proof with respect to most penalties. Rather, the citizen must prove the penalty does not apply. With this reversal of the burden of proof, the IRS is free to make wholesale assessments, most of which go unchallenged. If challenged, the IRS is assured the citizen knows little about how to argue a successful appeal of the assessment.

Just since May of 1992, we have received two very conflicting messages concerning the question of penalty assessments. The first message was sent by the IRS in May of 1992, when it adopted the sweeping changes to its collection mentality which I have come to recognize as the tax amnesty programs. The first message was the "good news."

The second message was sent by the Clinton administration, courtesy of the US Congress. It came with passage of the *Omnibus Budget Reconciliation Act of 1993*, the Clinton tax and spend package. The second message is the "bad news."

These two actions, totally at odds with one another, indicate the age of uncertainty in which we live. More than anything, they document the need for sweeping tax law changes. Nothing short of the measures called for in this book will be enough to rid the public of the contradictory, myopic, self-defeating programs put forth by Washington.

Let us examine the two measures which so radically contradict one another.

First - Sweeping Administrative Penalty Reform. Along with the many changes brought in with the IRS' new collection attitude, the IRS radically altered the manner in which it views penalties. On April 27, 1992, the IRS issued Policy Statement P-1-18, directed at the administration of penalties. In that statement, the agency admitted the past act of utilizing penalty assessments as a means to raise revenue. In the statement, the IRS confirmed my long-stated contention that improper penalty assessments do nothing to encourage compliance with the tax laws. In fact, they only make it worse. In many cases, penalties actually make payment of back taxes impossible.

The IRS observed:

> "* * *Penalties support the Service's mission only if penalties enhance voluntary compliance. Even though other results such as raising revenue, punishment, or reimbursement of the costs of enforcement may also arise when penalties are asserted, the Service will design, administer and evaluate penalty programs *solely* on the basis of whether they do the best job of encouraging compliant conduct." (Emphasis added.) IRS Policy Statement P-1-18, May 19, 1992.

In other words, when a penalty assessment does not serve the purpose of bringing a non-compliant citizen into compliance, no penalty should be assessed - period. This is true regardless of the fact the government may realize an increase in revenue from the the penalty.

In addition to the above significant development, the IRS issued a statement describing what the new penalty system will encompass. After I first read this, I noticed the presence of many issues I have been touting for years. The new policies were to:

a. Ensure consistency in assessments;

b. Ensure accuracy of results in light of the facts and the law;

c. Provide methods for the taxpayer to have his or her interests heard and considered;

d. require impartiality and a commitment to achieve the correct decision;

e. Allow for the prompt reversal of initial determinations when sufficient evidence has been presented to indicate that the penalty is not appropriate; and

f. Ensure that penalties are used for their proper purpose and not as bargaining points in the development of cases.

Each of the above points is an issue over which I criticized the IRS in the past. No guidelines existed to ensure that any of the above parameters were met.

Not surprisingly, this resulted in the assessment of about 30 million penalties per year.

In addition to inserting the above as guidelines for penalty assessments, the IRS created a new penalty handbook for use by its field agents in administering the new attitude. With over 150 different penalty provisions contained in the Code, it is hard to believe the IRS never bothered to write a definitive handbook setting forth guidelines for the assessment and abatement of those penalties. But it is true - until May of 1992, that is. The same policy statement mentioned above declares:

> "To ensure consistency, the Service prescribes and uses a single set of guidelines in a Penalty Handbook which will be followed by all operational and processing functions."

After years of complaining about the helter skelter manner in which penalties are assessed, the IRS finally responded with a concise handbook for administering penalties. The handbook, released on May 19, 1992, is incorporated into the IRS Manual, found at Part XX. Drafted by the national office, it was released to IRS offices and personnel nationwide for use in the penalty program described in Policy Statement P-1-18.

I viewed this as a major victory for taxpayers' rights. Finally, all citizens would have a guide for use in fighting the improper assessment of penalties, a problem of major significance. Most importantly, I viewed the adoption of Policy Statement P-1-18 as a commitment on the part of the IRS to abandon its long-followed practice of using penalties as a means of raising revenue. Such a practice constituted an improper, in fact, illegal use of the penalty provisions of the law. Worse, such tactics often made payment of the tax impossible due to the staggering escalations they cause.

Second - Clinton's Tax Bill on the Attack. The ink was not dry on these reforms when Bill Clinton was elected president in November of 1992. By the time he came forth with his proposal for tax and budget "reform" on February 17, 1993, his administration decided to resort to the old, Darth Vader way to doing business.

In the March and April, 1993, issues of *Pilla Talks Taxes*, I wrote detailed reports on what was then the Clinton proposed budget plan. It is, of course, now reality, with certain changes. One of Clinton's proposed tax increase programs was to broaden penalty assessments *purely as a means of raising revenue*. More specifically, Clinton's plan expressly provided that certain tax reporting requirements would be made stricter - more complicated - solely to allow a greater number of citizens to trip over the confusion. When mistakes were made, mistakes occasioned only by the change in the law, the IRS would be quick to assess penalties.

Under Clinton's plan, the IRS would use these new penalties to raise the sum of $8.35 billion over the four years of Clinton's administration. That amounts to a whopping 24 percent increase in penalty revenue per year. Sadly, this increase is projected exclusively because Clinton succeeded in making the law more complicated. On August 10, 1993, Clinton signed his reforms into law. At section 14252(a) of the *Omnibus Budget Reconciliation Bill of 1993*, the Clinton tax and spend measure, we find a revision specifically designed to "raise the standard for the accuracy-related penalty." The law increases the burden of proof necessary to avoid the penalty. With a higher burden of proof, more citizens will be stuck with the additional burden of paying the penalty. I discussed this in detail in Chapter Two.

The language of the Committee report accompanying the bill indicates plainly the measure was placed in the law *solely to raise revenue*. The measure is identified in the table of contents to the bill as a "Revenue Increase Provision." This further buttressed by a report issued from the Treasury Department on February 18, 1993, after the Clinton plan was released to the public. The report, entitled, *Revenue Provisions of the President's Economic Plan*, revealed the figure of $8.35 billion to be generated by "modified penalties" and "IRS compliance initiatives."

This is in direct contradiction to the IRS' administrative changes, which now *forbid* the use of penalties in that fashion.

So while we made great strides in 1992 to limit and decrease penalty abuse by the IRS, the Clinton administration opened the wounds to again allow an infestation of potential IRS abuse. The message sent by Clinton through this measure alone, never mind the other 81 tax law changes, is plain. Clinton intends an *attack* upon the American taxpayer, not a love affair, as he would have you believe.

Based upon the above, now more than ever, you must understand your right to cancel penalties. As the Clinton era progresses, you will be a penalty target more and more often because penalty assessments are viewed by the administration as a source of easy money.

How to Cancel Penalties

Every one of the penalty provisions of the Code contains a "good faith" or "reasonable cause" provision. It means when you act in good faith, and based upon a reasonable cause for your actions, the penalty does not apply. This is true even when your actions were incorrect.

My penalty-proofing techniques discussed in Chapter Two are designed to eliminate potential penalties for future tax returns. The premise holds that by making full disclosure of all the facts and circumstances regarding your claims, the law presumes the existence of good faith. The reason is, persons acting out of bad faith, or through a deliberate effort to mislead or deceive the IRS, do not willingly disclose the facts of their case. On the contrary, they attempt to conceal the facts and wrongfully color the circumstances.

Even though you may penalty-proof future returns, you remain at risk on returns already filed. The IRS, as explained in the previous chapter, may assess taxes and penalties anytime within three years of filing the return. Therefore, at any one time, you are exposed on at least two, and sometimes three previous returns. Therefore, be prepared to demand abatement, or cancellation, of assessed penalties.

The process for demanding abatement of penalties is incredibly simple. Given the overwhelming amount of money demanded through penalty assessments, and relative simplicity of the process, I am amazed everyone does not demand cancellation.

The process of demanding abatement begins with a simple letter. Direct the letter to the IRS office, usually a Service Center, which assessed the penalty. The letter must do the following:

1. State your name and address;
2. Contain a firm statement that you wish to have penalties abated;
3. State specifically which penalties and in what amounts, you wish abated;
4. Provide a detailed statement of the facts and circumstances which justify the abatement; and
5. Provide a declaration that your statement of facts is made under the penalty of perjury.

The fourth requirement is where most people have trouble. Let me simplify it. Your letter must be as detailed as possible. The details must set out facts that allow the reader to draw the conclusion you acted in good faith and based upon reasonable cause for your actions. Your facts must make it clear you did not attempt to avoid or defeat IRS' rules and regulations. Your presentation must assure the reader that, at all times, you made every effort to comply with your obligations under the tax law, but due to circumstances beyond your control, you were unable to.

I review many letters requesting abatement. I find a common denominator in each letter. It is that folks tend to err on the side of *incompleteness* when describing the facts. Folks tend to describe circumstances and events in very general terms, avoiding pointed specificity.

To be successful, a letter demanding abatement must be extremely specific on the facts. Give graphic details on the events leading to the assessment of penalties. You must firmly and boldly declare that the penalty does not apply and you are entitled to an abatement.

In the event the initial letter is unsuccessful, you enjoy the right to submit additional information, including further details on the facts. Also, you have the right to appeal a decision denying the request for abatement. Execute the appeal with a written protest letter as outlined in Chapter Five.

My own experience with letters demanding abatement indicates that you will be successful about 60 percent of the time. All it takes is a 29-cent postage stamp and 20 constructive minutes at the typewriter. Who would not invest such a small amount for a return of, say, $1,000?

These penalty abatement techniques may also be used in a routine tax audit. It is the wont of auditors to include an assortment of penalties in their tax increase recommendations. However, your right to challenge the penalties is on equal footing with the right to challenge the underlying bill. In fact, you may challenge penalties even when you concede your obligation for the underlying bill. Follow the steps in Chapter Five to challenge penalty assessments made in accordance with a face-to-face audit.

My book, *41 Ways to Lick the IRS with a Postage Stamp*, contains an entire chapter on abating penalties. I explain the various penalties commonly assessed and the process of winning an abatement. Also, I explore the prospect of winning an abatement of interest assessments. A right brought on by the passage of the *Taxpayers' Bill of Rights Act* in November of 1988.

CONCLUSION

The current administration is resorting to diabolical techniques to raise more revenue. Rather than attempting to reduce the burdens this tax system places upon citizens, it has increased them solely for the purposes of getting *more of your money*.

Truely, this underhanded tactic decries the need for sweeping changes - real rebuilding - to our tax collection system. Without them, more citizens will be abused and literally robbed by their own government.

In the meantime, it is fundamentally important to understand how to deal with penalty assessments since they can only be expected to rise in the coming years.

8

RIGHT NUMBER FOUR: THE INSTALLMENT AGREEMENT

Facing enforced tax collection is your worst nightmare. The vast number of horror stories we hear about IRS abuse, victimization of taxpayers and outright destruction of the lives of citizens often come at the hands of the Collection Division. Staffed with revenue officers whose job is to collect delinquent accounts, the Collection Division has the power to lien your assets, seize your bank accounts or paycheck, even sell your home or automobile. Very little is exempt from the reach of these officers and they seem to have little compassion for the problems delinquent paying citizens face in paying their taxes.

In this situation, installment agreements are often viewed by citizens as the only hope of paying the tax. When large sums of cash are unavailable or liquidated assets would yield insufficint revenue, the installment agreement seems the logical remedy. After all, it is the American way. Pay debt in installments, over time, the way you purchased your home and car. Why not pay taxes that way also?

One answer is the IRS does not fancy itself a bank. For that reason, historically, they have not looked kindly on installment arrangements. Because of that attitude, the IRS lied to taxpayers for years concerning such agreements. One revenue officer would explain no right to an installment agreement exists, while another would say installment agreements were good for just six months or a year. No consistency existed within the agency on this issue. That is the main reason why the issue of installment agreements was given such prominent attention in hearings before Congress on the *Taxpayers Bill of Rights Act* in 1988.

Since then, two significant improvements were made affecting the ability to win an installment agreement. The first was the actual passage of the *Taxpayers' Bill of Rights Act.* It squarely addressed the issue of installment agreements. I discuss this in detail later in this chapter.

Next came an administrative amendment to IRS procedures. In January of 1993, the IRS announced it was liberalizing its attitude toward payment arrange-ments. This attitude adjustment is part of the "new attitude" I discuss in the book, *How to Get Tax Amnesty.* The new procedures announced in January of 1993, are the most sweeping changes to installment agreement procedures enacted since the IRS has existed. I address them in detail here.

Automated Collection Sites and Delinquent Accounts

Delinquent tax collection begins with Automated Collection (ACS). The IRS operates some 21 ACS locations nationwide. They were designed and installed in 1984 as a means to, as the name suggests, automate the collection of delinquent taxes. ACS is initally responsible to issue tax due notices, file tax liens and execute levies. The horrible aspect of ACS is it is entirely computer driven. Very little of what eminates from ACS has touched human hands. Consequently, negotiating with this office or attempting to correct erroneous billings can quickly become a nightmare.

Demands from ACS must be taken very seriously and must be responded to immediately. Without prompt response, the IRS pursues enforced collection in a most uncomfortable fashion. Since early 1993, we have been presented with a most effective manner of handling ACS. The discussion follows.

New Form 9465

Shortly after announcing the news that installment agreements would be looked upon more favorably, the agency released new Form 9465, *Installment Agreement Request*. (Form 9465 is reproduced in this chapter as Exhibit 8-1)

Using this simple form, one asks the IRS to establish an installment agreement upon the terms set forth in the form. The citizen himself declares the amount he can afford to pay and the date on which the payment is made. This form is likely the closest thing to a self-executing installment agreement that we will see from the IRS.

Use Form 9465 upon receipt of your first bill from ACS. Also use it when filing your tax return if you do not have the money to pay the tax due. I learned from sources in Washington that the application is automatically granted when two conditions are met. First, the tax owed must be less than $10,000. Second, the amount of the installment payment must be greater than $100 per month.

That is not to say one cannot come to payment terms if he owes more or can pay less. If such is the case, the IRS asks to review financial information through a completed financial statement. I discuss this process later. When your application is accepted, you are notified and the installment process begins.

The new attitude and form have made the process of negotiating installment agreements vastly easier. Even before the formal procedures were placed into effect, the IRS began in earnest in mid-1992 negotiating more in good faith on installment agreements. As a result, the number of installment agreements accepted in 1992 increased by 38 percent to 2.5 million. This is up from 1.8 million in 1991.

In addition, during 1992, the IRS collected 24 percent more revenue through the installment agreement process than it did the year before. Approximately $2.3 billion was collected in 1992, compared with $1.3 in 1991. IRS *1992 Annual Report*, page 8.

This evidence confirms a point I have made all along. I insisted the IRS'

Darth Vader approach to tax collection actually *cost* the agency more money than it collected. By refusing to negotiate with citizens in good faith, the IRS succeeded only in driving them underground. This of course makes collection of any amount much more difficult, or impossible.

Certain critics of my book *How to Get Tax Amnesty* claimed it would encourage wholesale tax cheating. The suggestion was if citizens believed they could simply use the amnesty programs to "get out" of paying taxes, they would deliberately stop paying. The above numbers prove this assertion is entirely incorrect. Americans want to pay what they owe. They resist, however, when they are forced to make a choice between paying their taxes and feeding their families. No person should ever have to make such a choice.

Exhibit 8-1

Form **9465** (Rev. December 1992)	Department of the Treasury – Internal Revenue Service **Installment Agreement Request**	OMB Clearance No. 1545-1350 Expires 12/31/93

General Information

If you can't pay the amount you owe in full at this time, please request an installment agreement by completing this form. Specify the amount of the monthly payment you propose to make in the block marked "Proposed monthly payment amount."

We encourage you to make your payments as large as possible to lower penalty and interest charges. Under law, these charges continue to increase until you pay the balance in full.

Please attach this form to the front of your tax return or to the notice we sent you, and mail it to the appropriate IRS office.

Make your check or money order payable to the Internal Revenue Service, and mark the payment with your name, address, taxpayer identification number, form number and tax period. If you have any questions about this procedure, please call our toll-free number 1-800-829-1040.

Within 30 days, we will let you know if your request for an installment agreement is approved or denied, or if we need more information.

Taxpayer name(s) as shown on the tax return	Taxpayer identification number *(SSN for primary & secondary filers)* or EIN		
Address	City	State	ZIP Code
Business telephone number *(include area code and extension number, if any)*	Most convenient time for us to call you	Home telephone number *(include area code)*	Most convenient time for us to call you
Form number and tax period	Amount paid with return	Amount owed on return	Proposed monthly payment amount
			Amount I am able to pay each month	Date each month I am able to make the payment *(Must be the 1st through the 28th day)*
Your signature		Date	
Spouse's signature *(joint returns only)*		Date	

Privacy Act and Paperwork Reduction Act Notice

We ask for the information on this form under authority of Internal Revenue Code sections 6001, 6011, 6012(a), 6109, and 6159 and their regulations. We use this information to process your request for an installment agreement. The principal reason we need your name and social security number is to secure proper identification. We require this information to gain access to the tax information in our files and properly respond to your request. If you do not disclose the information, the IRS may not be able to process your request.

The time needed to complete and file this form will vary depending on individual circumstances. The estimated average time is 10 minutes.

If you have comments concerning the accuracy of this time estimate or suggestions for making this form more simple, we would be happy to hear from you. You can write to both the **Internal Revenue Service**, Washington, DC 20224, Attention: IRS Reports Clearance Officer, T:FP, and the **Office of Management and Budget** Paperwork Reduction Project (1545-1350), Washington, DC 20503. DO NOT send this form to either of these offices. Instead, refer to the instructions above.

How to Win an Installment Agreement

At some point in your quest for an installment agreement, it may become necessary to do more than complete Form 9465 and mail it with your best hopes sealed inside. You may likely be confronted, either by ACS personnel, or a revenue officer who shows up at your door. To neutralize the contact and win the agreement, you must assert your need for an installment agreement. More importantly, you must know exactly what it takes to prevail on the issue.

Prior to passage of the *Taxpayers' Bill of Rights Act*, there was absolutely no written authority, either in the form of a statute or regulation, permitting the IRS to enter into installment agreements. Accepting an agreement was purely discretionary with the revenue officer and his immediate supervisor. Often, the agreement was looked upon by the Collection Division as a form of "favor" granted to the citizen. It does not require much experience to know the IRS is not routinely in the business of granting "favors."

Therefore, installment agreements were difficult to come by. It required intensive negotiation to achieve one. Once instituted, the IRS was notorious for arbitrarily increasing the installment payment amount or worse, disregarding the agreement altogether. These facts were considered by Congress when it passed the *Taxpayers Bill of Rights Act* in 1988.

One provision of the Act created Code section 6159. Section 6159 represents the sum and substance of the written authority for the IRS to enter into installment agreements. The statute reads, in relevant part, as follows:

> "The Secretary is authorized to enter into written installment agreements with any taxpayer under which such taxpayer is allowed to satisfy liability for payment of any tax in installment payments if the Secretary determines that such agreement will facilitate collection of such liability." Code section 6159(a).

You no doubt noticed the above provision of law *does not* contain any specific statement saying installment agreements are a matter of *absolute right*, expressly offered for the benefit of a financially strapped taxpayer. The language of the law seems to clearly communicate the notion that discretion to permit an installment agreement remains in the hands of the IRS.

Yet, the presence of the law itself provides substantial benefit to a citizen who, through no fault of his own, finds himself behind the eight ball. In the first place, a previously prevalent problem created by the lack of specific authority is gone. That is, the IRS cannot now claim, as it did so often in the past, overdue tax accounts must be satisfied in full–now–without delay, or else. The presence of the statute affords the citizen full latitude to negotiate an installment agreement.

Second, and perhaps more important, a request for an installment agreement must be considered by the Collection Division on its merits. They can no longer be summarily rejected as in the past. This is because the Problems Resolution Office may now step in to order or otherwise provide for an installment agreement. We discuss the Problems Resolution Office later in this chapter.

I am always concerned the lack of objective statutory standards often vitiates the import of the supposed right. In this case, however, we can nevertheless force the IRS to the bargaining table on the issue of installment agreements. If nothing else, Form 9465 makes this possible. Furthermore, when the issue is negotiated properly, you will walk away with an agreement which will, at least for the short term, be responsive to your needs.

How to Establish the Installment Payment Amount

The heart and sole of any collection case is the financial statement. The first job of the RO (or ACS representative) in a collection case is to obtain a financial statement if the citizen expresses inability to pay the tax in full. The IRS does not entertain alternative payment methods unless you provide a full and complete financial statement.

Financial statements are submitted on IRS Form 433-A (individuals) or 433-B (businesses). In Chapter Five on *How to Get Tax Amnesty*, I provide copies of these forms with more details on their use.

The purpose of the statement is two-fold. You must understand both purposes when completing either form. First, the IRS determines from the financial statement whether, in fact, you are unable to pay the tax. The RO considers all income and assets to ascertain whether you can pay. If the statement reveals sufficient income and assets from which to pay, negotiating any long-term installment agreement will be most difficult.

However, short-term arrangements are yet possible. A short term agreement enables you to selectively liquidate certain assets or otherwise make arrangements to raise the needed funds. Of course, along with revealing your income and assets — and their locations — you provide the RO with possible sources of levy action. This may be an unavoidable risk since you cannot win an installment agreement without a completed financial statement. Further, the financial statement must be true and accurate lest you risk prosecution for submitting a false document to the IRS.

Next, the RO analyzes your expenses and liabilities to determine the amount of the installment payment you can afford. You are not at liberty to declare, "I will pay you $100 per month," and expect the RO to accept such a payment without question. The financial statement is used to determine the amount of your payment. Understand, however, the amount demanded by the RO is entirely negotiable.

Pay particular attention to the portion of the financial statement seeking information concerning your present income and expenses. This information should be complete and accurate. For example, do not list items of income which are not certain and recurring money *each month*. In addition, be careful to examine each item on which you spend money *every month*. These items, your monthly expenses, play a prominent role, as we shall see, in determining the amount of your payment. You must be prepared to verify any expense claimed on the form for reasons you are about to learn.

The IRS manual for revenue officers stipulates the amount of the monthly payment "will be at least the difference between net income and allowable expenses." IRM 5323(4)(e). Net income is determined based upon amounts withheld for federal and state income and social security taxes and all mandatory retirement contributions. The difference between gross pay and these withholdings is considered "net income."

Determining what constitutes "allowable expenses" is another matter. It involves a wide range of discretion on the part of the RO. The RO has the power to disallow, for purposes of determining the amount of the installment payment, certain expenditures you incur from month to month. By disallowing certain expenditures, the RO demands that funds otherwise committed to those items be used to increase the payment to the IRS. Such disallowance of payments is made without regard to the effect on other creditors. After disallowing such payments, the RO advises you to "make such arrangements as are necessary" with those creditors whose obligations you are instructed to ignore.

This power is not unchecked, however. Understanding its limitations spells the difference between an installment agreement which chokes you and one under which you can actually survive. There are two general categories of expenses which, according to the manual, "constitute allowable expense items." The first is expenses necessary for the production of income. These include union or professional dues, child care payments which allow you to work each day, expenses for commuting to and from work, and any other costs directly associated with earning income.

Self-employed persons must pay particular attention to this element of determining "allowable expenses." Naturally, the tendency of the IRS is not to consider all expenses. Be prepared to assert and prove the existence of all expenses and that they constitute allowable expense. See IRM 5323(4)(a)(1).

The second category of non-disallowable expenses includes those which provide for the health and welfare of your family. Expenses must be reasonable, based on the size of the family and geographic location. These expenses include rent or mortgage payments, food, clothing, transportation expenses including insurance, car payment, gasoline, etc., home maintenance expenses including utilities, insurance, etc., medical expenses and health insurance, *current tax payments*, life insurance payments (but not to the point of constituting an investment), and, alimony, child support or other court ordered payments.

As you see, these two categories provide much in the way of latitude in negotiating the installment payment amount. For example, if the difference between your net monthly income and all monthly expenses (within the two categories described) is just $125, yet the RO demands $300 per month, you have every right to stand firm on the $125 figure. On the other hand, if the difference between the two figures is $300, you will have a hard time justifying your demand for a $125 per month payment.

In any event, be prepared to prove two things. First, that each of the expenses claimed is both a legitimate, recurring expense. And second, the expense is necessary to earn income or is essential to provide for the health and welfare of your family. Prove the points with invoices, checks or other documents showing the amount of the payment and to whom paid, with explanations for the purpose of each item.

There are two further categories of expenses we should address. They constitute generally "allowable items" when determining the installment payment amount. Minimum payments on secured, legally perfected debts are generally allowed. However, if the payment is for a luxury item such as a boat, expect the RO to ask you to sell the asset, then commit the additional revenue to the IRS, including the profit, if any, from the sale of the item.

The IRS generally attempts to classify as unallowable, monthly payments due on unsecured debts, such as credit cards. Look for the RO to ask you to discontinue payments to these entities if by doing so, the IRS is paid in full within 90 days. However, if such action does not pay the tax debt within 90 days, argue that minimum payments to unsecured creditors must be allowed. If they are not, those creditors could commence legal action against you. That can impair your ability to pay the tax.

In some cases, a fixed, level monthly payment cannot be determined. Those in business for themselves, or those working on strict commission, do not always realize the same cash-flow or profits from one month to the next, or from season to season. If this is the case, make the point clear to the RO at the outset of negotiations. I find it helpful to prepare a detailed cash-flow projection showing your expected income and expenses for the ensuing 12- or 24-month period.

By doing this, the RO, who probably has no understanding whatsoever of how real-world businesses operate, is taken by the hand and shown how your business, and hence, income, fluctuate. From this, you can structure an elastic payment plan which expands and contracts with your income.

It is within the framework expressed above that you negotiate to determine the amount of your monthly payment. During these negotiations, never lose sight of the fact that the RO's job is to *get the money!* Everything he says and does revolves around that general goal. As a practical matter, he attempts to reach that goal by doing the following:

1. Obtaining information on all possible sources of levy, including the location and value of all assets, bank accounts, etc. The Financial Statement serves this purpose.

2. Obtaining a Signed Form 900, *Tax Collection Waiver*, if the financial statement indicates immediate or short-term collection is not possible.

3. Filing a *Notice of Federal Income Tax Lien* with the county recorder in and for the county in which you live. By filing the lien, the IRS' interest in your assets is protected and to a certain extent (subject to limitations expressed in the Federal Bankruptcy Code), the interest is "secured."

4. After analyzing the financial statement, expect the RO to seek to liquidate any assets in which there is an equity interest sufficient to generate positive revenue. If, for example, you own a lake home and would realize substantial revenue by selling it, the RO will want it sold. He may threaten to levy the asset if you do not willingly list it for sale.

He will wish to explore the possibility of obtaining a loan from a bank by remortgaging property. Be careful, however, not to use credit card credit as a means to raise cash for *partial* payments to the IRS. That merely increases your monthly expenses without eliminating the IRS collection problem.

Before finalizing the agreement, it is submitted to his immediate supervisor for approval. You *may* be forced back to the table. On the other hand, you have the right to appeal to the supervisor if you cannot agree with the RO.

I caution any citizen who is currently under an installment agreement or contemplating such an agreement. Use that tool in conjunction with other techniques which more fully address the problems a past due citizen faces. The installment agreement is not an end in itself because accumulating interest and penalties almost always negate any nominal monthly installment payment. The result is that the liability continues to build even while making payments.

The installment agreement is an important tool used to stabilize an otherwise volatile collection situation. Once in place, you may pursue other techniques to resolve the delinquency entirely. The techniques to which I refer are the tax amnesty programs explained in *How to Get Tax Amnesty*. Only by resolving the delinquency entirely do you finally eradicate the threat of enforced collection.

EMPLOYMENT TAXES AND THE INSTALLMENT AGREEMENT

Employment tax delinquencies present special problems. The IRS views them in a much more serious light. Consequently, it moves to enforce collection of employment taxes much faster and with more tenacity. As a result, there are special problems associated with employment tax delinquencies which are outside the scope of this essay. However, I do address them in great detail in Chapter Five of *How to Get Tax Amnesty*. Anybody facing employment tax debts should consult that discussion.

The substantive negotiation on the actual amount of the installment payment for employment tax liabilities is no different from that used for personal income taxes. The heart of the process is the financial statement. When a business is involved, the applicable financial statement is Form 433-B, which reveals business income and expenses. From there, you ascertain the amount of the monthly payment as outlined earlier. Unlike personal income taxes, however, RO's generally do not allow substantially protracted payment arrangements. This is particularly true with an operating corporation. To settle the manner purely in the installment arena, be prepared to make aggressive payments, while at the same time, remaining current with all filing and payment obligations.

THE PROBLEMS RESOLUTION OFFICE

I declared earlier the presence of the Problems Resolution Office (PRO) often helps hasten IRS' acceptance of installment agreements. PRO has the ability to issue what is called a Taxpayer Assistance Order (TAO). The TAO is designed to prevent or correct IRS actions, or lack of actions, the effect of which is to cause a "significant hardship" to the citizen. PRO has the power to intervene in installment payment negotiations to assist in arranging a workable plan.

Recent changes in the regulations governing the TAO reflect the IRS' "new attitude." The new regulations define a "significant hardship" as a "serious privation caused or about to be caused to the taxpayer as a result of the manner in which the tax laws are being administered by the IRS." Revenue Regulation section 301.7811-1(a)(4). Mere personal or economic inconvenience does not rise to the level of "hardship." However, financial hardship created by wage or bank levies does constitute "significant hardship."

Under regulations existing before March 20, 1992, financial hardship alone did not constitute "significant hardship." Of course, no other hardship is created by wage and bank levies. That quirk in the regulations operated to deprive citizens of the relief they will probably now win, given the "new attitude."

I find PRO to be quite effective in achieving installment agreements under emergency circumstances. For example: if a citizen under levy is unable to win an installment agreement with the RO, a PRO can step in to order release of the levy and help the citizen negotiate an installment agreement. Bring your case to the attention of PRO through the use of IRS Form 911, *Application for Taxpayer Assistance Order.* More detailed discussion of the Form 911 and PRO can be found in *How to Get Tax Amnesty*, and the *Taxpayers' Ultimate Defense Manual.*

Conclusion

If not handled properly and quickly, enforced collection action can kill you financially. That is why it is so important to employ the technique of first slowing the train, then stopping it, when you face a tax delinquency. If you attempt any challenges of the liability or the system while the assessment is under collection, you have nothing to look forward to but liens, levies and seizures.

Because of the excessive lattitude afforded the IRS by the federal courts, it enjoys collection powers no other creditor in or out of government could dare attempt. These powers often reduce delinquent citizens to a condition of abject poverty. Ironically these citizens are reduced to poverty in the name of preserving a system which has, as its primary purpose, the elimination of poverty.

Something is seriously wrong with a system which allows a gainfully employed person to be put out of a job for not paying a tax which goes to fund benefits for other persons who are themselves out of a job. But this is exactly what happens when enforced collection drives citizens underground.

Enforced collection of this magntude is no small matter. For example, during 1992 alone, the IRS executed 3.25 million wage and bank levies. This is an increase of *19 percent* over 1990 levels. In that same year, 1992, the IRS filed 1.45 million federal tax liens and seized 11,000 homes, businesses and automobiles. All of these actions were taken, for the most part, without court orders.

To make matters worse, they were taken *not* against citizens who would not pay their tax bill. Rather, they were taken by and large, against citizens who *could not* pay their tax bills. If the United States is to preserve the legal and Constitutional characteristics which set it apart from every nation in the world, our tax system must be radically altered to prevent such actions from continuing.

9 RIGHT NUMBER FIVE: THE CORRESPONDENCE AUDIT
STAY OUT OF THE IRS' CLUTCHES

Earlier we discussed several telling statistics regarding face-to-face tax audits. We learned that about 88 percent of all returns audited end up with additional taxes due. And we learned the additional bill is, on the average, over $5,800. Sadly, just 10 percent of the affected citizens appeal the adverse decision. I firmly believe these results do not occur solely because citizens are making wholesale mistakes in their tax returns, or are cheating.

In large part, the statistics arise because of the great level of bluff and intimidation used by agents in the audit process. If this were not the case, the large appeal reversal rate of 69 percent would not exist. The right to a correspondence audit plays an important role in erasing the abuse which occurs at the examination level.

An important byproduct of my audit-proofing techniques plays directly into this critical right. The right to a correspondence audit is fundamental to tax audit fairness, but is virtually unknown. Not only is the average citizen unaware of this right, tax professionals almost never discuss it.

By audit-proofing your tax return with all relevant explanations, including copies of appropriate documents, you can effectively eliminate the need to ever meet face-to-face with an IRS agent. By avoiding the audit meeting, you avoid the risk of being trapped or taken advantage of by a plotting agent. Still, how do we eliminate the need for a meeting? After all, in any audit, the IRS practically insists on the presence of the "victim."

The answer lies in the audit principles outlined earlier. As explained, the only legitimate purpose of an audit is to determine the correctness of the tax return. That goal is accomplished by reviewing all documentation and evidence in support of the claims made. When such evidence is provided as attachments to the tax return, what possible need is there for meetings? If all relevant documentation is provided with the return itself, what additional information is available to disclose in a subsequent audit?

The answer, of course, is nothing constructive can be accomplished through subsequent meetings or disclosures. Granted, there may be occasions in which the agency has legitimate questions concerning your documentation. Surely it is much easier for the agent to transmit those questions in writing, rather than set aside part of his day for lengthy meetings. More important than that, how much easier and less tension-filled is it for you to merely respond in writing to a letter? That way, you avoid the need to take a day off work or hire a professional, travel downtown and face the hassle and anxiety of meeting with the agent.

All aspects considered, the scales tip decidedly in favor of the correspondence audit. The next question, then, is why does the IRS not talk about the correspondence audit? In the first place, the right of a correspondence audit is discussed in Publication One. (See Chapter Five, Exhibit 5-1.) What is written there, however, is the sum and substance of the IRS' coverage of the right.

The IRS wishes to ignore the right simply because the agency has much greater success in face-to-face audits than it does in correspondence audits. We know the average tax assessed in face-to-face audits is over $5,800. However, in correspondence audits, the average falls to $2,206. 1992 Annual Report, Table 11.

During face-to-face audits, citizens are largely intimidated, somewhat frightened, and tend to talk too much but say the wrong things. Generally in that environment, they are willing to do anything to end the ordeal. Of course, "doing anything" means you pay more. Versus a correspondence audit, they pay about 2.5 times more.

Even if you did not audit-proof your return, you nevertheless can benefit from the safety of a correspondence audit. When the IRS sends an audit notice, it generally specifies the issues in question and establishes a date for a conference. You can transform your meeting into a correspondence audit by following a few very simple steps.

First, respond quickly to the request for a conference. Explain you cannot meet on that day because you need additional time to locate all necessary records and prepare for the audit. Be very courteous and professional. Explain you understand your obligation to verify the items in question and you stand prepared to do so. State you will contact the agent when you are prepared.

Next, immediately begin to gather and organize all records needed to verify the items in question. When ready, photocopy all relevant documents and prepare a detailed written explanation of their contents. It is a good idea to have your explanations notarized, thus making them sworn statements. Affidavits are discussed in Chapter One.

Next, mail the photocopies (*never send original documents*) to the agent with your notarized explanation. In a cover letter, explain you are sending copies of all documents in your possession relative to the items in question. Direct his attention to the explanation. Conclude by saying you hope this clears up all his concerns. Lastly, invite him to write you with any further questions or concerns. Be careful to note that you will respond in writing to all his questions.

Through this process, you undergo a tax audit without ever leaving your home. You avoid suffering the anxiety of a face-to-face meeting and do not risk failing under pressure. At all times, you enjoy the ability to think clearly and rationally before making any statements. You also enjoy the luxury of consulting counsel, if necessary, before responding to any questions. Most importantly, by transmitting the documents with explanations through the mail, you create a precise and uncontrovertible record of the process. Explanations carefully written are clear and cannot be misunderstood. By contrast, oral statements can either be inherently or deliberately misunderstood.

You are probably asking, "What if the agent demands a face-to-face meeting?" To answer the question, I draw back to Right Number One, Chapter Five, and ask you, "Who has the power and who does not?" I hope you remember there is nothing the agent can do to force his will upon you. The likely response from a belligerent agent is to disallow certain of your deductions. But if he does so, *appeal his decision!* By mailing copies of your documentation, you create a record of cooperation and establish your entitlement to the deductions he disallowed. Certainly, no reasonable Appeals Officer will sustain such a decision!

Conclusion

Tax audits and the fear of being in debt to the IRS are among the two chief sources of anxiety for Americans. This does not have to be. If the IRS were forced by citizens to deal more honesty with them, most of the abuses seen in face-to-face audits would disappear. For one thing, you cannot expect agents to freely put in writing the kind of threats and intimidation tactics they use verbally, behind closed doors.

In the context of the potentially abusive tax audit, you effectively Fire the IRS when you demand a correspondence examination. You fire an abusive tax auditor when you choose to avoid meeting him face-to-face. You fire a system which is designed to bluff you, intimidate you, and take money from you which you do not owe.

10

Right Number Six: Challenging IRS Computer Notices

In discussing Right No. One, I state the right of appeal is perhaps the most important right citizens enjoy. In this chapter, we discuss the process of challenging computer notices. The computer has become a major enforcement tool for the IRS in the past ten years. I explained earlier how the IRS has computerized the collection process through implementing its ACS operations. But much more is done with computers.

We examined the IRS' Information Returns Program, Non-filer Program, DIF program, and other ways the agency uses computers to attack the public. Another major aspect of the IRS' computer power is its ability to link data bases both in and out of government, to gather, assimilate and utilize information about and against American citizens. Largely due to IRS demand for more and greater computer power, your right to privacy is practically a thing of the past.

In its 1991 Annual Report, the IRS boasted of mailing some 100 million (that is not a misprint) letters and notices to the public. See 1991 *Highlights*, page 7. Considering there were only 112 million individual returns filed in 1991, I would say that was quite a feat. As incredible as this may sound, you should look for the IRS' blizzard of computer notices to get worse. Since 1984, the IRS has been beating a drum it refers to as Tax System Modernization (TSM). The purpose of TSM, according to the agency, is to bring out of date computers up to industry standards. That may seem reasonable enough, but the IRS has already spent some $8.5 billion in the past 10 years doing so. Still, there is no end in sight.

When my first book *The Naked Truth* was published in 1986, the IRS Strategic Plan showed a desire of the agency to expand its computers into virtually every area of private life. The IRS expressed the goals of auditing every taxpayer for every year, to eliminate the paper income tax return by the year 2000, and most ominously, to "create and maintain a sense of presence" in the lives of all Americans. These goals are not attainable unless the IRS creates a ubiquitous computer tracking system. Many called me paranoid when I made those claims.

But there is no better, more objective judge of one's accuracy than history. In *41 Ways to Lick the IRS with a Postage Stamp*, and in the Introduction to Part

I of this book, I chronicle the events which update my earlier claims. I add to those earlier remarks by illustrating how President Clinton's budget intends to broaden the IRS' reach, scope and presumably, its authority.

In the *Pilla Talks Taxes* newsletter, March, 1993, "Special Report on the Clinton Budget Plan," I explained one of the President's "economic stimulus proposals" was to provide additional funding to the IRS in the amount of $192 million over four years to "Accelerate Tax System Modernization." See *A Vision of Change for America*, at page 132. However, the Clinton Administration was not being truthful with the public in terms of that declaration.

The House Ways and Means Committee issued a report on the President's proposed budget in the spring of 1993. There it is revealed that some *$1.7 billion* will be dedicated to tax systems modernization over the next four years! See *Bender's Federal Tax Week*, No. 10, March 11, 1993, page 119.

In the past, I reported that overall spending for computer upgrades would cost about $8.5 billion. However, more recent insider reports from Washington put the spending more on the level of $21 billion plus. Ibid, at page 119. This an incredible amount of money for computers and begs the question, what on earth are they doing with this kind of power?

The answer lies in three areas. First, I harken back to the 1984 Strategic Plan. Chief among the facets of the plan is one to link the nation with a hardware system allowing the IRS instant access to virtually all data bases maintained in the country. The goal is to give IRS agents instant access to all the financial data needed to "compute tax liabilities on the spot." The Bender's report explains the purpose of the $21 billion program as "a modernization effort intended eventually to give the IRS employee almost instant access to necessary taxpayer information." Ibid, page 119. This is entirely consistent with the 1984 Plan.

Second, I point to the Clinton-Gore campaign document entitled, *Putting People First*. (The book is more accurately entitled, Putting Government First, as that is what it proposes from first page to last.) On page 144, within the chapter entitled, *Rebuilding America*, we find the following statement:

> "Create a door-to-door *information network* to link every home, business, lab, classroom, and library by the year 2015. Put public records, databases, libraries, and educational materials on line for public use to expand access to information." (Emphasis in original.)

Here we see virtually the same lofty goal as expressed earlier by the IRS. At least a portion of the Administration's "stimulus program" is intended to make the IRS the most thorough, well-equipped, high-tech spy organization in the world. The bad news is the IRS spies only upon American citizens.

Third, the report of the Ways and Means Committee indicates the long-term $21 billion spending spree on computers is designed to "give the IRS employee almost instant access to necessary taxpayer information." The phrase "necessary taxpayer information," in the government lexicon, really means "all taxpayer information."

By linking "every home, business, lab, classroom, and library," and by putting all the nation's "data bases" on line for "public use," you can well imagine how the IRS may wish to immediately access your bank records, employment records, records on your home and other mortgages, credit card balances and credit card purchase records, IRA or 401(k) information, medical records including records regarding the immunization of your children (necessary to enforce socialist health care reforms), all state and local licensing data, data concerning the education of your children, insurance information, data concerning the purchase and sale of real estate, automobiles and other title property, records of the purchase of guns or ammunition, all stock, bond and commodity transactions, records evidencing cash transaction such as IRS Form 4789 and 8300, Passport and Visa data, and records revealing your membership or association with groups, organizations, churches or clubs. Did I miss anything?

This is fascism, folks. It plainly evidences the tendency of a government without God, to become, in itself, a god. Because any god worth its salt must be "all-knowing and all-seeing," modern high technology is about to become the eyes and ears of the god of Washington. As technology will be the eyes and ears of this government, the IRS will be its arms. The IRS is the natural choice because no other agency of government has the legal latitude or claim to involve itself - without cause or justification of any kind - directly into the affairs of one's daily life.

No doubt you are suggesting I may be over-reacting. After all, any government desiring to "Put People First" would never carry out the ideas I outline above. Don't be so sure about that. For one thing, I already pointed out in Chapter Two how the Clinton administration plans to "reduce the deficit" by stealing more of your money under the guise of tax penalties. The targeted sum is about $8.35 billion over four years. Who do you believe will be paying that money? You will. Unless, of course, you understand how to deal with bogus IRS penalty assessments.

Beyond that, however, we have the small matter, also disclosed in the Ways and Means Committee report on the Clinton plan, of some $633 million additional revenue to the IRS to fund "additional IRS compliance initiatives." Do you know or can you imagine what a compliance initiative is? As succinctly as possible, it is the means to *police* the American taxpayer. By *police*, I mean, spy upon and, more specifically, *extract from* American taxpayers. Without a doubt, the lion's share of this activity will involve computer contacts with citizens.

There are 11 specific enforcement initiatives. They include $31.6 million to fund a "large increase" in employment tax audits; $22.4 million to pursue past due tax bills; and $12 million to increase audits of high income returns, bankruptcy cases and tax return non-filers. Interestingly, the IRS also gets an additional $10 million to cope with the new changes in the tax laws! See Bender's *Federal Tax Week*, No. 15, April 15, 1993, page 178.

Within the pages of the 1992 Annual Report, the IRS explains some of the terms of a new contract with AT & T "for computer equipment." According to the agency, the contract will:

> ". . .permit the IRS to acquire more than 3,000 mini computers and 50,000 work stations. The systems will give front-line employees improved access to taxpayer data. . ." 1992 *Highlights*, page 16.

The report goes on to explain the details of a new contract awarded to TRW, Inc., the giant computer designer. The IRS explains the TRW contract this way:

> "This contract provides for services to integrate large-scale automated systems - including electronic filing, converting data received on paper to electronic format through imaging, organizing tax information into integrated data bases, and making tax information readily available through computer terminals - to make certain TSM delivers expected benefits and efficiencies." 1992 *Highlights*, page 17.

The conclusion of the IRS 1992 report is an explanation of the "IRS of the Future." Among the goals listed are:

> "* 100 million electronic returns and a dramatically reduced reliance on paper submissions of any kind;

> "* all tax payments received by electronic funds transfer;

> "* *instant access to all relevant information*." (Emphasis added.) 1992 Highlights, page 23.

Without a doubt, the IRS is building the incredible computer monster I foresaw seven years ago in *The Naked Truth*. There should be no question as to what the agency intends to do with that monster. The IRS dressed the beast in a shirt and tie to hide the bolts in its neck, but make no mistake about it. The beast has the power to disrupt your life in profound ways and you must know how to deal with it.

With each new computer terminal, with each new program, with a new plan for achieving "voluntary compliance," you face electronically created demands for more of your time and money. These facts speak persuasively of the need to kill this beast before it has an opportunity to ravage the countryside. This is but one more case against the present system and in favor of the changes I propose in this book.

THE RIGHT OF APPEAL IN GENERAL

Let me first point out some general rules. The general rule with respect to IRS decisions is simple: All decisions are subject to review - period. The review process is what we refer to as the appeal. Regardless of what you now believe or were led to believe, if the IRS demands additional taxes, penalties and interest, those demands are appealable.

If this is so simple, why so much confusion? The confusion arises when we discuss the process of appealing the computerized, or non- face-to-face audit. The IRS routinely assesses taxes, interest and penalties through the mail without providing the citizen with a face-to-face meeting. These notices (*demand notices*) are referred to as mathematical recomputations, tax recomputations based upon allegedly unreported or under-reported income, and of course, penalty and interest computations. During 1992, the IRS mailed millions of such notices, demanding billions in additional revenue. For example, a total of 6.36 million citizens were contacted under just the non-filer and underreporter programs.

Each computer generated assessment is unquestionably subject to the right of appeal. However, we must now stir into the pot the fact that IRS mails millions of *collection notices* each year. Collection notices are mailed only after a tax is assessed and the case is in the hands of the Collection Division.

Collection notices closely resemble, in form if not substance, the demand notices mentioned above. This is where the confusion lies because collection notices are not generally subject to the same clear-cut right of appeal as demand notices. Moreover, when one attempts to utilize procedures prescribed for *demand* notices to handle a *collection* notice, or vise versa, he runs into a stone wall. This leads to the frustration normally realized when dealing with an oversized, often insensitive, too powerful, computer-oriented bureaucracy.

Here we deal with identifying the difference between the garden variety *demand* notice and the garden variety *collection* notice. I also explain the appeals procedures available with the various demand notices.

DEMAND NOTICE OR COLLECTION NOTICE? WHO REALLY KNOWS?

Let us begin at once to point out certain distinguishing features of the two potentially perplexing documents. Ask yourself these questions:

1. Is this the first notice received from the IRS concerning that particular tax year? Usually, the first notice received is *not* a collection notice. Rather, before a case goes to collection, *demand* notices are mailed. Thus, the first notice received is likely a demand, not a collection notice. Hence, it is subject to the right of appeal.

The *exception* (unfortunately, there are some exceptions to these general rules) is if you filed a tax return but did not pay the tax in full with the return. If this is the situation, your case is handed immediately to collection personnel. The first notice received is a *collection* notice.

2. Does the notice state the reasons you owe additional taxes? As a rule,

demand notices provide some information as to why the tax is owed. Even the so-called arbitrary notice, which presents precious little information whatsoever, claims "an error" was made leading to a recomputation of your tax bill. The notice describes the amount owed, with interest and penalties included. Any notice which provides details of even the slightest nature concerning the source of the tax must be considered a *demand* notice. A collection notice does not explain the source of the tax. It merely states the total due, the year in question and demands payment immediately.

3. Does the notice offer any alternatives to paying the tax? Demand notices issued by the Examination Division or Appeals Division typically explain the alternatives to paying should you disagree. The alternatives vary, hinging upon the specific notice involved. However, if the notice explains you have the right to submit additional information, you have the right to request a conference with a supervisor, you have the right to file a protest letter or otherwise appeal the decision, the letter is a *demand* notice and not a *collection* notice.

4. Does the letter include schedules or worksheets justifying the amount sought? Notices issued from Examination and Appeals usually contain detailed worksheets and analyses of the tax, penalties and interest. Such work sheets are *never provided* with collection notices.

With the foregoing features of a *demand* notice firmly in mind, let us now turn our attention to the contrasting features of *collection* notices. Ask yourself this question:

Does the letter abruptly and pointedly demand payment of taxes without supporting explanations?

Such a letter is a computerized billing notice generated from the Collection Division. Collection of tax begins at the Service Center or ACS with a series of four letters. Each is a one-page document setting forth, in the upper right-hand corner, the year involved, the date of the letter and the type of tax in question.

The first of the four letters is the more polite of the series. It states "the federal tax shown below has not been paid. It is now overdue. Please pay it today." The letter explains the total amount due, including interest and penalties. It explains further interest will accrue if the tax is not promptly paid.

The second letter is more pointed. It follows the first by approximately 30 days. It states "we have previously written you about the federal tax shown below. Additional interest and penalties are included. Please pay it now." This letter restates the information provided in the first letter, updating the balance of the tax, interest and penalty due.

The third letter depicts a nastier attitude. It follows letter number two by approximately 30 days. It states, "Your full payment of the federal tax shown below has still not been received. We have previously billed you for the overdue tax and must now consider filing a notice of federal tax lien and seizing your property, wages or other assets to satisfy your unpaid tax." The letter shows a balance due with additional interest and penalties included.

The fourth and final letter arrives via certified mail, return receipt requested. It follows letter number three by approximately 30 days. It is downright terrifying. The letter reads, "This is your final notice. Your full payment of the federal tax shown below has still not been received. If full payment is not received within 30 days from the date of this notice, we will begin enforcement proceedings."

If any or all of these letters were sent to you, you *are not* dealing with an examination matter which can be handled with a simple appeal. Rather, your case is in collection. The IRS, acting on the belief you owe the tax, has undertaken to collect it with all the enforced collection tools available. That, of course, includes liens, levies and seizures of property.

When faced with such a letter, take immediate steps to minimize the effects of potential enforced collection action. See Chapter Eight for more details.

APPEALS PROCEDURES: THE MAIL ORDER AUDIT

Since my first book, *The Naked Truth*, was released in October of 1986, I have faithfully criticized the IRS and its computerized examination and billing practices. I accused the agency of deliberately establishing procedures designed to collect taxes it knew or should have known were not due. I claimed it continues to permit its system to operate after being placed on notice, not only by me but by the General Accounting Office of the United States Government, that its system was defective at best, and an outright fraud at worst.

In 1988, the GAO issued a report claiming that fully 48 percent of all IRS notices and demands for payment of taxes were either wrong or incomprehensible. In 1990, the GAO, in a follow up report pointed out the IRS has done nothing to correct the problem. Therefore, the letters continue to pour forth from a computer no one seems to know or care how to turn off.

The April, 1990, issue of *Money* Magazine reported the results of a Gallup poll conducted of *Money* subscribers. The report indicated that of the persons receiving correction notices from the IRS, 69 percent were incorrect.

Interestingly, in April of 1991, I received a copy of the April 1991, *TAXFAX* newsletter, published by the IRS' Ogden, Utah Service Center. Now I must tell you, I did not even know the Ogden Service Center published a newsletter, so I was most curious when an unsolicited copy suddenly appeared in my mailbox.

As I perused the pages of the document, I was astonished to find that the premise of the entire 12-page newsletter was that the Ogden Service Center was *cleaning up its act* respecting correspondence! As a matter of fact, the title of the lead article is, *"IRS Cleans up its Correspondence."* The newsletter went on, page after page, explaining how the IRS is testing and developing new computer systems and techniques. Their purpose is to ensure its correspondence and billing practices would be better and *more accurate* in the future.

Despite the Ogden Service Center's efforts, the mail order audits continue, and at record levels. The IRS has yet to institute the reforms it claims will help.

That means only one thing: unless you understand your right to appeal such audits, and unless you understand how such appeals are perfected, you will simply pay more taxes than you owe! Let us address the appeal procedures.

1. Mathematical Recomputations. The most common form of mail-order audit is the mathematical recomputation, more accurately referred to as a correction notice. For the sake of economy, I treat all forms of correction notices as a recomputation. You should know, however, that not all correction notices involve mathematical errors. Essentially, there are four forms of these notices I have seen over the years. They are:

a. Mathematical recomp. This notice is sent when a math error is found in the return. The error is corrected and the notice demands payment of additional taxes. We may also include in this category letters proposing a mechanical correction to your return. For example, should the IRS determine you failed to include a necessary schedule with your return, or placed an entry on an incorrect line, a correction notice is mailed.

b. Underreported income. This notice is sent when IRS believes you did not report the full amount of your income. The agency adds the alleged unreported income to your return, computes the new tax liability and sends a bill. These notices grow out of the Information Returns Program. In a GAO study released in March of 1991, it was revealed that of the 6.2 million underreporter notices mailed in 1987, approximately "one half were unproductive." In other words, they were *wrong*. The citizen did not owe additional taxes as claimed. During 1992, some 5.3 million of these notices were mailed.

c. Non-filing of tax return. This notice is sent when the IRS believes you failed to file your income tax return. Using available information, such as Form W-2 or 1099, it computes your income tax liability without a return, then sends a demand for payment of the taxes. My experience indicates the same error rate, at least one-half, exists with regard to claims the citizen failed to file a tax return. Some studies put the error rate even higher, perhaps as high as 90 percent with respect to these demands. During 1992, the IRS sent non-filer notices to 4.6 million individuals and businesses.

d. The arbitrary notice. This notice is so named by me because it fails to provide any explanation whatsoever why additional taxes, interest and penalties were assessed. The letter merely states an error was made, your taxes were recalculated after correcting the error and now you owe more.

The appeal procedures for these notices are quite simple. Before we review them, let me reemphasize an important premise upon which the appeal right is based. That premise is, the IRS cannot alter your tax liability without following very carefully prescribed procedures. Those procedures, known as the deficiency procedures, insure that if you disagree with IRS proposals, you have the right to appeal. Without affording a citizen an opportunity to contest the proposed assessment through the deficiency procedures, that assessment is simply invalid.

Alterations to your return made through any one of the above four methods are subject to the deficiency procedures, but only if you challenge the assessment at the time it is made. The objection must take the form of a letter written in response to the demand notice. The letter is very simple, but must be mailed within 60 days of receiving the notice. It must clearly and unequivocally state you disagree with the IRS' determination. You must also demand an *abatement*, or cancellation of the liability. Conclude by saying if the IRS believes you do indeed owe the taxes, you demand it issue a notice of deficiency so you may exercise your right of appeal. We discuss the notice of deficiency in more detail later. For more information on the letter demanding abatement, please see *41 Ways to Lick the IRS with a Postage Stamp*, Chapters Two and Three.

At this point, suffice it to say when the notice of deficiency is issued, the IRS is barred from making any alterations to your return or from assessing or collecting the tax until *after* you exercise all your appeals options.

2. Penalty Assessments. The error rate on penalty assessment is at least as great as that relative to other forms of computer notices. For example, in the 1992 Annual Report, the IRS discusses employment tax penalty assessments. The rules covering the requirement of employers to deposit employment taxes are quite complex and have been changed regularly over the years. The result is a vast number of employment tax penalties are assessed against confused business owners each year. During 1992, the IRS assessed 1.5 million such penalties against businesses, large and small. In describing the abatement rate, the agency explains:

> "However, we abate more than 20 percent of the penalties and 60 percent of the penalty amounts when taxpayers request abatement and provide sufficient justification." 1992 *Highlights*, page 9.

The assessment of most penalties is not subject to the deficiency procedures applying to tax assessments. This means the IRS may assess the penalty and include the amount with a tax bill without first providing an opportunity for review. However, that does not mean there is no opportunity for review subsequent to the assessment. As discussed in Chapter Seven, all penalty assessments are subject to abatement, or cancellation, when the citizen challenges them properly.

Challenging a penalty assessment begins with a written request for abatement. Your letter must set forth facts which allow the reader to conclude you acted in good faith and with a reasonable cause for your actions, rather than out of deliberate disregard for the IRS' rules and regulations. When such a showing is properly made, the IRS is obligated to abate the penalty.

The time for making a penalty abatement request is not nearly so limited as with the case of mathematical recomputations. In general, the penalty is subject to abatement at any point while it is legally collectible. A tax (or penalty) is collectible any time within 10 years of the date it was assessed, unless that time is extended for some reason. See Chapter Six for details on the collection statute of limitations. Thus, as long as the case is open for collection, penalties are subject to cancellation without regard to any 60-day limitation.

But what if the IRS refuses to abate the penalty? A decision against abating the penalty is not final. First, a decision rendered by a Service Center or by a Revenue Officer is subject to appeal. Any time within 30 days of the IRS' letter denying the abatement, you enjoy the right to submit a written protest letter to challenge the determination. The protest letter should explain why you disagree with the decision to deny the abatement and should specifically ask for an Appeals Division conference on the matter. See IRS Publication 5, Exhibit 5-2 in Chapter Five.

An Appeals conference is conducted before an Appeals Officer. His responsibility is to review the entire matter and make his own decision. It is to be based upon the facts of the case and applicable law, independent of the previous decision.

Another highly successful tactic is to merely resubmit a revised request for abatement after the first is denied. This is effective for a number of reasons. First, there is no limitation on the number of requests for abatement a person is permitted to present. Therefore, if you are unsuccessful the first time, provide more details and more clearly present your argument in a second demand. That often meets with success.

Additionally, the second request may find its way to another IRS officer or employee who sees the facts and applies the law in a more favorable way. Much of the penalty abatement process involves the application of subjective issues. Thus, two people may very well see the same events in a much different light.

If all else fails, penalty assessments are subject to the refund procedures set forth in the tax Code. Those procedures provide for the ability to sue the IRS in district court for a refund of any taxes, interest or penalties paid or collected illegally or erroneously. The refund procedures are utilized after paying all or a legally divisible portion of the penalty assessed. Thereafter, one must file a claim for refund. If the agency denies the claim, the citizen is free to sue the IRS. The refund procedures, including sample forms and detailed instructions, are provided in Chapter Five of the *Taxpayers' Ultimate Defense Manual*.

3. Interest Assessments. According to the IRS, $4.3 *billion* in interest was collected in 1989. (I do not have a more up-to-date number.) What the IRS does not tell us, however, is interest, like penalties, is subject to the right of abatement. The latitude to win such an abatement is, though, much narrower than with penalties.

There are just two reasons to justify an abatement of interest. The first is if you can demonstrate the interest is attributable to *IRS error*. If, for example, the IRS advised you to file your return in a particular manner which later proved to be incorrect, all interest should be canceled.

Second, interest is subject to cancellation when it is attributable to *IRS delay*. I must clarify this rule. The delay which leads to the assessment of interest cannot be a mere calendar delay. Rather, the delay must occur while the IRS is performing a "ministerial act" as opposed to an act involving the use of discretion. The difference is best illustrated by example.

Cases settled one way or another by a particular division of the IRS must be handed to the next level within IRS structure for appropriate consideration and handling. If delay occurs while the case is handed from one division to another, such as delay while performing a ministerial act (an act involving the administration of the case). Interest which accumulates during this period is subject to abatement.

On the other hand, delay which occurs while an IRS officer is utilizing his discretion is not subject to abatement. Let us assume you submit your arguments to an Appeals Officer for review. After meeting and submitting all documents, he spends eight months making his decision. These eight months is considered time expended during the exercise of the officer's discretion. Thus, the interest which accumulates during that period is not subject to abatement.

Another reason for abating interest arises when the IRS issues an erroneous refund check. Clearly, this type of interest is subject to abatement because of IRS error. However, due to the frequency of the occurrence, it deserves separate treatment.

One of the provisions of the *Taxpayers' Bill of Rights Act* holds that when the IRS issues an erroneous refund check and the citizen to whom the check was issued in no way prompted the refund, the IRS cannot charge interest. Routinely, however, the IRS does so, beginning with the date the refund was issued. Under these circumstances, a letter demanding abatement of interest must be mailed promptly (of course the principle amount due must be repaid). The IRS cannot charge interest on an erroneous refund until after it issues a final notice and demand for payment (the final *collection* notice discussed earlier).

Procedurally, winning an abatement of interest is precisely the same as for penalties. However, great care must be taken to be sure your argument presents facts and circumstances which paint a picture entitling you to the abatement. For example, do not spend time arguing facts leading the reader only to conclude the delay involved the officer's exercise of discretion. The argument must focus upon delay in the process of a ministerial act or you must illustrate IRS error. Please see Chapter Seven of *41 Ways* for more details.

4. The Seized Refund. Another way the mail order audit is manifested is through the seized refund. A phenomenon I tied a can to some time ago, the seized refund occurs when the IRS sends a notice with a refund check. The notice explains the refund is reduced due to an error (mathematical or any of the other reasons discussed here) in the return. The error, it is claimed, was corrected and the additional tax was taken from the original refund amount due. Often, the initial notice does not even explain the error. Rather, it states that follow-up correspondence will explain the error.

Before we go any further, I must draw a distinction between two potential reasons for a seized refund. First is that to which we have already alluded. It relates to errors, real or imagined, in the return for the *year in question*. When a refund is seized for reasons relating to the correctness of the return in question, this discussion controls.

It is quite common, however, for the IRS to seize refunds and apply the proceeds to some other tax year for which there is an outstanding balance. For example, your 1992 refund was supposed to be $1,000. When you receive your check, you find the IRS applied $400 to tax year 1989, for which there was an outstanding balance. When this occurs, the appeals procedures discussed here do not apply. The reason is I am drawing the assumption that there did indeed exist an outstanding balance for the previous year. If that is not the case, however, then you should challenge the IRS' actions.

The first step to take when confronted with a seized refund is to make a demand for abatement (this assumes there was no valid assessment pending). The abatement letter is simple and was outlined earlier. To review, state firmly that you disagree with the IRS' determination. Demand an abatement or cancellation of the alleged assessment to which your refund was applied. Lastly, demand a *refund* of the amount seized.

I would not let the matter die with the first demand for refund. I would follow with two letters. The first would be a formal claim for refund following the appropriate claim for refund rules and regulations as set forth in Chapter Five, *Taxpayers' Ultimate Defense Manual*. The second would be to Problems resolution. Remember, PRO has the authority to step into any controversy between the IRS and a citizen.

You may ask why I would take such aggressive action in this scenario as compared to when the IRS merely issues a demand notice? The answer is simple. When the IRS issues a mere demand notice, you still have the money! You have the luxury of taking remedial steps while you are yet in possession of your property. On the other hand, when the IRS seizes your refund, the agency has the money! Common sense tells me the matter is worthy of more decisive action when you are separated from your property.

Another consideration is, when the IRS has your money, the time limitations governing formalized claims for refund begin to tick. Generally, you have two years from the date the tax is paid or seized to make the claim for refund. When you allow that period to lapse without making a claim, a serious uphill fight is ahead of you if you wish to pursue the matter. Therefore, I recommend firing all guns as quickly and accurately as possible.

CONCLUSION

Computerized contacts have been a thorn in the side of the American public since they began in earnest in 1984. Those contacts can only be expected to expand both in number and in scope. At the same time, despite overwhelming evidence of the error rate in these contacts, do not look for Congress to limit the IRS' undertakings in any way.

Remember, Congress is the institution handing this power and equipment to the IRS. They do so solely because the agency has it convinced it will collect more money in the process. The fiscal irresponsibility of Congress alone implies it will do nothing to stop the high-tech rip offs.

As a result, you must educate yourself in the manner of dealing with these contacts. But it goes beyond that. We will not terminate this nonsense unless and until we adopt the rebuilding measures I call for in this book. If my program of true, honest, sweeping tax change is put into place, no American will ever again face an erroneous computer notice. He will never again experience the fear and frustration that go with attempting to correct it.

11

RIGHT NUMBER SEVEN: RECOVERING THE COST OF WINNING
END HARASSMENT BY MAKIN' 'EM PAY

One of the most frustrating aspects of dealing with the IRS is the cost of defending one's self, win or lose. Many audit victims have told me, "I won, but I lost." In other words, the cost of defense was such that the victory was hollow, at best. This reality fosters the IRS' relentless pursuit of taxpayers, even when the agency is flat wrong. It also buttresses the attitude, which I have long assailed, suggesting it is cheaper to *lose* when dealing with the IRS, than it is to win.

Keeping the IRS out of your life, and consequently, the lives of all honest, hardworking Americans, means you cannot surrender in the battle for your paycheck. You must fight when faced with illegal, unreasonable or improper demands. At the same time, however, it is not necessary to *eat* the costs of doing so. Two specific provisions of law allow you to recoup all or part of the costs of battling unreasonable IRS claims. Most individuals have no idea these provisions are available. Most professionals are equally unknowing. If this were not true, they would not continue to advise their clients to "just pay the bill because it is cheaper than fighting."

I have long taken the position that it is cheaper to *win* when doing business with the IRS, than it is to *lose*. Each time someone yields in the face of an unjust claim, the IRS gains more power. With every increase in power, the agency becomes more and more bold. As bad as the U.S. tax situation is, it would not be nearly this bad if the IRS simply *obeyed its own laws!* However, because the public is horribly ignorant of this, it is fully convinced it cannot win the battle. Thus, the IRS inflicts far more damage upon the nation than might otherwise be the case.

Each time somebody yields in the face of an unjust claim, the IRS feels at liberty to go back for more. Consequently, you can expect to be greeted with annual demands for audits, penalties, additional taxes and interest when you just cave in. On the other hand, when you fight - and win - you force the IRS to reconsider spending further time and effort in your case. You must recognize that like you, the IRS does not have unlimited money and manpower with which to fight its battles. It is for that reason the IRS spends so much of its efforts bluffing and intimidating the public. Like the schoolyard bully, the IRS reigns largely because it has gone unchallenged, not because it is unbeatable.

Still, there is no getting around the fact that fighting can be expensive. That is why we must understand how to recapture the costs of fighting. When we recapture these costs *directly from the IRS itself*, we send a loud and clear message that its crime no longer pays. When it is more expensive for the agency to abuse citizens than it can hope to gain through the abuse, we will see the abuse evaporate.

I have long said the way to stop a runaway train is *not* to stand in front of it. You must first *slow it down* to bring it under control. Only then can it be disabled and do no further harm.

This discourse addresses the two provisions of law which make it possible to recover costs when battling the IRS. My hope is to educate more and more citizens and professionals alike on this issue so we can turn the tables on the IRS. My goal is to make unlawful harassment, vexing audits and claims, and other improper tactics simply too expense for the agency to continue.

1. GETTING INTO THE IRS' POCKET THE EASY WAY

If I said you could fight the IRS in your audit and force the agency to pay a portion of the fees and costs incurred in the fight - *win or lose* - would you fight back against an unreasonable claim? Most people would. However, they have no idea they own the legal right to recover a portion of the cost. Most citizens have no idea the tax law allows a *deduction* for the costs of fighting the IRS.

It is true! Under the law, when you fight the IRS, you can force them to pay a portion of the cost. Consider the language of Code section 212(3). It provides as follows:

"In the case of an individual, there shall be as a deduction all the ordinary and necessary expenses paid or incurred during the taxable year-

"(3) in connection with the determination, collection, or refund *of any tax*." (Emphasis added.)

Under the language of this section, fees, costs and expenses incurred in connection with defending a tax audit, collection matter, or pursuing a refund or abatement, qualify as an itemized deduction. More specific guidance on what items are covered is provided below. IRS regulation section 1.212-1(1) provides this insight on the matter:

"Expenses paid or incurred by an individual in connection with the determination, collection, or refund of any tax, whether the taxing authority be Federal, State or municipal, and whether the tax be income, estate, gift, property, or any other tax, *are deductible*. Thus, expenses paid or incurred by a taxpayer for tax counsel or expenses paid or incurred in connection with the preparation of his tax returns or in connection with *any proceedings involved in determining the extent of tax liability or in contesting his tax liability are deductible*." (Emphasis added.)

Without question, the deduction is available for fees paid to a tax professional to prosecute or defend your case. Such fees include tax return preparation fees, legal fees paid to an attorney, fees paid to an accountant, and fees paid to any other tax practitioner in connection with your case.

Expenses, other than professional fees, are also deductible if incurred in connection with the preparation of tax returns, or in connection with the determination, collection, or refund *of any tax*. Examples of the type of expenses which are deductible include court or administrative filing fees, duplicating costs, postage expenses, witness fees and their travel expenses, and transcript costs. Other expenses you may claim include your own travel or mileage expenses, parking fees and similar disbursements.

From the moment you become embroiled in a dispute with the IRS, begin counting the costs of battle. Keep receipts for parking costs, track your mileage, log the number of photocopies you must make, save postage receipts, and otherwise record and be prepared to prove the amount and nature of any other expense you might incur. When you pay a professional to represent you, that of course falls into the category of deducible fees. However, the cost of your own time is *not* deductible.

The deduction under Code section 212(3) is *not limited* to just the cost of battling the IRS. I already mentioned tax preparation fees are deductible under this code section, but the benefit goes beyond that. Also deductible are the costs of educational material designed to provide tax advice. Under this category, text material used or useful in the preparation of your tax return is deductible.

In addition, any material you purchase which is used or useful in connection with the determination, collection or refund of any tax you may owe is also a deduction. In this regard, all of the material published by Winning Publications, Inc., including this book, is tax deductible under Code section 212(3)! Without a doubt, all of my books and monthly newsletter are designed to provide help and guidance concerning tax collection issues. If you have not done so, your annual newsletter subscription fee and book costs should be deducted. The expenses are deductible in the year paid.

Deducting the cost of battling the IRS, as well as the costs of learning how to battle the IRS, is the easy way to get into the agency's pocket. It is the quickest way to force the IRS to pay a portion of the cost with which they burden us. The deduction under Code section 212(3) is considered a miscellaneous itemized deduction. To claim it, you must file a Schedule A with your Form 1040.

To be deductible, miscellaneous itemized deductions must exceed 2 percent of your adjusted gross income. For example, if your adjusted gross income were $25,000, you would be entitled to deduct miscellaneous expenses which exceed $500 ($25,000 x .02). Further illustrating, if you incurred $2,000 in various fees and costs in fighting the IRS, you are entitled to deduct $1,500 as miscellaneous expenses.

The ability to deduct the cost of fighting the IRS certainly does not remove all the sting from the outlay. After all, even if you were allowed a one hundred percent deduction for the expense, the money is nevertheless gone. I am sure you would rather have spent it on, say, a root canal. Still, it does represent at least some measure of a hoist by the agency's own petard when you claim this deduction.

2. GETTING INTO IRS' POCKET THE COMPLETE WAY

One of the focal points of dispute in crafting the *Taxpayers' Bill of Rights Act* was the claim that some citizens were deliberately abused or unreasonably pursued by the IRS, but had no recourse. Even if they prevailed, these citizens generally incurred such overwhelming legal expenses that the ability to deduct them under Code section 212(3) was not enough to correct the injustice. As a result of compelling testimony by average citizens on the nature and extent of such abuses, Congress expanded section 7430 of the Internal Revenue Code.

Code section 7430 goes far beyond the scope of section 212(3). Section 7430 allows you to *recover* fees and costs when you prevail in your tax case. Stated more simply, section 7430 forces the IRS to reimburse you for all fees and costs incurred under certain circumstances. We shall examine what those circumstances are.

Section 7430 is a hammer which has been available to citizens since 1988, when former President Reagan signed Public Law 100-647 on November 10, 1988. The right applies to any case *commenced after* that date. Without a doubt, this code section is one which must be applied by citizens across the nation. This section is in a category with precious few other legal options. When used broadly but properly, it sends a clear message to the IRS. The message, like that communicated from Moses to Pharaoh, is simple: "Let my people go."

In order to recover fees and costs under section 7430, the following elements must be established:

a. You were involved in litigation or an administrative proceeding with the IRS in which you were the "prevailing party." Subsection (c)(4)(A) defines a "prevailing party" as one who has "substantially prevailed with respect to the amount in controversy, or has substantially prevailed with respect to the most significant issue or set of issues presented." You are the prevailing party when you win based upon either, the amount in controversy, or the most important issue or set of issues presented in the case.

b. The position advanced by the IRS through its representatives in the case was substantially "unjustified" based upon the law and facts of the case. Code section 7430(c)(4)(A). To be justified, the IRS' position must have a *reasonable basis* both in law and fact. When the position is not well-founded in law and fact, that is, it cannot satisfy a reasonable person as to its validity, the position is unjustified. The burden of proof is on *the IRS* to establish that its litigation position was substantially justified based upon the law and all facts of the case.

The following factors bear upon the reasonableness of the government's case: whether the government used expenses of litigation against its position to extract concessions from the citizen that were not justified under the circumstances; whether the IRS failed to adequately investigate its case before asserting a claim; whether the government pursed the litigation for purposes of harassment or embarrassment, or out of political motivations; and such other factors as may be relevant under the circumstances of each case.

c. You exhausted all administrative remedies under the Code and did not unreasonably protract the proceedings. Code section 7430(b)(1) and (b)(4). Where it is shown that the citizen "unreasonably protracted" portions of the proceeding, he will not be allowed to recover costs for such portion. He may, however, yet recover costs for the portions which he did not unreasonably protract. Revenue Regulation section 301.7430-2(d).

d. You must of course establish the nature and extent of the fees and costs in question. This is done through an affidavit presenting testimony as to the nature of the fees and the purpose of the expenses you incurred. Code section 7430(c)(1).

e. The final element in recovering fees and costs is to prove your net worth does not exceed $2 million. This requirement is lifted from the *Equal Access to Justice Act*, Title 28 USC, section 2412. Under the Act, a person whose net worth is in excess of $2 million, or a business whose net worth exceeds $7 million or has more than 500 employees, cannot recover any fees or costs under Code section 7430. The only option is to deduct the expenses under Code section 212(3).

CASE STUDIES ON RECOVERING FEES AND COSTS

Since Code section 7430 was added to the law in 1988, there have not been a great deal of cases in which demands for fees and costs have been presented. The few which clearly establish the right to recover and the grounds upon which one may recover deliver a *decisive blow* to the arbitrary powers of the IRS. By publicizing these cases and the circumstances behind them, I hope to turn the fear game around on the IRS.

These cases, more than anything I could ever say, perfectly illustrate the point I have been making for years. When you know your rights and understand the IRS' limitations, you never have to become a tax collection statistic. Beyond that, the cases graphicly illustrate the point I made earlier in this text. It is indeed cheaper and more beneficial for all of us to *win* when dealing with the IRS, than it is to lose.

Case Study No. One - *Abernathy v. United States*, 93-1 USTC 50,108 (U.S. Bankruptcy Court, Northern District of Illinois) (February 16, 1993).

Faced with 10's of thousands of dollars in growing tax assessments they could not possibly pay, Bill and Peggy Abernathy filed a Chapter 7 bankruptcy petition in June of 1986. In October of 1986, the Bankruptcy Court issued a general discharge order. As a result of the discharge, all the taxes they owed for the years 1979 through 1982 were eliminated.

Despite the discharge order, the IRS continued sending notices demanding payment to Bill and Peggy. Collection notices were mailed in 1987 and 1988. In addition, the IRS followed an annual practice of seizing their tax refund and applying it to the discharged taxes.

By September of 1988, they had enough of the IRS' disregard of the bankruptcy court's discharge order. They filed an adversary proceeding within the bankruptcy court to enforce the discharge order. An adversary proceeding is a civil suit filed under the jurisdiction of the bankruptcy court. It is the manner in which issues collateral to the bankruptcy itself are resolved.

Amazingly, the IRS' deliberate wrongful collection efforts continued even after the adversary proceeding was commenced. The IRS issued a final notice, notice of intention to levy in June of 1989. In an effort to stop the IRS, the court entered an order holding it in contempt of court for violating the discharge order. The contempt order was entered on June 20, 1989.

This did little to slow down the illegal actions. In June, November and December of 1991, more final notices were issued warning of enforced collection if the discharged taxes were not paid. In February of 1992, the IRS seized their 1991 income tax refund, then issued still another final notice, notice of intent to levy.

The IRS' actions in this case can be described only as bureaucratic madness. For even while the Abernathy's motion for fees and costs under Code section 7430 was pending, the IRS issued *yet another* collection notice. In January of 1993, while the court was considering the motion for sanctions, the IRS seized their 1992 tax refund and applied it to the discharged taxes.

As you might hope, the court was incensed by the IRS' bold, defiant actions of violating not one, but two court orders. The court observed:

"* * *In its more than two decade-long involvement as a practitioner, professor and judge in the bankruptcy court system, this court has never encountered a more *egregious flaunting* of the bankruptcy system as that which it has seen by the IRS in this case. For some five years, the constant position of the IRS has been that it is free to ignore the Debtors' bankruptcy discharge of certain taxes as it sees fit. *However, the IRS cannot act with impunity*, like a rogue elephant. It is not free to simply proceed as if the taxes the Debtors owed the IRS had never been discharged in bankruptcy. The IRS, like any other person or entity involved in a bankruptcy case, *must obey the rule of law* in this bankruptcy case, which is that the income taxes it seeks to collect have been discharged in bankruptcy and that the IRS is *enjoined from trying to collect the taxes, period.*" (Emphasis added; footnotes omitted.)

The court found that "without a doubt," the IRS' position in this case was arbitrary and unjustified. In fact, the court pointed out the IRS position was not just substantially unjustified, rather, it was "completely unjustified."

The court found that Bill and Peggy Abernathy were entitled to recover all the fees and costs they incurred as a result of the IRS' continued wilful, arbitrary and defiant disregard of the bankruptcy discharge. The Abernathy's have submitted a claim for fees and costs. The amount they will recover has yet to be determined by the court. You can bet the illegal actions will cost IRS dearly.

Case Study No. Two - *Christensen v. United States*, 93-1 USTC 50,246 (U.S. District Court, District of Delaware) (March 10, 1993).

Jim Christensen operated a construction company in Colorado during 1982. In 1983, the business went under. After a perfunctory employment tax audit in 1986, the IRS determined Jim paid employees of his company a total of $424,000 in wages. The IRS claimed he failed to withhold or pay any of the required employment taxes. As a result, it assessed a 100 percent penalty against Jim in the amount of $91,946.

There was a simple problem with the IRS' determination. Jim *had no employees whatsoever*. Records examined by the court indicated the IRS never completed a proper examination of Jim's operation. Instead, the agency made an arbitrary determination as to his alleged payroll.

Subsequent to the assessment, the IRS seized income tax refunds and applied them to the 100 percent penalty assessment. In October of 1991, Jim filed a suit in the United States District Court seeking return of the seized refunds, and a determination he was not liable for the 100 percent penalty. After lengthy proceedings in court, the government conceded Jim was not responsible for the penalty. In September of 1992, it agreed to abate the penalty and refund the money seized. The IRS refunded $4,837. Jim then filed a motion seeking attorneys fees and costs under Code section 7430.

In opposition to the motion, the IRS argued it secured the "actual payroll records" from Jim's company. According to the agency, those records constituted the evidence supporting its claim. From such evidence, the IRS submitted its position in the case was "substantially justified" and therefore asserted it was improper to award fees and costs under section 7430.

The court pointed out that in order to be substantially justified, the government's litigation position must be based upon information "which would satisfy a reasonable person to go forward with the proceedings." In other words, the government's evidence must have substance. It cannot be concocted or imagined. It must be capable of persuading a reasonable person as to the merits of the claim. The position does not necessarily have to *be correct*. But it must have *substance*.

Upon careful examination of the documents submitted by the IRS, the court found the government's evidence entirely lacking. For example, none of the documents indicated Jim's role in the company. The documents did not identify the number of employees in question or their names and addresses. Thus, the IRS was unable to show Jim actually paid a dime in wages to any person.

Most importantly, however, the government's claim that the true company payroll was gleaned from these records was simply incorrect. The audit report stated "actual payroll records" were obtained. However, the court pointed out, "There are no payroll figures in the record." In reality, the government had absolutely no evidence upon which to support its claim. As a consequence, the court held the government's evidence "does not show that the position of the IRS was justified to a degree that could satisfy a reasonable person."

The court ordered the IRS to pay attorney fees in the amount of $10,741 and costs in the amount of $238.40. What began as a claim against Jim for $91,900, ended up costing the IRS $15,816, including the money it agreed to refund.

Case Study No. Three - *Kreidle v. Department of Treasury, Internal Revenue Service*, 92-2 USTC 50,449, 145 BR 1007 (U.S. Bankruptcy Court, District of Colorado) (June 23, 1992).

Jim Kreidle operated a number of businesses and was involved in a partnership during 1986. At that time, he was liable for about $8 million in non-tax partnership debt and other personal guarantees. As a consequence, he was forced by his creditors into an involuntary bankruptcy. After negotiations with creditors, all agreed Jim would be given a crack at a Chapter 11, Reorganization.

In October of 1986, subsequent to the agreement to file in Chapter 11, the clerk of bankruptcy court inadvertently issued an Order for Relief under Chapter 7. That order gave the appearance a Chapter 7, Liquidation proceeding was in motion, rather than the reorganization. The IRS received the Order for Relief, but never acted on it. In addition, they never made an appearance in the case and failed to file a proof of claim with the court.

Shortly after discovering the erroneous order, the clerk corrected the mistake. The IRS was notified of the correction. Later, it was given notice of all relevant events as the Chapter 11 progressed. At no time, however, did it ever participate in the proceedings. In November of 1987, the court confirmed Jim's Plan for Reorganization. He was on his way to working out of financial trouble.

In the meantime, Jim and his wife filed their federal income tax returns in a timely and proper manner. Returns for 1986 and 1987 were filed and the tax was paid. From 1987 until October of 1990, Jim was making his plan payments and all was progressing smoothly. He was, however, being audited for 1986, 1987 and 1988.

The trouble began on October 5, 1990. On that date, the IRS issued a notice of deficiency to Jim for the years mentioned. The IRS alleged Jim owed an additional $1.5 million in taxes due to unreported income. The alleged income was based upon two theories.

First, the IRS claimed Jim filed an important election improperly. The election, submitted under Code section 1398, entitled him to terminate his tax year as of the date of filing Chapter 11. That effectively pushed income out of the 1986 year and into the 1987 year. If the IRS were correct on the issue, Jim would have substantially more income in 1986 than he reported on his return.

Second, the IRS contended Jim realized income from the discharge of indebtedness. Initially, the IRS claimed this income to be $5.3 million. Later, the IRS reduced the claim considerably, but maintained its insistence that Jim realized substantial unreported income from the discharge of indebtedness.

The above determinations were made by a tax auditor and the notice of deficiency was issued without being reviewed for correctness. As it happens, both determinations were grossly in error.

As to the first issue, the IRS maintained Jim's election was filed late and that is why they readjusted his income. However, the IRS used as its starting point, the date the bankruptcy court erroneously issued the Chapter 7 order. Remember, this was not a Chapter 7 case. It was a Chapter 11 reorganization. All parties, including the IRS, knew the Chapter 7 order was issued erroneously. Yet, the IRS auditor maintained such date dictated when Jim's election should have been filed.

There were two glaring problems with the second issue. First, Jim did not realize any income from discharge of indebtedness because he filed a Chapter 11, not a Chapter 7. Next, even if substantial debts were canceled by the bankruptcy, Code section 108(e)(2) expressly states that no discharge of indebtedness income arises as a result of cancellation of debt, which if paid, would lead to a deduction. All Jim's debts were business debts. Thus, if all debts were paid, they would have been deductible. The IRS attorney later admitted this section of the Code was "overlooked."

After trial on the issues, the court found Jim did not owe the $1.5 million sought by the IRS. In fact, Jim was owed a refund for both the years 1986 and 1987. Jim then submitted a motion for fees and costs. The IRS asserted its position was reasonable, but the court rejected that contention. Specifically, the court stated:

> "* * *IRS' failure to confirm the accuracy of its audit before trial supports a finding of unreasonableness. Overall circumstances, including the IRS' unfavorable settlement during trial on the amount of cancellation of debt income, also demonstrate the unreasonableness of the IRS position on this issue. The IRS was not substantially justified in its position on the amount of cancellation of debt income."

Both the auditor and the IRS' attorney "overlooked" a key provision of the tax code when issuing the notice of deficiency to Jim. That, by itself, is not unusual. It happens all the time. So much so that I have come to believe most tax auditors do not know or care about the tax law. They want only to collect more money. In this case, however, the IRS was forced to pay the price for its ignorance of Code section 108. The Court ordered the IRS to pay Jim's costs and fees, *in the combined amount of $192,817.23!*

Case Study No. Four - *Powers v. Commissioner of Internal Revenue*, 100 T.C. No. 30 (United States Tax Court) (May 25, 1993).

Melvin Powers was a real estate developer in Houston, Texas. He owned and operated five office complexes in the Houston area. He leased office space to tenants within those buildings.

During 1982, IRS audited Mel's tax returns for the years 1976 and 1977. At issue were Mel's business expenses in connection with the office buildings. The IRS had also looked at Mel's returns for the years 1978 and 1979. However, it made the decision it *would not* conduct a full scale audit of the two latter years.

Despite this fact, the IRS asked Mel to sign Forms 872, waiving the time period on the assessment statute of limitations. Mel agreed to sign the forms. What he did not know, however, is the IRS had already made the decision *not to pursue* 1978 and 1979 if he refused to sign. Thus, if Mel had refused to sign Forms 872, he would never have had any problems with the IRS.

The IRS did nothing for three years after obtaining Mel's agreement to extend the statute. In March of 1986, Mel's attorney counselled him to terminate the waiver in order to get the matter closed and behind him. Mind you, Mel and his attorney still had no idea the IRS made the decision *not to pursue* the matter. Up to March of 1986, no effort whatsoever was made to audit Mel's records for the two years mentioned. Neither did the agency make any contact with him.

After Mel terminated his waiver, the statute of limitations was set to expire in June of 1986. In April of 1986, the case was assigned to an auditor who discussed it with the attorney representing the IRS in the 1976/1977 case. The auditor proposed to disallow all Mel's deductions in excess of $9,000. The agent's reasoning was because of, "lack of time on the statute." The agent claimed to be protecting "the government's interest" by disallowing all deductions in the returns.

The IRS' attorney reviewed the agent's proposal and approved the issuance of notice of deficiency. This was done despite the fact that an earlier decision was made *not to pursue* Mel for those years. Furthermore, there was "nothing in the file suggesting that (Mel) had improperly claimed deductions." In fact, IRS counsel knew better as a result of his involvement with the two earlier years.

Nevertheless, IRS issued a notice of deficiency and Mel ended up in Tax Court. Subsequent to filing the petition, another agent was assigned to assist in reviewing Mel's records. By the time the case was called for trial in February of 1991, Mel and the IRS were in agreement that he was entitled to all the deductions claimed in his returns. In fact, through the simple verification process, Mel proved he had losses in each of the years. As a result of this process, the parties agreed Mel owed no income taxes or penalties for either the year 1978 or 1979.

Mel then filed a motion in the Tax Court seeking an award of fees and costs under Code section 7430. The IRS opposed the motion, claiming its position was substantially justified. In defense of the claim, IRS counsel asserted that because a notice of deficiency is, under the law, "presumed correct," such presumption by itself constitutes "substantial justification." The Tax Court disagreed.

To be substantially justified, a legal position must have "substantial evidence to support it." In this case, there was no evidence at all. Furthermore, the IRS made no effort to gather any evidence. During the three-year period of time in which the assessment statute was suspended, the IRS did nothing. They failed to act because of an administrative decision specifically to not act. Still, they asserted in a notice of deficiency Mel was not entitled to any of his deductions.

In rejecting the IRS' claims, the court declared:

"In the instant case respondent's position had no factual or evidentiary basis. If some relevant evidence is required (to support a claim) *then none is surely not enough.* [How's that for sound judicial reasoning? Author.] In addition to having no relevant evidence about the case, (IRS) had specifically decided not to contact (Mel) to seek any. It has been held that the Government does not have a reasonable basis in both fact and law if it does not diligently investigate a case." (Emphasis added; footnotes omitted.)

The mere fact IRS may assert a claim in a notice of deficiency does not make it immune from an award of fees and costs under Code section 7430. It is true, the notice of deficiency is presumed correct. But the presumption acts only to place the burden of proof on the citizen. It does not allow the IRS to make unreasonable, arbitrary, meritless claims with impunity. As the court observed:

> "The fact that the Commissioner has the right to maintain a position does not bar a taxpayer from receiving an award for litigation costs if the position is unreasonable."

The IRS makes a practice of disallowing all deductions in a tax return simply because the statute is about to expire. Despite the fact the IRS has absolutely no evidence to support its disallowance, the citizen is placed in the position of having to prosecute a Tax Court case to prove his innocence. In this case, it came back to haunt the IRS in a big way. Mel was awarded attorney's fees, accountant's fees and related costs to the tune of $55,707.

Case Study No. Five, Six, Seven. . .

My list of case studies on Code section 7430 could, I am happy to say, go on and on. As I stated earlier, the number of cases is not great as compared to the number there could be, but they are growing. As you can see, they are very, very promising! I see a trend which, frankly, I never expected. I see the courts hammering the IRS when it pursues a course which is unreasonable, unfounded, arbitrary or without justification.

Most importantly, the courts are hammering the IRS because citizens are forcing them to hammer the IRS. Code section 7430 is an important right. But you cannot exercise that right if you are ignorant of it. Each time the IRS is hit with an award under Code section 7430, the agency will surely become more wary of its actions.

As evidenced by the case studies discussed above, the IRS is simply not at liberty to arbitrarily harass and intimidate the citizens of this country any longer. This change in judicial attitude has been a long time in coming, but is now upon us. You must take advantage of it.

One final case note. The Supreme Court has considered the issue of "substantial justification" under the *Equal Access to Justice Act*. The Supreme Court's insights on the matter have been applied universally to cases involving Code section 7430. I recommend reading the case of *Pierce v. Underwood*, 487 U.S. 424 (1988), for further guidance on this subject.

PROCEDURE FOR RECOVERING FEES AND COSTS

Internal Revenue Regulations specify the procedure for making a claim for fees and costs. In essence, there are two forums available for making the claim. The first is the administrative forum. This involves a case before the IRS which did not proceed into the courts. The second is the judicial forum. This involves a case, such as those cited here, which did proceed into the courts. I address each one individually.

1. The Administrative Claim for Fees and Costs. Under Revenue Regulation section 301.7430-2(c), an application for fees and cost must be made in writing. It must be sent to the chief of the division of IRS with jurisdiction over the claim. For example, audits are the jurisdiction of the Examination Division. Collection cases are the responsibility of the Collection Division. If you are in doubt as to which division is responsible for your case, send the claim to the district director.

The written request must contain the following information:

a. A statement showing the underlying tax liability issues have never been presented to a court. If the tax issues were decided by a court, the IRS will not decide the question of fees and costs. It must then be presented to the court which decided the underlying questions.

b. A clear and concise statement as to why you believe the position of the IRS was not substantially justified.

c. A statement showing you substantially prevailed in the case, either with respect to the amount in controversy or with respect to the most significant issue or set of issues in the case.

d. A statement showing that you did not unreasonably protract the portion of the proceedings for which you are seeking costs and fees.

e. A detailed statement showing the nature and amount of fees and costs you incurred, for which you are seeking recovery.

f. An affidavit stating you meet the net worth requirements of the *Equal Access to Justice Act.* Those requirements were outlined earlier.

g. Copies of any bills, receipts or other documents evidencing your claim for fees and costs.

h. Lastly, the address at which you wish to be notified of the ruling on your claim.

Your claim should be notarized or contain a declaration that it is made under the penalty of perjury. Each of these requirements is taken from Rev. Reg. section 301.7430-2(c)(3).

Timeliness in making the claim is very important. Under section (c)(5) of the above-cited regulation, the claim must be made within "90 days after the date the final decision" covering all tax, interest and penalty issues is either "mailed, or otherwise furnished" to the citizen.

The IRS has six months to rule on your application. If the application is either denied or no action is taken within that time, you have the right to appeal to the Tax Court. Failure to respond within six months is tantamount to denial of the claim. The appeal is taken by filing a petition with the United States Tax Court in accordance with the Rules of Procedure for the Tax Court. Rev. Reg. section 301.7430-2(c)(6) and (c)(7). For more information on the Tax Court, please see Chapter Four of *Taxpayers' Ultimate Defense Manual.*

2. The Judicial Claim for Fees and Costs. When a court, such as the Tax Court, passes upon the correctness of the IRS' claims, it is that court, and not the IRS, which has the authority to decide an application for fees and costs. For example, suppose the Appeals Office rules against you, then issues a notice of deficiency. You in turn file a petition in the Tax Court and eventually win your case. Under that scenario, you must file your application directly with the Tax Court, and not the IRS.

When a judicial application is made, the rules for making the claim are the same as those outlined above, with one important exception. Under Code section 7430, you must file the claim within *30 days* of the court's final decision on the merits of the case. Chapter Four of the *Defense Manual* offers more information on the application itself, including a sample application form. That form can be adapted for use either within the IRS itself, or in the Tax Court. When adapting the form for use within the IRS, be sure to meet the content requirements of Rev. Reg. section 301.7430-2(c)(3), which are listed above.

CONCLUSION

Would you like to stop IRS abuse in its tracks? Then make 'em pay for their improper or abusive tactics! Using the two techniques discussed in this article, you can both recover the costs of fighting abuse, and send a clear message to the IRS in the process. The message is simply that we will not tolerate the agency's illegal actions any longer!

CHAPTER

12

Right Number Eight: Punishing Individual Agents How to Stop the Lies

The most prevalent feeling experienced by victims of IRS abuse is that of helplessness. Faced with the awesome power of a $7 billion per year bureaucracy and the notion that you cannot fight city hall, most people just take their lumps. It is not that folks will do nothing about abuse, rather, they feel there is nothing they can do to make a difference. Litigation is too costly, so lawsuits are out. Complaining does no good, because those to whom you complain have no power either.

Consequently, IRS abuse continues. Agents regularly lie to citizens concerning their rights and obligations under the code. Others violate laws or regulations while in the conduct of their duties. Some forms of abuse are even more grave, causing serious disruptions in peoples' lives.

Is the ability to lie to taxpayers written in the job description of IRS employees? You can bet it is not. Has Congress expressly given the IRS the right to lie to taxpayers? Of course not. Does the institution openly teach its employees to lie to taxpayers? No again. If the answer to these questions is so emphatically "no," what allows IRS as an institution and individual employees in general, to get away with it?

They get away with it simply because they have gone unchallenged for so long. While lying and violating the law is not directly taught, it is certainly encouraged. If this were not the case, we would not see widespread abuse in these areas. Let me give an illustration of how the tacit imposition of these ideas leads individual agents to lie and violate laws on a broad scale.

A man I will call Bill went to work for the IRS upon leaving college. Unable to find work suitable to his accounting background, he reasoned a job with the IRS was a good starting point. He was hired by the agency and began his training as a tax auditor. During his training, IRS instructors preached a general principle. Sticking to the principle was to ensure all taxpayers were treated equally. The principle was "apply the code." Whatever the situation, auditors were to "apply the code." What the code says is what governs. It did not matter what anybody "thought" the law might be. Only the law determines the outcome of the case.

That seemed mighty reasonable to Bill. Bill was a man of high moral values. He was fully capable of applying the law to all situations. If, in doing so, the taxpayer was found to owe more money, so be it. The law is the law. We all must obey the law.

Bill's training was eventually complete. He became a full-fledged revenue agent. Before long, he found himself hip-deep in his first tax audit. Bill took his training very seriously. He made every effort to do a conscientious job. "Apply the code," he told himself, as he paged through stacks of receipts and canceled checks. "Apply the code," he repeated silently, as he questioned the citizen and reviewed the return.

Finally, Bill completed the audit. He wrote a preliminary report and presented it to his supervisor. The supervisor could not believe his eyes. You see, in Bill's first audit, he ascertained that the citizen was due a small *refund*.

"How did you come up with this?," the supervisor asked incredulously.

"I applied the code," Bill responded, "just as I was instructed to do. This man is due a refund."

The supervisor gave Bill the training of his life. He explained he could not approve the audit findings. Bill was specifically instructed to "get something" from the citizen.

Remember I told you Bill was a man of high moral standards? Well, to his tribute, he did not attempt to "get something" from a man whom he knew darned well had a refund coming. Instead, he quit his job. Bill, tax auditor for a day, learned a lesson I have been teaching throughout this text. Tax auditors simply want to get the money. This is what they are taught in the field and that is why lying is so prevalent in the audit environment. Because so few citizens ever contest IRS decisions or actions, this kind of behavior feeds upon itself.

Many high officials within the IRS insist my story about Bill and others like him is purely anectdotal. They say such instances are rare. They assert the IRS maintains high standards of ethical conduct and does not condone such behavior. It is true, the agency's *public* declarations do not condone such behavior. But what happens in *practice* is another matter. Let me provide some more examples, these of much more severe abuses.

A Phoenix businessman was approached by a local revenue officer early one morning. After identifying himself to Dave, the collector demanded full and immediate payment of an alleged $12,000 debt.

In response, Dave asked to see a copy of the assessment documents. The IRS officer refused to provide them. Dave asked to see a copy of the tax lien. That request was refused. Dave asked for an explanation of his rights under the circumstances. None was given. Dave inquired whether an installment agreement was possible. The collector insisted one was not. In fact, the only response of any kind was a belligerent demand for payment of the "full amount and nothing less."

Dave eventually worked his way around to asking whether it was true his tax bill could be discharged in bankruptcy. At that, the officer began a yelling tirade of threats. The display of unprofessional anger was witnessed both by Dave's 19 year-old son and two neighbors.

As the argument raged, Dave attempted to close his garage door, which was open at the time of the collector's arrival. As he did, the collector stepped forward and the two men - the collector, 260 pounds, and Dave, 220 pounds - bumped stomachs. After closing the garage door, Dave led the way to the street. As he did, the collector followed and the argument raged. Both men well heated at this point. Dave continued to insist on an explanation of his rights, explaining full payment was impossible. The collector repeated his bold demands for nothing less than full payment.

Later, the agent filed a false report with his supervisors. He claimed Dave "provoked, challenged, and impeded him" while in the act of performing his duties. He went so far as to say, "if I were not working, I would have hit him." As if that were not enough, the collector had the nerve to falsely report that Dave "forcibly assaulted and resisted, opposed, impeded, intimidated and interfered with" him while in the act of collecting taxes. In his blindness, however, the collector neglected to take into account the presence of the three eye-witnesses who watched the entire episode. Between their testimony and the continued arrogance of the collector throughout the whole affair, Dave was found to have done nothing wrong.

A similar event played out in southern California. This time two female revenue officers walked into the pawn shop owned by Chris. They requested full payment of Chris' tax debt. Chris explained he did not have the money. Some cordial conversation followed and the collectors soon left. They parted by saying, "Have a nice day."

When the two women got back to the office, they filed a false report. In it, they claimed Chris threatened them with a gun. The collectors explained that Chris revealed a hand gun he was carrying. According to the report, he placed his hand on the gun, and stated, "What do you want me to do, kill?" The report explained that the two collectors walked out of the store "with their backs against the door." Based upon this report, Chris was charged with the felony offense of "assaulting" the federal agents with a firearm. Chris faced five years in prison if convicted of the charge.

The lying agents failed to take one small factor into consideration before making their fabricated report. Dave's southern California pawn shop was equipped with video surveillance equipment! In living color complete with audio, the entire event was recorded for the world - and federal prosecutors - to see. Here we have the IRS' answer to the Rodney King beating. When it was made clear the two agents lied through their teeth, the charges were dropped.

Let us consider another story from southern California. Dion worked as an electronics repairman for a mom-and-pop operation. Rosa owned the repair shop. Dion also rented a small apartment from Rosa, located behind the store. Rosa took in telephones, answering machines, tape recorders, etc. Dion repaired them.

Years earlier, Dion operated his own repair shop, but it failed. He went out of business owing the government several thousand in employment taxes. After seven years, the IRS showed up at Rosa's shop to collect Dion's past taxes.

The revenue officers on the scheme assumed Dion owned Rosa's shop and its contents. In fact, most of the items in the store did not belong to either of them. They belonged to customers who left them for repair. These facts were explained to the collectors. Proof of the shop's ownership was provided, with copies of the claim checks given to customers for their items. The agents were unimpressed with any of it.

One agent explained to Dion, "we came here to get this property and we're going to get it." The agent even declared, "we are not here to collect taxes, we are here to close you down." As Rosa protested the seizure of her property, she was physically pushed out of the building. She suffered a back injury in the process.

After they finished cleaning Rosa's shop to the bare walls, they turned their attention on Dion's apartment. They took everything. By everything, consider these entries on the Notice of Seizure documents prepared after the affair:

"1 standing Eureka vacuum cleaner; 1 standing Regina electric broom; 1 lot assorted blankets, pillows and sleeping bag; 1 upright plastic 3' tall trash can; 1 lot assorted papers and misc items; misc personal items."

I want you to imagine selling those items to pay a tax debt. What do you suppose a 3-foot tall plastic trash can would fetch at your average garage sale? Fifty cents?

The collectors knew full well they were taking business property which they had no right to take. Even if they had cause to believe it belonged to Dion and not Rosa, they also knew customers' property was among the items seized. On the official seizure report, we find the following listings:

"assorted customers' property; misc customers' telephones, answering machines, laser disc player"

It seems the declarations of the collectors were quite accurate. They were not there to collect taxes. They were there to put Dion out of business, even if they had to close Rosa's repair shop to do it.

In the two months preceding this writing, I spoke with three people who had loved ones driven to suicide over tax problems. In each case, I heard stories of IRS agents - usually collectors - wielding arbitrary and unreasonable powers. I was told of the mindless manner in which collection was pursued, almost as though the goal of the process was not to collect taxes at all. As a matter of fact, I have previously written that often the collection function becomes a sort of punishment. Rather than work reasonably with a citizen to facilitate collection, the collector takes on the role of executioner. His job is to punish the poor fool who managed to get himself into tax debt. At that point, collection is purely secondary.

The process is what IRS refers to as "encouraging and achieving the highest possible degree of voluntary compliance" with the tax laws. It is precisely why so many people have gone into hiding when they find themselves owing money. People are not stupid. They will not willingly subject themselves to such treatment if there is some other reasonable alternative. For too many citizens, hiding - some for years at a time - has become a viable alternative to living through an IRS-induced hell.

The fact is, official declarations made by the IRS for public consumption deplore such behavior. The IRS' *official view* is that such behavior is neither encouraged or tolerated. In practice, the opposite is true. So the question is, how can we stop it?

To answer the question, let us recognize some realities. First, such behavior is widespread. Second, the IRS would never dare admit such behavior is taught or encouraged. We can therefore conclude that if this behavior is brought to light through an effective complaint process, the IRS would be forced to do something about it. If it did not, it runs the substantial risk that America would lose what little faith it has in the tax system. This would render the IRS ineffective as an enforcement agency.

As I shall prove in a moment, the IRS recognizes as a fact of life what I have just declared. What we must do therefore, is to utilize an effective complaint process to shine the light of truth upon outrageous IRS conduct. In this way, we can force the IRS to deal internally with those actions which it has silently endorsed in the past.

The third reality is this: it is the nature of despotic government to express a willingness to sacrifice one or more of its own pawns in order to foster the goals of the organization. The IRS would think nothing of offering up one of its own agents as a sacrificial lamb if, in doing so, it believed it was helping the security of the agency. Public perception in the integrity of the IRS is of paramount importance. If any individual agent is seen publicly as posing a threat to that perception, he shall surely be brought down by his own agency. This is true despite the fact the agency itself has allowed, or even taught, that agent to act improperly.

The reason the agency has not routinely disciplined outrageous behavior in the past is because it seldom comes to light. But when it does, correction action must be taken in order to preserve the public perception that government is concerned about honesty and integrity in its operations.

THE OFFICIAL REQUIREMENTS FOR IRS BEHAVIOR

In 1978, Congress passed the *Ethics in Government Act*. 5 USC section 7351. In broad terms, the act requires all federal government employees to act in a manner which bespeaks the trust relationship in which they are placed. The regulations under act provide a clear definition of this public trust. In 5 CFR section 2635.101(a), we find the following:

"(a) Public service is a public trust.
Each employee has a responsibility to the United States Government and its citizens to place loyalty to the *Constitution, laws and ethical principles* above private gain. To ensure that every citizen can have the complete confidence in the integrity of the Federal Government, each employee shall respect and adhere to the principles of ethical conduct set forth in this section, as well as the implementing standards contained

in the part and in supplemental agency regulations." (Emphasis added.)

The regulations go on to describe 14 specific ethical principles. These principles form the basis of the standards of ethical conduct. The significant items within the list of 14 are:

1. Public service is a *public trust* requiring each employee to place loyalty to the Constitution, laws and ethical principles above private gain.

2. Employees shall not hold *financial interests* that conflict with the conscientious performance of their duty.

4. An employee shall not solicit or accept *any gift or other item of monetary value* from any person seeking official action, doing business with, or conducting activities regulated by the employee's agency, or whose interests may be substantially affected by the performance or nonperformance of the employee's duties.

5. Employees shall put forth *honest effort* in the performance of their duties.

7. Employees shall not use public office for private gain.

8. Employees shall act *impartially* and not give preferential treatment to any private organization or individual.

11. Employees *shall disclose* waste, fraud, abuse, and corruption to appropriate authorities.

14. Employees shall endeavor to avoid any actions creating the *appearance* they are violating the law or the ethical standards set forth in this part. Whether particular circumstances create an appearance that the law or these standards have been violated shall be determined from the perspective of a reasonable person with knowledge of the relevant facts. Executive Order 12674, signed in April of 1989, published in the Federal Register on August 7, 1992.

In February, 1993, the Office of Government Ethics (OGE) produced a report based upon Executive Order 12674. That report is entitled *Standards of Ethical Conduct for Employees of the Executive Branch*. IRS Document 9077. At the same time, the OGE released an ethics *Self-Study Guide* for IRS employees. IRS Document 9076. The study guide confirms my observations concerning the importance of maintaining the public's confidence in the agency. Consider this statement from the Introduction to the study guide:

> "The basic mission of the IRS is to foster, to the fullest extent possible, voluntary compliance with all revenue laws and regulations. Confidence in the Service and faith in its dependability, integrity and high ethical standards are factors having a major impact on our ability to carry out our mission. We can maintain the public's confidence only to the extent that every one of our contacts with the public reflects the highest ethical standards." Document 9076, page 2.

The study guide mandates IRS employees put forth an "honest effort" in carrying out their day to day activities. They must conduct themselves in accordance with the ethical directives of the law. They are to "display a conscientious effort" to carry out the IRS' mission. Document 9076, page 7.

The "mission" of the IRS as of September, 1992, is as follows:

"The purpose of the Internal Revenue Service is to collect the proper amount of tax revenue at the least cost; serve the public by continually improving the quality of our products and services; and perform in a manner warranting the highest degree of public confidence in our integrity, efficiency and fairness." 1992 IRS Chief Financial Officer Report to Congress, page 5.

All behavior of individual agents must foster this mission statement. If any act does not, an ethical violation occurs.

The study guide demands all IRS employees disclose any "information or allegation coming to their attention which indicates that another employee may have committed a crime, including violation of tax laws, or any IRS, Treasury, or OGE conduct provision." Document 9076, page 8.

IRS employees are under a firm directive to police one another. Violations of ethical standards are presented as serious matters which must be attended to promptly and properly. Failure to disclose, is itself an ethical violation.

An issue of particular importance in the study guide is the need to avoid actions "creating the appearance that they are violating the law or these Standards of Ethical Conduct." Document 9076, page 9. The appearance of a violation can be as "detrimental as actually violating the law." IRS employees are therefore counselled to use "good judgment" in avoiding circumstances which could be construed to be a violation of ethics or law, even if it is not.

The question of whether the "appearance" clause is violated is judged upon the "reasonable person" standard. The question is whether, from the perspective of a reasonable person with knowledge of the relevant facts, one might construe the conduct to constitute a violation of law or ethical standards.

When a violation of law or any of the 14 ethical standards is shown, an employee is subject to disciplinary action. Such action can include dismissal from the IRS or criminal prosecution.

The IRS produced a handbook which addresses the ethical rules outlined by the OGE. The handbook is entitled *Handbook for the Rules of Conduct*. Internal Revenue Manual part 0735. The Introduction to the handbook uses pointed language to express the need for high ethical standards on the part of IRS employees. Consider this:

"In order for the Service to serve the public interest, the Service and its employees must hold and maintain the confidence and esteem of the public we serve. To achieve this, employees are expected to conduct themselves in their official relations with the public and their fellow employees, in a courteous, businesslike, and diplomatic manner. Conduct which does not conform to these rules, or related statutes or regulations, which directly impacts on an employee's position, official duties, or the Service, may subject the employee to appropriate disciplinary action. The absence of a specific rule relating to an employee's action which may impact on their official duties or the

Service does not mean that such an act is either condoned or may not result in disciplinary action.* * *" Handbook for Rules of Conduct, section 211.

The Rules of Conduct handbook contains prohibitions which directly pattern the 14 specific points expressed above. But it goes farther. Listen:

"False Statements - Service Rule

"Employees *will not* intentionally make false or misleading verbal or written statements in matters of official interest." Handbook section 214.5. (Emphasis added.)

The handbook itself is based upon federal regulations which address themselves to Treasury employees. They were promulgated under the authority of the Civil Service Commissioner. See 31 CFR Subtitle A, section 0.735.

With respect to making false or misleading statements, the regulations are more telling than is the handbook. Section 0.735-54 declares the following:

"Falsification of Official Records

"Employees shall avoid making false, misleading or ambiguous statements, deliberately or wilfully, whether verbal or written, in connection with any matter of official interest. Some of these matters of official interest are: *Transactions with the public,* other Federal agencies or fellow employees; application forms and other forms which serve as a basis for appointment, reassignment, promotion or other personnel actions; vouchers; leave records; *work reports of any nature or accounts of any kind; affidavits;* entry or record of any matter relating to or connected with the employee's duties; and reports of any moneys or securities received, held or paid to or on behalf of the United States (18 USC 1001)." (Emphasis added.)

At last we find clear, uncontrovertible proof from two sources that *it is not proper* for IRS employees to lie or mislead citizens in any particular. We know from the Introduction to the handbook that violation of this rule is actionable, possibly leading to dismissal. The handbook expressly demands that employees "promptly report" any information or allegation which indicates another employee "may have" violated any law or other provision of the Rules of Conduct. Handbook, section 214.31. All IRS employees are required to sign a statement acknowledging receipt of a copy of the Rules of Conduct. The signed statement is to be maintained in the employee's personnel file at all times. Handbook, section 212.2.

Finally, we turn to IRS Publication 1, *Your Rights as a Taxpayer*. (Reproduced in Chapter 5 as Exhibit 5-2) The opening remarks in Publication 1 hold:

"As a taxpayer, you have the right to be treated fairly, professionally, promptly, and courteously by Internal Revenue Service employees. *Our goal at the IRS is to protect your rights so that you will have the highest confidence in the integrity, efficiency, and fairness of our tax system*. To ensure that you always receive such treatment, you should know about the many rights you have at each step of the tax process." Publication 1, page 1. (Emphasis added.)

As you see, the IRS places the idea of *public perception* of its legal and ethical function on highest priority. Should the public begin to believe such is not case, IRS authority is directly undermined. As people begin to lose faith in the system, they stop adhering to the rule of law. In this regard, government is very much the teacher. If it teaches lawlessness, citizens respond with lawless actions.

Despite all the talk about ethics, we know individual agent abuse is widespread. The reason is the agency gives these ethical considerations mere lip service because nobody effectively complains about their violation. We must begin to complain loudly and properly to hold individual agents accountable for their lies and improper or illegal conduct.

LEGAL REQUIREMENTS FOR **IRS** BEHAVIOR

Actions for which IRS employees may be punished go beyond ethical standards. IRS employees are subject to criminal prosecution for violation of law to the same extent any other person is subject to those laws. In addition to the typical criminal laws covering tax fraud and evasion, a family of criminal statutes is pointed squarely at IRS employees. Section 7214(a) of the tax Code provides for criminal prosecution in nine specific instances. They are:

1. Extortion or willful oppression under color of law;

2. Demanding other or greater sums than are allowed by law, or receiving a fee or commission for the performance of a duty;

3. Failure to perform any required official duty with the intent to defeat the application of any law;

4. Conspiracy to defraud the United States;

5. Knowingly making the opportunity for another person to defraud the United States;

6. Acting or failing to act with the intent to enable another person to defraud the United States;

7. Making or signing any fraudulent entry in any book, certificate, return or statement;

8. Failure to report in writing the violation of any revenue law when such person has knowledge or information concerning such violation;

9. Demanding or accepting any bribe. Code section 7214(a)(1) - (a)(9).

Each of these is considered a felony offense. Upon conviction of one of them, the perpetrator can be imprisoned for up to five years and fined up to $10,000. He is also to be dismissed from office. The court may award a portion of the fine to the injured person to compensate for his damages.

Section 7213 of the code provides criminal sanctions against any IRS employee or former employee who discloses the confidential tax return or return information of any person without proper authority. This is a felony offense carrying a penalty of up to five years in prison and a $5,000 fine.

Under the United States criminal code, Title 18, section 1905, the unauthorized disclosure of trade secrets or proprietary business information and the like, is a crime. Upon conviction, one can be imprisoned up to one year and fined up to $1,000.

The solicitation or receipt of bribes is a crime under 18 USC section 201. Conviction under that statute carries the penalty of a $20,000 fine and up to 15 years in prison.

An important point bears repeating. Under all the regulations we have examined, including the IRS' Rules of Conduct handbook, IRS employees are *absolutely mandated* to report information relating to the violation of law or the Rules of Conduct by another employee.

Such a report does not have to be based upon personal knowledge. The report can be based upon "information" available to the reporting employee. See, for example, the Rules of Conduct, section 214.31. Under that section, the report must be made when any "information or allegation" of wrongdoing comes to the attention of the particular employee. Section 214.32 requires such reports to be made "promptly," either orally or in writing.

Later, I address the process of making complaints. My suggestions are based squarely upon the regulations and handbooks we have just examined. The process is designed to ensure that complaints of misconduct such as those exposed earlier in this chapter do not go unpunished. By using these procedures, we quite literally FIRE the offending IRS employee!

WHERE TO COMPLAIN ABOUT IRS ABUSE

Every police force has a department which investigates police conduct. Generally, that department is known as Internal Affairs. The IRS has its own version of Internal Affairs. It is known as the Inspection organization. Officers within Inspection, police the police. Their job, among other things, is to investigate all allegations of misconduct on the part of IRS employees. The IRS manual which addresses Inspection describes the function as follows:

> "* * *[A]n investigative service which will assure the maintenance of the *highest standards of honesty*, integrity, loyalty, security, *and conduct among Internal Revenue Service employees* and which will protect the integrity of the Service from attack by outsiders who seek to compromise it through attempted bribery or other illegal or improper acts. . ." Internal Revenue Manual, (10)-44, section (10)131.1(1)(b). (Emphasis added.)

The Inspection organization is divided functionally into two divisions - the Internal Audit Division and the Internal Security Division. It is the Internal Security Division which focuses upon employee misconduct. Two types are mentioned. Criminal misconduct implies violation of one or more criminal statutes. Administrative misconduct implies a violation of the ethical standards or Rules of Conduct.

The IRS uses its Inspection function against its own employees in much the same manner it uses the Examination and Criminal Investigation functions against the public. The purpose of the latter functions is to create and maintain a sense of "presence" in the lives of all Americans. The IRS wants you to feel its presence at all times. This acts as a deterrent. In fact, criminal prosecutions are carried out against the public almost exclusively for the purpose of generating a deterrent effect in the community.

The Manual calls upon the IRS to undertake a "proactive Inspection program" for the same reasons. Manual section (10)133.1. The specific objective of Inspection's security programs is to "detect instances of fraud or corruption, and to provide a *deterrent effect through high Inspection visibility*." Ibid. at 133.2(1)(b); (emphasis added). The agency keeps individual agents in line by making them believe there is an Inspector behind every corner. This "high visibility" is designed to keep employees in line.

The reality of what I just outlined offers a prime opportunity to legally and effectively retaliate against IRS abuse. First off, Inspectors have no job if they have nobody to investigate. Just as tax auditors and criminal investigators "uncover every stone" to determine whether tax law violations have occurred, I must believe Inspectors function the same way. The only difference is they are investigating their own agents, not honest citizens.

Secondly, there can be no deterrent effect created if an occasional victim is not sacrificed on the alter of obedience. The presence of Inspection and its function would become entirely hollow if those "inspected" did not occasionally fall. Creating deterrence is simply impossible if no visible punishment is dealt to offending employees.

Therefore, I conclude the Inspection Division needs cases to investigate if its prime functions of "high visibility" and creating "deterrence" are to be met. I suggest we help them do their job! I suggest we use the Inspection function as a means to complain against individual agents who abuse taxpayers, who lie in connection with a matter of official interest, who violate tax laws or regulations while in the act of collecting taxes. We have been frustrated in the past by such actions, but we have not complained to the proper police force. The Inspection Division is the proper police force and they are driven by such complaints. I have every reason to believe they will take such matters seriously.

How to Complain About IRS Abuse

All complaints to Inspection concerning the conduct of IRS employees are to be investigated. Manual section (10)332.1. When a complaint is received which alleges criminal or administrative wrongdoing, the Internal Security Division commences a "conduct" investigation. The conduct investigation is designed to determine whether that employee is suitable "for retention in the Service and for necessary action by management to separate or otherwise discipline or clear the employee, as the case may be." Manual section (10)331.1.

Original complaints should be made in writing to the Inspection function, Internal Security Division. Each local IRS office has an Inspection function staffed with Inspectors. Mail a copy of your complaint to the Regional Inspector. He is the Regional Commissioner of Inspection with charge over your entire revenue region. A revenue region encompasses several states. The address of the Regional Inspector can be obtained from your local IRS office.

A copy of the complaint should also be mailed to the employee's immediate supervisor and to the District Director. The District Director is the top manager within the revenue district. A revenue district generally consists of one state.

The idea of sending copies of the complaint to so many managers is simple. As we studied earlier in this chapter, each IRS employee is mandated to complain when he has any "information" concerning misconduct on the part of another employee. By spreading the complaint broadly, we ensure that more than one complaint on that particular employee is filed with Inspection. When Inspection receives more than one complaint about a given employee, the chances increase substantially that a serious investigation will grow from the process.

I wish to offer a word of caution before we go any further. The complaint process should, *under no circumstances*, be abused. Complaints must involve only serious violations of either the tax laws or regulations, or express violations of the Code of Ethics, or Rules of Conduct. Complaints should be well-grounded in fact and you must by ready and willing to offer testimony and evidence to support the claim.

Be aware of the fact that filing a false complaint with Inspection could be considered a criminal violation under either 18 USC section 1001 or 26 USC section 7206(2). Do not take lightly the obligation to base your complaint upon the truth. At the very least, filing frivolous complaints for vexatious or harassment purposes could potentially lead to civil action against you by the government.

The sanctity of the complaint process must be preserved. That way legitimate complaints are treated seriously. If frivolous complaints are showered upon Inspection, it may come to summarily reject all complaints. This would operate to deprive citizens truly wronged by IRS abuse of an opportunity to correct the injustice.

How to Draft the Complaint

The IRS provides no specific form on which to submit a complaint. I suggest the following format.

1. State your name, full address and telephone number.

2. Give the name, office address, title and employee number of the IRS employee in question.

3. Provide a clear and concise statement of the background facts. The statement should allow the reader to learn of the relevant circumstances behind the employee's actions.

4. Provide a clear and concise statement of the specific violation of tax law or regulation alleged, or the violation of Ethical Standards or the Rules of Conduct. When alleging criminal or administrative misconduct, be specific. Vague or general allegations are insufficient.

5. Provide copies of any documents or other tangible evidence to support

your allegations. This may include affidavits or statements from third parties having relevant testimony.

6. Provide a declaration stating that under penalty of perjury, the facts contained in the complaint are true and correct to the best of your knowledge and belief.

7. Sign and date the complaint.

The original signed complaint should be mailed to Inspection by certified mail, with return receipt requested. Mail copies to each of the other offices outlined above, also via certified mail, with return receipt requested.

FIRING IRS EMPLOYEES

IRS employees who violate the tax laws, regulations, ethical standards or rules of conduct should be fired. This is particularly true when those violations cause serious hardship to the citizen involved. For example, there is no imaginable reason why the two IRS collectors who lied about the threat on their life should work another day for the United States Government. That kind of behavior is absolutely intolerable. If I understand the IRS documents outlined earlier in this chapter, a complaint to Inspection should lead to a full investigation of the matter and discharge of the employees. They expressly violated the rules prohibiting making a false report on a matter of official interest.

Many complain that it is impossible to win the discharge of any civil service employee because the laws make it so difficult. *The Civil Service Reform Act of 1978* was designed to change that. See 5 USC sections 1110-8913. Specifically, the procedures under the act are intended to simplify and accelerate the means by which to fire incompetent employees. The procedure, as outlined in the *Civil Service Reform Act*, has been implemented by Federal regulation. Furthermore, it is incorporated into the employment contract between the Internal Revenue Service and the National Treasury Employees Union. The terms of that contract are published in IRS Document 6647.

Under section 4303 of the *Civil Service Reform Act*, 5 USC section 4303, a federal employee can be removed or reduced in grade "for unacceptable performance." Under section 7503 of the act, 5 USC section 7503, employees may be disciplined for "discourteous conduct to the public." Specifically, if an immediate supervisor confirms "four instances" of such conduct "within any one-year period," that employee can be suspended.

The contract between IRS and its employees specifies that agents may be fired when the performance of their duties does not meet acceptable levels. The specific levels are known as performance standards. The performance standards are set by the IRS and must be adhered to by the employee. These include the ethical standards and Rules of Conduct. An employee may suffer "removal, reduction in grade, or reassignment if the employee's performance is unacceptable and does not improve. . ." Document 6647, Article 17, section 3.

Constructive complaining through Inspection insures that troublesome employees are ferreted out and fired. The manual states that "Sufficient investigation will be conducted *in every case* to establish proof or disproof of the allegations. . ." Manual section (10)332.5(1); (emphasis added).

CONDUCT INVESTIGATION AND IRS EMPLOYEES

When the conduct investigation begins, Inspection contacts the employee implicated. He is to be read his rights. When the investigation involves administrative misconduct, the employee has the right to counsel and may refuse to answer questions. However, he is advised that the mere refusal to answer any questions could by itself lead to dismissal.

The employee is required to sign IRS Form 8112, *Statement of Rights and Obligations*, which acknowledges his rights have been explained. If the facts and information warrant, the employee can be suspended during the pendency of the investigation. Manual section (10)332.6.

If the conduct investigation takes a criminal turn, Inspection is instructed to consult the United States Attorney to ensure that all aspects of the criminal statutes are explored. The employee is read his Miranda rights before any direct questioning begins. The Miranda warning explains the right to counsel, the right to remain silent and the fact that any statements may be used in court.

After receiving the warning, the employee is given IRS Form 5228, *Waiver of Right to Remain Silent and of Right to Advice of Counsel*. If the employee chooses to waive his rights to counsel and to remain silent, he must sign the written waiver in Form 5228. The waiver is witnessed and questioning begins.

At the conclusion of the investigation, Inspection makes a full written report of the matter. The report explains the allegations and evidence developed during the investigation. It includes the employee's statements and defense to the charges. If the defense was investigated, the findings are reported.

The report is then submitted to the top IRS manager having disciplinary authority over the employee. In administrative misconduct cases, that person makes the determination of what specific action is to be taken. If the charges are criminal in nature, the United States Attorney's office decides whether to prosecute the employee for a crime.

USING THE MEDIA TO COMPLAIN

By now, there should be no question about the fact that the IRS is dependent upon favorable public perception of its actions in order for it to survive. When the public becomes disenchanted on a broad scale, the IRS will become ineffective. It will lose its ability to persuade Congress to continue to fund it. In short, it will have to be eliminated and our tax system rebuilt. That of course, is the most desirable outcome possible.

As I explain in Part III of this book, we all will be much better off if we fire the IRS entirely. But we must build up public support for the idea. We do that by publicizing more broadly the incidents of abuse along with actions taken to defend against it. Merely focusing upon abuse does nothing but scare more people. It serves to advance the notion that the IRS is unbeatable. Therefore, the need to communicate the idea we are fighting back *successfully* against IRS abuse is paramount.

The media concentrates on victims of IRS actions because the IRS systematically releases news stories about them. When Leona Helmsley, Red Foxx, Willie Nelson and others were raked over the coals, the media hyped the reports because it received information from the IRS on the details. We can accomplish the same thing where complaints to Inspection are concerned.

Let us begin to use the media to expose abusive IRS agents and their actions. In this way the media becomes our tool of justice used in the same manner as the IRS. Use it to communicate the notion that illegal or abusive conduct will no longer be tolerated. When that message is communicated in print or over the airwaves, individual agents will have no alternative but to obey the law.

Every city has a talk radio station which discusses national and regional issues. I have appeared on thousands of talk radio shows throughout the nation. Whether the host is liberal or conservative, considers himself a Democrat or Republican, all have one thing in common. They recognize the IRS is an agency with too much power and is likely out of control. These talk shows provide a perfect opportunity to air complaints and stories about the activities of a particular IRS employee. Phone the show and tell your story on the air. Give the details. Get the truth out. By shining the light of truth upon illegal IRS actions, we effect the very thing the IRS is most frightened of - *public opinion.*

Most local newspapers and television stations feature a consumer reporter who covers stories of fraud, etc. in the marketplace. Some even feature reporters who concentrate on government mishaps. Complaints against individual agents should be shared with these reporters. Give them the facts and details of the case so they can run stories about the illegal or improper actions. This will put great pressure on the agency to clean up its act, punish the offending agent and stop its practice of abusing citizens.

Most importantly, it sets the public's awareness of the issue at a heightened level. It makes the public more sensitive to the problem. It eliminates the notion that such abuses are few and far between. That, in turn, reinforces the idea that sweeping change must be made if the problem is to be solved.

In doing research for this chapter, I read hundreds of pages of IRS manuals, regulations and other documents, much of which I reference here. The one point that comes through time and again in those documents is this: *The IRS is afraid of public opinion.* Public opinion directly controls the agency's effectiveness. The IRS is desperate to keep the public believing that all is well with both our nation's tax collection system and agency. We must change that. We can do so with the same tools the IRS uses to foster the misinformation in the first place. We must use the media.

CONCLUSION

In our nation, everything turns on public opinion. The IRS knows this as well or better than anyone. The Declaration of Independence recognizes that governments exist only with "the consent of the governed." Without that consent, government loses its effectiveness and the ability to control its people.

The IRS maintains the "consent of the governed" by carefully contriving the appearance of propriety in its actions. People go along with the system as long as they perceive there are no serious deficiencies in it. When that perception is lost, major changes must be made or the public loses all confidence in its government.

In my heart I believe this to be one reason IRS installed programs of tax debt forgiveness as discussed in my book *How To Get Tax Amnesty.* Today nearly 20 million people owe the IRS money they can't pay. That number is too great - nearly three times the stated number of unemployed in this country. Were they not to address this horrible situation, it is easy to see how widespread public opinion of the agency would be destined for the commode.

We've also learned that the IRS must punish willful violators of law, regulation, ethical standards or rules of conduct in order to preserve the notion that it does not tolerate such conduct. If it fails to punish such violations, and if such violations are made public on a broad scale, the IRS will simply be unable to function.

The fact that agents have largely gone unpunished to this time is not testimony to the fact that my thesis is incorrect. It is merely testimony to the fact that citizens have not effectively taken action in public view and shined the spotlight of truth upon agency conduct. This failure must be corrected. The sooner they are corrected, the sooner we will see IRS abuse stop entirely.

In April of 1992, after appearing on the popular *Point of View* Radio Talk show with Marlin Maddoux, I received a letter from a former IRS employee. Ruth worked for years in the Problems Resolution Program and as a Training Coordinator in the Kansas City Service Center. She responded to my radio claim that IRS agents "lie" to the public on a regular basis. Ruth stated:

> "Most IRS employees that have 'lied' to taxpayers are operating on misinformation. They have been given that 'information' by their managers or instructors, and they do not have the time, experience or availability of the appropriate Internal Revenue Manual to verify the facts. However, I will admit that there is a strong resistance to change on all levels. When a piece of misinformation is discovered, it is very difficult to get the changed information put into practice."

Ruth explained that while the IRS instituted a number of programs designed to elevate the quality of its performance, she pointed out that the programs "provide no measure or consequence if a quality product is not achieved. Employees are told to produce a quality product and told by the directors of the quality programs that they will be given the means to do the job. Meanwhile, local management will hand out a memo encouraging quality while telling an employee to forego quality to produce quantity."

According to Ruth who is a former training instructor for the IRS, "The system is designed to produce substandard taxpayer service."

Ruth concludes as follows:

"You have explained to people how to deal with the IRS when they have a problem and how to avoid that problem in the first place. That is a very important thing to do. Average people need to have the knowledge of how to deal with the IRS bureaucracy, which people with means can buy from an experienced accountant. Everyone needs a fair chance to work within the system, but they also have the responsibility to contact the Commissioner of Internal Revenue and their Congressmen when they have had an encounter in which the IRS was wrong. *Unless the people at the top know the extent of the problem, they will not produce the massive changes needed* for the IRS to be the organization it was meant to be." (Emphasis added.)

Ruth provides very sound advice in her sincere letter. Unless we begin to complain in an effective way, no changes will take place. I can imagine no better forum for launching a complaint than with the IRS' Inspection division. It is the police force which polices the IRS. If we can take its manuals and directives at their word, it will punish IRS employees who abuse taxpayers, violate laws and regulations, ignore ethical standards and disregard the rules of conduct for Treasury employees. By prosecuting the complaints outlined in this discourse, we will make great strides toward bringing IRS abuse to an end forever.

3

ELIMINATE THE IRS
ONCE AND FOR ALL

America's tax collection system is built upon animosity. To establish tax policy, Congress uses class envy to enflame the passions of the public against a particular group. Generally, the "rich" are the target of the attacks. The reality, however, is tax increases, justified by attacks upon the rich, always end up hurting the middle class and the poor.

In the meantime, the IRS' arsenal of enforcement tools is built up year after year. The potential for audits, enforced collection, and penalty assessments, as well as recordkeeping and reporting burdens grow each time Congress imposes more statutory restraints. These tools are not used only against the rich. They are used against middle class taxpayers, small businesses and self-employed individuals, most just eking out a living in an increasingly hostile business environment.

The reason the attacks center upon the middle class, while the political justification centers upon the rich, is quite simple. Rich people are in a minority. Consequently, they make an easy target for rhetorical political assault. However, the reality of their numbers makes them an impractical target for *true* revenue increases. Let me illustrate.

The top two percent of all income earners in the nation are those earning over $200,000 annually. Given the fact that 114 million tax returns were filed in 1992, we are talking about just 2.28 million families earning that kind of money. The remaining 98 percent of all taxpayers represent 111.72 million families.

If you were in charge of tax policy, from which group do you suppose you could extract the most money? The reality is you have a far better chance of raising substantial sums from the latter group, the middle class, than you do from the "rich." Allow me to illustrate. By extracting just $1,000 per family from the middle class, you raise over $111 billion in revenue. On the other hand, by increasing the burden on the rich by as much as $10,000 per year (assuming you could get away with it), the revenue increase is just $22.8 billion. That is barely one-fifth what is realized by hitting the middle class in a "small" way.

Congress is keenly aware of this reality and so is the IRS. That is why Congress *talks* about raising taxes on the "rich" but *actually* raises taxes on the middle class. That is why the IRS *talks* about pointing its enforcement weapons at the "rich" but *actually* points them at the middle class. Those who can least afford to pay the price of increasing government costs and debt are those who end up paying the price. Ironically, the middle class accepts the idea only because they are *told* and *believe* the "rich" alone will pay more.

At work with the tax policy of envy, is the propensity of Congress to spend at a level far greater than the nation is capable of supporting. Since 1980, total federal debt has increased more than four-fold, growing from slightly under $1 trillion, to its present level of nearly $4.5 trillion. The ironic truth about the growth in debt is it did not occur at a time when tax receipts suffered.

No indeed! During the same period of time, federal tax collections from all sources more than doubled. Revenues rose from just under $500 billion in 1980, to $1.1 trillion in 1992. Thus, it is fair to say that the fiscal problems faced by the United States are caused largely by spending, not by tax collection. As we shall examine in the coming chapters, our tax policy over the past 20 or so years is also largely to blame for the economic problems we now suffer.

What is needed in this nation is not more debate about who is to blame or which income group we must penalize to "get even." What we need is the guts to own up to the problem, the foresight to develop a plan for a real, honest-to-God solution, and the courage to implement the plan.

We need a new tax system because the current system does not work. The current system is too cumbersome, too costly for both the government and the private sector, and subject of too much abuse at the hands of both the IRS and Congress. We need a system which is truly simple not one which boasts of simplicity while increasing the compliance burden for all.

We need a system which is fair for all citizens. A tax system which penalizes one group in order to subsidize another is not fair - period. We need a tax system which encourages savings, investment and productivity. Our current system penalizes these attributes and as any responsible economist will tell you, when these three attributes are encouraged, the economy flourishes. When they are penalized, the economy stagnates.

What we need is the *American Reconstruction Act*. The American Reconstruction Act is my proposal to eliminate the personal income tax system as we know it and replace it with a system which is inherently fair and balanced for all citizens. With the elimination of income taxes comes the elimination of the Internal Revenue Service. Under my system, tax audits, liens, levies and seizures of property, arbitrary penalty notices and the incredible cost of complying with our tax laws will be a thing of the past.

The need for liberty's sake to eliminate the Internal Revenue Service is written plainly in the faces of all citizens who have ever faced enforcement action. But recently, even more compelling testimony was offered suggesting the time is now ripe to rethink the way we collect taxes.

On August 4, 1993, the General Accounting Office released its findings on the first ever audit of the IRS. Standing alone, the fact the IRS has been audited just once in its 80-year history is amazing enough. The findings of the audit, however, are shocking - even to me. The findings prove conclusively and irrefutably that our present system of tax collection is too complex even for the IRS. GAO Report to Congress, *Examination of IRS' Fiscal Year 1992 Financial Statements*, June, 1993, GAO/IAMD-93-2.

Addressed in the audit is the IRS' outstanding accounts receivables - the tax gap. As you recall, the tax gap is the amount of money reported by the IRS to be owed and unpaid after the IRS collects all revenue. The tax gap is referred to often by the IRS in their requests for more money and manpower. It is claimed, without more money and manpower the tax gap may remain uncollected.

In testimony to Congress on the issue, U.S. Comptroller General Charles A. Bowsher explained the audit found all previous IRS reports to Congress on the tax gap to be unverifiable. In his findings he stated that only "reliable estimates" of actual accounts receivable were able to be provided to Congress. The estimates were "tens of billions of dollars less than what had been reported by the agency in the past" (Bowsher, *First Financial Audits of IRS and Customs Revealed Serious Problems*, August 4, 1993, page 2.)

Of course the question arises, why only estimates? Bowsher goes on to explain:

"We were unable to express an opinion on the reliability of IRS' fiscal year 1992 financial statements because critical supporting information for *billions of dollars* was either not available or was unreliable. *Preparation of financial statements presented a substantial challenge to IRS.*"

The GAO was also unable to "express an opinion" on the validity of IRS' financial statements because "critical supporting information for billions of dollars was either not available or was unreliable." Ibid, page 7.

I want you to ponder for a moment what you have just read. The Internal Revenue Service - the agency which holds you personally accountable for compliance with 17,000 pages of complicated tax law and regulation - itself cannot compose a financial statement of its activities which meets normally acceptable accounting standards. While the IRS is quick to crucify those who misplace a canceled check or lose a receipt, it cannot begin to provide records to support the propriety of its own financial declarations.

On the validity of IRS' accounts receivable declarations, Bowsher observed in his testimony:

"After performing a detailed analysis of IRS' receivables as of June 30, 1991, we estimate that only $65 billion of about $105 billion in gross reported receivables that we reviewed were valid and that only $19 billion of those valid receivables were collectible. At the time, IRS had reported that $66 billion of the $105 billion was collectible." Ibid, page 8.

The conclusion I reach is, IRS exaggerated its accounts receivables by 165 percent in order to induce Congress to hand it more power, equipment and money it would then use to chase middle-class Americans.

Even more troubling is the GAO's inability to examine the IRS' operating budget. Bowsher explained that "We were unable to audit approximately $4.3 billion, or 64 percent, of the reported spending of $6.7 billion from IRS' operating appropriations because IRS could not reconcile the total of detailed spending information. . .with summary amounts reported. . ." Ibid, page 14.

Stated very simply, the IRS cannot show where it is spending the money given it by Congress.

Of a more serious nature was the finding that IRS was simply cooking its books to make them balance. On this account, Bowsher explained:

> "We found, for instance, that the IRS had several billion dollars in unresolved cumulative gross differences between its records and Treasury's cash records at the end of the fiscal year. Also, as of September 30, 1992, IRS had not resolved $53 million in unmatched expenditures which were in a suspense account. To clear the account, *IRS arbitrarily charged* the $53 million to three appropriations (each appropriation was allocated one-third of the amount), causing IRS' report to show that it had exceeded the budget authority for one of its appropriations. However, *to eliminate the appearance* that it exceeded such authority for this appropriation, *IRS recorded an unsupported receivable* from another appropriation." Ibid, page 15 (emphasis add).

I want you to imagine with me for just a moment that you are the Chief Financial Officer of a large corporation - somebody like, oh, I don't know, say, *Leona Helmsley*. I want you to suppose that during the course of a tax audit, the IRS finds evidence that your records were falsified. Suppose they found you had "arbitrarily charged" certain personal expenses to your business account. Suppose further that in order to "eliminate the appearance" of such wrongdoing, you simply "recorded an unsupported receivable" in your books to offset the fabricated expense.

What do you suppose the IRS would do upon discovering these accounting glitches? As I am sure you know, at this very moment, Leona Helmsley is in jail for doing with about $3 million precisely what somebody in the IRS did with *$53 million!*

But it does not end there. Throughout the report we find examples of other overpayments and duplicate payments combined with a myriad of recordkeeping shortfalls. Literally billions of dollars have vanished over the years. In this report, we see clear, uncontrovertible evidence that the IRS has gone too far. Our system must be rebuilt and the agency must be eliminated in the process.

The *American Reconstruction Act* proposes to do just that. In addition, it provides the added important features of favoring savings and investment and encouraging production. The combination of these three factors is alone what leads to sustained growth and prosperity in a nation. I refer to these three factors as the three necessary elements to a sound economy.

Make no mistake about it. Government cannot create jobs. Government can only transfer jobs from one economic group to another. Government cannot create wealth. It can only transfer it from one economic group to another. Only the free market can create wealth and jobs. The free market can operate to its fullest potential only when government takes its hands off the economic controls.

If our nation is to survive as a free society, we must create an environment in which *people* can live freely. Government is only a reflection of its people. If our nation is to remain free, our people must be free. The *American Reconstruction Act* is the means of freeing society to save, invest and produce. Government cannot do these things, but it can create the circumstances which allow people to do them. Conversely, it can create circumstances in which the necessary elements to a sound economy are ignored. That is precisely what has happened during the past two or so decades. That is why we face economic stagnation today.

When we implement the three necessary elements mentioned, we will see a major reduction in the level of unemployment. We will see a major reduction in the tax burden imposed by government on all families. And, we will see a substantial increase in the flow of revenue to the federal government. Both our nation and our people will end the pattern of debt which has sapped our productive strength.

In the next several chapters I explain the reasons why America does not need an income tax to survive. In fact, you will learn that the income tax and the IRS themselves are responsible for much of the economic uncertainty in which we now live. You will read of my plan for a stronger future, one in which all Americans have a meaningful opportunity to build for tomorrow. Most importantly, you will read of my plan to implement this program on a national level.

I need your help. The decision you make on this matter will affect your children and grandchildren for decades to come. I ask you now to do something for your country. Help ensure the blessings of liberty to our posterity.

13 WHAT IS WRONG WITH THE INCOME TAX

No reasonable person will argue that we need some kind of tax system to support the legitimate functions of government. Only an anarchist would suggest no system of taxation is acceptable. I am not an anarchist. I believe in our Constitutional system of limited government. I recognize the need to support its rightful undertakings. That being the case, we must devise a system which is capable of obtaining the revenue the government needs, but which does not in the process, offend any rights guaranteed under the Constitution.

Any system of taxation must also be as close to neutral as possible in its effects on the economy. Every tax has a negative effect on the economy. When government takes a portion of your earnings and spends it in ways that you would not, certain distortions result. This is unavoidable. The challenge is to develop a system with the least amount of distortion possible. The challenge is to create a system which imposes the least burden on the citizens. This leaves citizens the greatest opportunity to invest, produce and save.

I submit to you, the income tax structure we currently labor under is the most invasive form of tax system possible. It is the most offensive to our Constitutional system of government. It is the most costly, both to business and government. It creates the broadest possible economic distortion, leading to the greatest amount of negative impact on savings, production and investment. The following is a careful discussion of these points.

PRACTICAL PROBLEMS CREATED BY THE INCOME TAX

The most significant practical consideration evidencing the need to trash our present system is its *complexity*. When the 16th Amendment took effect in 1913, the Bureau of Internal Revenue was born. The income tax was then administered with just 170 pages of law and regulations. Since that time, the tax code has grown to encompass over 17,000 pages of law and regulations. Literally 100's of thousands of pages of court decisions interpret the law. In addition, we are burdened with IRS revenue rulings, revenue procedures, opinion letters, information letters, technical advice memoranda, private letter rulings, Chief Counsel orders and notices, and General Counsel memoranda.

We are showered with thousands of pages of tax forms which change each time the tax laws change. For example, in 1986 the "simplification" process which led to the most sweeping tax law change in 30 years, created more than 200 new forms. The IRS produces thousands of pages of instructions to teach us about these forms, and hundreds of booklets to teach us about the instructions. The law is so confusing that two people of reasonable intelligence can read the same provision of the tax code and come away with differing conclusions as to its meaning. This spells trouble for the average citizen.

In the 1990 IRS Annual Report, then Commissioner Fred T. Goldberg reported the following:

> "* * *The past decade has witnessed substantial growth in both the size and complexity of our tax system. The Internal Revenue Code has been amended *more than 100 times since 1980*. Tax law changes have affected thousands of sections of the law requiring modifications to existing forms and instructions, development of nearly 100 new forms, annual reprogramming of computer systems and the need to constantly re-train our employees." 1990 Annual Report, page 7 (emphasis added).

These tax law changes cost America a fortune. Billions are spent annually by the private sector keeping up with the changes, trying to understand the new laws and the obligations they create, and attempting to comply with them. More and more people just throw up their hands in the process. This accounts for the rapidly growing number of citizens who turn to paid preparers for help. In 1985, 45.22 million citizens used paid preparers. In 1991, some 55.7 million used a professional. This is a 19 percent increase during a period when the tax laws were supposedly simplified.

The continuing changes in our tax laws account for the next significant problem with the system - *compliance*. Let's face facts, when the tax system consists of 17,000 pages of law and regulation, compliance is no easy matter. Most Americans make every reasonable effort to comply with the law. Often their efforts are defeated by one of two factors. Either they simply do not understand what the law requires, or they cannot afford to pay what they owe.

In her 1992 testimony to Congress on the administrative changes giving rise to tax amnesty, former IRS Commissioner Shirley Peterson explained the impact of the law's complexity upon the issue of compliance. She stated:

> "The Service's basic approach to tax administration has not changed in four decades. During that time, society, the economy, and the statutes we administer have undergone many changes. The law is now so complex that it affects taxpayers' ability to comply - and often affects their willingness to comply, as well. * * *

> "...a good part of what we call non-compliance with the tax laws is caused by taxpayers' lack of understanding of what is required in the first place. Once you acknowledge that reality, it makes good business sense to increase our efforts to help taxpayers comply rather than

relying solely on after-the-fact enforcement.* * *" Testimony to House Government Operations Committee, June 3, 1992, page 2.

On the question of those who simply cannot afford to pay, Mrs. Peterson stated:

"Many taxpayers fail to comply because they are unaware of the requirements of the law or because they cannot easily understand what they are supposed to do. To help these taxpayers, we must first ascertain why they did not comply. Then, we must modify our instructions and our systems and processes so that they can comply. Many taxpayers may want to comply, but cannot because they don't have the money to pay the tax due. When this happens, they often decide not to file a return. They may eventually drop out of the system altogether.* * *" Ibid, page 3.

At current estimates, there are about 17 million citizens who faithfully file their tax returns each year, but do not have the money to pay the tax. When delinquencies arise, the IRS swings into the enforcement mode, using its powers of lien, levy and seizure to collect the tax. Piling interest and penalties on the bill only adds insult to injury, often making it impossible to settle the account.

Many of the these citizens find themselves on what I have termed the tax debt treadmill. Even as they somehow find the money to pay off an old debt, they are faced with a new one. Year after year, the pressure of IRS pursuit and mounting interest and penalties take their toll. Many of these people do in fact "drop out of the system," as suggested by Commissioner Peterson. I have spoken with thousands over the years who were forced underground, not by a conscious decision to evade the IRS, but out of a need to just feed their family. The IRS now estimates as many as 10 million citizens have stopped filing altogether. In virtually every case, the *system* is to blame.

Yet the IRS and Congress continue to heap one additional requirement after another upon citizens, without regard to the burdens created. Even for those who can pay and do file, the burden is staggering. Added recordkeeping and information reporting requirements continue to grow at breakneck speed. Businesses never know from one moment to the next what new requirement will be laid upon them. This makes planning next to impossible and administrative costs outrageous.

There is no better example than in the area of employment taxes. The deposit rules on employment tax withholdings have been changed no less than four times in the past four years. Each change is designed to "simplify" the process but does nothing more than stir the pot. In Mrs. Peterson's June, 1992, testimony, she pointed out that the deposit rules have become so complicated that "one in every four" businesses was assessed a deposit penalty despite the fact that "some had fully paid the amount of tax due with their returns." Testimony of Commissioner Peterson, page 5.

In the 1992 Annual Report, the IRS itself recognizes that the payroll tax deposit system is "complex and burdensome, particularly for small businesses." 1992 Annual Report, page 9. Each year over 1.5 million businesses are penalized under a program nobody can figure out. The IRS solution to the problem? Change the rules yet again! In 1992, an entirely new payroll deposit mechanism was set up and installed. History will judge whether the new system is a lick better than any of its predecessors.

Mrs. Peterson brought to the commissionership a singular understanding of the burdens this system places upon the average citizen. Her tenure as Commissioner was marked by specific strides to lighten the load for citizens. The administrative changes she was responsible for are well-chronicled in *How to Get Tax Amnesty*. However, the IRS Commissioner does not write the tax laws. If she could, Mrs. Peterson would have gone much farther than she did. In an interview with *Forbes Magazine*, she explained what must be done to fix the system. "I would repeal the Internal Revenue Code and start over." *Forbes*, September, 1992, page 44.

Mrs. Peterson hit squarely upon the problem of attempting to improve the system we now have. In a word, it cannot be fixed. In fact, you should have noticed that *I have not* in this text referred to my proposals as "tax reform" proposals. The reason is "tax reform" implies that the foundation of the tax system is sound and can be built upon or improved. Such is not the case with our system.

You remodel a home when the foundation is sound. But when the foundation is crumbling, or sitting on poor soil, or constructed improperly in the first place, you cannot build upon it. You must bulldoze it and start over. That is precisely what must be done with our current system. The foundation is not sound. It is based upon an inherently flawed premise. That premise is the idea of taxing gain or profit as a means to raise revenue. When you *tax* gain or profit, you *inhibit* gain or profit. Do not lose sight of the single most basic economic reality. What you tax, you get less of. What you subsidize, you get more of. Under the current system, savings, investment and productivity, the three cornerstones of a sound economy, all suffer because they are taxed.

The third practical problem with the income tax law is the matter of the *cost* of compliance. The IRS brags that it is a most efficient and effective government agency. It claims that in 1992, the cost of collecting $100 in tax was just 59 cents. It arrives at that figure simply by dividing the agency's operating budget by the total tax collected.

With this kind of productivity, it is easy to see why Congress is so willing to fund the IRS' every whim. Congress, as we all know, is driven by the need to collect more money in the fastest, cheapest way possible. If the IRS is able to collect $100 with an investment of just 59 cents, why would Congress not give it everything it needs and more?

Before we go on, let's acknowledge the fact that the GAO has proven the IRS really doesn't know how much anything costs. If they do know, they can't prove it. If it is accurate this cost analysis still ignores a very important consideration. That is, what does it cost *society* to comply with the law. What is the cost to the American economy of dealing with the tax law, understanding the changes, keeping records, supplying information, filing returns, hiring professionals, handling audits, challenging penalties and computer notices, coping with collection, and just generally suffering under the agency's enforcement thumb? The IRS and Congress seem oblivious to these costs but they are real and quantifiable. They must be considered if we are to paint a true picture of the compliance burden.

Independent research economist Dr. James L. Payne did an exhaustive study of the cost to the public of complying with our tax laws. His findings are published in a book entitled, *Costly Returns - The Burdens of the U.S. Tax System* (1993, Institute for Contemporary Studies). Payne's study focused upon the quantifiable aspects of complying with the system. Specifically, he addressed:

- The enforcement costs of audits and appeals;
- The costs of tax litigation and enforced collection;
- The economic disincentive costs;
- The costs of tax evasion and avoidance; and
- The costs to government of administering the system.

Payne's conclusion is shocking. His findings establish that the total cost of compliance with our tax laws is 65 percent of the amount collected. For every dollar paid into the system, it costs the economy another 65 cents to pay it! In 1992, the IRS collected a total of $1.1 trillion from 204 million business, personal, estate and gift, and employment tax returns. The cost to America to file these returns amounted to *$720 billion!*

Payne's study was based upon 1985 conditions. I feel the cost of compliance is likely higher than 65 percent simply because of the changes that have occurred since 1985. Most notably, the *Tax Reform Act 1986* so confused millions of citizens that record numbers turned to tax professionals for preparation help. In 1985, some 45.22 million citizens used professionals to prepare their returns. By 1987, the first year in which the 1986 reforms took effect, the number had increased to 49.35 million. This alone has increased the cost of compliance.

The IRS itself admits the percentage of citizens who use paid preparers is a "good indication of the complexity of tax laws, tax reforms, and the instructions we give to the 'average' taxpayer. This performance indicator is a good measure of the amount of burden we place on the taxpayer." (IRS 1992 Financial Statement to Congress, page 17.) By this standard alone, tax compliance is becoming more costly with each passing year.

Do not believe that just "rich" people need or use tax professionals. IRS figures indicate the opposite is true. Of the returns filed with paid preparers, "slightly more than 80 percent" were for "taxpayers with less than $50,000 of Adjusted Gross Income." Ibid, page 17.

There is something drastically wrong with a law which cannot be complied with unless the average person hires a specialist to help him figure out what it means. Given the problems of complexity, compliance and cost to society of complying with the system we now have, it is clear that radical changes must be made, and soon.

LEGAL PROBLEMS CREATED BY THE INCOME TAX

The federal income tax is the most litigious area of law in our nation. Not only is the law changed many times each year, but thousands of court cases are generated as a result of disputes over what the law means. Each year, about 40,000 citizens end up in Tax Court contesting audit determinations. Each year, some 2,500 citizens are dragged through the criminal courts over alleged violations of the tax laws. The Justice Department handles thousands of cases each year involving refund suits, collection matters, 100 percent penalty cases, tax shelter litigation, tax protester litigation, summons enforcement proceedings, and other related matters. In 1992, over 970,000 individuals and businesses filed bankruptcy. You can be sure the lion's share of those bankruptcies was motivated, at least in part, by the IRS. Since 1986, the IRS' involvement in bankruptcy litigation has doubled.

All this proves that as laws becomes more complex and costly, the courts become more and more burdened with the task of policing the system. That certainly increases the cost of administering the system, but there is a more far-reaching problem associated with it. I have stated many times in the past the court takes an extremely paternal view of the IRS and taxes. One court refereed to taxes as "the life blood of government." As a consequence of this desperate view, courts are reluctant at best to curtail the IRS' growing powers. What suffers is the very premise upon which our system of government was built.

The Constitution of the United States represents the first time in the history of modern civilization a government was established with expressly limited powers. The Bill of Rights sets clear boundaries for government and established that the people are the ultimate proprietors of all power. Under a constitutional system of limited government, our nation became the richest, freest, most powerful nation in the world. Our legal system was the envy of the world because of the assurance that a citizen's basic rights could never be infringed.

Over time, however, the imposition of income tax laws and government's need to enforce them has attacked and eroded our unique system. Despite the fact that our court system is set up to operate independently of other branches of government, the reality is that all government employees, including federal judges, see the need for more money. The unfortunate outgrowth is our constitutional system of limited government has been the principle victim of growing IRS power and of a Congress with an insatiable need for more of your money.

The federal income tax laws have been challenged on numerous constitutional grounds over the years. With very few exceptions, all such challenges have failed. This is true despite the fact that in several ways, the federal income tax system is a direct affront to the legal protections it guarantees. One can go down the list of guaranteed rights and find a court decision growing from a tax dispute which undermines it in favor of tax collection. There is no need to provide a line-by-line empirical analysis to prove my point. All that is necessary are some of the more glaring examples.

Consider the case of *United States v. Doe*, 104 S.Ct. 1237 (1984). There, the court considered the question of whether a person could be forced by the IRS to produce his private books and records in the face of a 5th Amendment claim against self-incrimination. The state of law prior to *Doe* was quite settled. The well-travelled path was hacked out by the Supreme Court nearly 100 years prior to the *Doe* decision. In the 1886 decision of *Boyd v. United States*, 116 U.S. 616 (1886), also a tax case, the Supreme Court held that the Fifth Amendment created a "zone of privacy" protecting an individual and his personal records from compelled production. In short, the IRS could not force a person to produce his personal books and records any more than it could force him to give testimony against himself.

Literally hundreds of court decisions followed the *Boyd* logic to a point where, by the time *Doe* was presented to the Supreme Court, a legion of well-grounded case authority and the plain language of the constitution, weighed against the idea of forcing a person to produce his own books and records against his will. But *Doe* was a tax case. The IRS was fishing for information which "might reveal" whether any taxes were owed. That fact, it seems, called for more direct judicial action.

In *Doe*, the Supreme Court "sounded the death knell" for *Boyd*. It held that a person has no right to privacy with regard to his private papers. To quote Justice O'Connor in her concerning opinion, "The Fifth Amendment provides absolutely no protection for the contents of private papers of any kind." With the stroke of a judicial pen, your right of privacy, a right plainly in existence since the inception of our nation, was destroyed. As such, the law seems to permit any government agency to force you to reveal your private records for whatever reason it deems appropriate. Once surrendered, they apparently can be used against you in whatever way that agency deems appropriate.

The rationale used to arriving at this decision is even more offensive to reason than the decision itself. Justice Powell rendered the opinion of the court. In it, he observed that the Fifth Amendment protects a person only from "compelled incriminations," i.e., statement he is forced to make. However, he observed that since one is not *forced* to prepare private papers, the protections of the Fifth Amendment do not extend to those papers.

What the Justice's sophomoric logic overlooks is that it is the act of transmitting the documents to the government which is protected. One does not become a witness against himself by preparing documents. He becomes a witness against himself when his documents end up in government hands. Whether a person has or has not voluntarily prepared that information is not the issue. The question is whether or not he is forced to transmit data to government authorities against his will.

The Fifth Amendment states that no person shall be compelled to "be a witness against himself." That is to say, one cannot be forced to give any information about himself to any government agency. To say that forced transmittal of one's private papers does not violate the right because he voluntarily prepared those papers strains the limits of reason and common sense.

Another telling example is found in the decision of *United States v. Lee*, 102

S.Ct. 1051 (1982). In that decision, the court seems to have unceremoniously stamped out the last vestige of any claim we have to individual liberty. As hard as that is to believe, the Supreme Court nonetheless has declared that individual rights must yield to the state when "an overriding governmental interest" is present. In the *Lee* case, that interest was money.

Lee involved a member of the Old Order Amish. Lee was a self-employed farmer and carpenter employing several persons. Because the Amish are religiously opposed to the kind of benefits offered by social security, Lee did not withhold or pay either the employee's or employer's share of social security taxes. He was assessed several thousand dollars by the IRS and, after paying a portion of the tax, sued for a refund. After initial success, Lee found himself before the Supreme Court.

In its opinion, the court specifically found that because of the Amish faith, "compulsory participation in the social security system interferes with (Lee's) free exercise rights" under the First Amendment. But the court rationalized the direct infringement of those rights by claiming the government's "overriding interest" in collecting taxes permitted the violation. Going on, the court stated that "mandatory participation is indispensable to the fiscal vitality of the social security program." Citing the questionable financial soundness of the system, then Chief Justice Berger observed that "widespread individual voluntary coverage under social security...would undermine the soundness of the social security program."

In no uncertain terms, the Supreme Court said that because "we need the money," it is permissible to violate the constitutional rights of a citizen to get it. Thus, the only "overriding governmental interest" involved here is financial. To allow the Amish their absolute right to freedom of religion would threaten the program's image of fiscal soundness. Therefore, the court held that they cannot be allowed to practice their religious principles any longer.

It is important to note that Lee and his religious brethren demanded nothing from the system in the first place. They established a program which provided for the needs of their families as well or better than the government could.

In concluding, Berger reasoned that religious beliefs "can be accommodated, but there is a point at which accommodation would radically restrict the operating latitude of the legislature." According to the Supreme Court, the Congress must have free rein - absolute freedom - in passing laws. Religious and presumably other constitutional rights cannot be permitted to exist if they threaten the government's ability to create laws.

Have you read the Bill of Rights lately? Evidently the Supreme Court has not. Form beginning to end, the document places *express restrictions* upon the government's ability to pass laws. Without such restrictions, this government is no better than any other dictatorship which has ever existed.

The First Amendment states in part:
"Congress *shall make no law* respecting the establishment of religion, or prohibiting the free exercise thereof. . .(Emphasis added.)

These restrictions directly and simply forbid the invasion of individual rights by government eager to pass laws. Yet the Supreme Court held that all limitations are to be placed upon the *individual*, not upon *government*. The Supreme Court said that the government must have absolute authority to pass any law it deems appropriate so long as an "overriding governmental interest" is shown. When that interest is "we need the money," then the individual's rights simply can no longer be "accommodated."

In just these two cases we see strong evidence of a process of encroachment upon the liberties of the individual. Where our nation began as one in which the citizen was free of governmental intrusion into his private affairs, it has been transformed by judicial edict into just another police state with absolute authority vested in the hands of the government. This has all happened in the name of tax collection.

The courts have abandoned a strict reading of the plain language of the constitution in favor of judicial creativity designed specifically to achieve the pre-determined goal of getting into your pocket. Strict adherence to the letter of the document was insisted upon by Hamilton and Jefferson. Hamilton spoke loudly on the subject, saying:

"If we set out with justice, moderation, liberality, and a scrupulous regard to the Constitution, the government will acquire a spirit and tone productive of permanent blessings to the community. If, on the contrary, the public counsels are guided by humor, passion, and prejudice; or from resentment to individuals, or a dread of partial inconveniences, *the Constitution is slighted, or explained away, upon every frivolous pretext*, the future spirit of government will be feeble, distracted and arbitrary. The rights of the subjects will be the sport of every party vicissitude. There will be no settled rule of conduct, but everything will fluctuate with the alternate prevalency of contending factions." *The Basic Ideas of Alexander Hamilton* (Pocket Books, 1957) (Emphasis added.)

The message of Hamilton's remarks is simple. Continuity of the moral fabric of society is dependent upon legal absolutes, especially where citizens' rights are concerned. If the government is free to "explain away" the protections of the constitution, in the end there will be no constitution. If the rights of the citizens are made the "sport" of every governmental opinion change, in the end, citizens will have no rights.

Using the need for revenue as its compelling justification, the courts have caused our precious constitutional system of law and government to deteriorate. There is no system of taxation so important that we must sacrifice our precious liberty to save it. In fact, as I have stated, freedom and the income tax cannot exist side by side. One must necessarily drive out the other. We find substantial proof of that fact in the two case studies just examined.

At present, the courts are using the expedience of judicial fiat to extinguish our liberties. Do you feel so strongly about saving our income tax system as to be willing to sacrifice your constitutional rights to do it? I didn't think so.

ECONOMIC PROBLEMS WITH THE INCOME TAX

The three cornerstones of sustained economic growth are savings, investment and productivity. Savings provide the source of funds used by business to make investments. Businesses invest in things such as machinery, raw materials, facilities and labor to produce goods and services. If the national savings rate is low, it follows that the nation's rate of investment, and hence, productivity will also be low. When productivity is low, what follows is a corresponding decline in wages. Then the standard of living under such a scenario is reduced.

Bear in mind the basic economic premise I have repeated throughout this discourse. What you tax you get less of; what you subsidize you get more of. The current income tax system penalizes investment and savings. This leads to a reduction in productivity. That in turn causes a reduction in real wages.

Savings are penalized by taxing them as ordinary income. The higher the savings, the more tax liability one incurs on those savings. This was especially troublesome when our tax system was laden with a series of escalating tax brackets. Prior to Reagan taking office in 1981, there were 14 different tax brackets. Even a slight rise in one's income level often pushed him into a higher bracket. This phenomenon was known as "bracket creep." It had the direct impact of discouraging any increases in income.

With the *Tax Reform Act of 1986*, the number of tax brackets was to be reduced to just three. Plus, they were indexed for inflation. This largely eliminated the effect of bracket creep and false, inflationary increases in income. But under Clinton's tax plan, two more brackets have been added. The top bracket is back up to 39.6 percent. The trend under Clinton is to return to a law consisting of a wide variety of rates which operate to discourage increases in income.

According to Professor Lawrence Kotlikoff, professor of economics at Boston University and independent researcher for the National Bureau of Economic Research, our national savings rate is at a "crises level." During 1991, the net national savings rate was just 1.7 percent of net domestic product. He declares this to be "the lowest rate observed in the post-World War II period." Kotlikoff, Cato Institute Policy Analysis Report No. 193, April 15, 1993.

During each of the six years preceding 1991, U.S. savings was just 4 percent of net domestic product. Ffrom 1950 through 1970, U.S. savings averaged 9.1 percent. During 1970 through 1980, the average savings rate was 8.5 percent.

Investment is penalized in three ways. First and most important is through limited depreciation. Depreciation and depletion are the legal mechanisms under which investors recapture their capital investment. Our law does not tax the return of capital, but it greatly limits the investor's ability to recover his investment. Under the *Tax Reform Act of 1986*, depreciation schedules were greatly modified, extending recapture periods for years in some cases, decades in others. In addition, the Alternative Minimum Tax (AMT) was greatly strengthened. The AMT was specifically designed to *prevent* companies from eliminating their income tax liability through capital investment.

This has had the direct negative effect of discouraging capital investment.

Investment by its very nature is speculative. Profits are not assured. Therefore, venture capitalists require a quick recapture period in order to minimize their risk. When the tax law pushes the recapture period out several years, or even decades, this creates substantial disincentive to invest.

The lack of investment capital is especially hard on upstart businesses with no track record of profits. Existing businesses can somewhat offset the prolonged recapture period by paying current income on the profits generated by the investment. But what happens if there are no profits? The investor's ability to recapture his capital is greatly limited.

The Clinton tax plan makes an already difficult situation even worse. Under prior law, nonresidential real estate could be depreciated over 31.5 years. A company which invested in buildings was limited to recovering its capital investment over that lengthy period. However, under the new law, the recovery period is pushed to *39 years*. There is now even less incentive for business to invest in manufacturing or office facilities.

Let me illustrate how these recovery periods adversely affect the whole economy. According to the National Association of Home Builders (NAHB), construction starts of multi-family housing dropped from 669,000 units in 1985, to 372,000 units in 1989. Note that prior to 1986, real estate projects such as multi-family housing received favorable depreciation and capital gains tax treatment. Through the 1986 act, both these advantages were eliminated. The multi-family housing industry went south with the tax incentives. The NAHB expected a further decline to 350,000 units by the end of 1990. *Impact, Effectiveness and Fairness of the Tax Reform Act of 1986*, Hearings before House Committee on Ways and Means; March 5, 1990, page 579.

As rental property becomes more scarce, what is available naturally is more expensive. According to NAHB, the hardest hit segment of the housing industry was low- and moderate-income rental housing. The number of rental units available for less than $350 per month "declined by 75 percent from the first half of 1986 to the first half of 1989." Ibid, page 580. With nearly all incentives to invest in low- and moderate-income housing projects removed from the tax law, actual investments in such property virtually dried up. Those who suffer are the low- to moderate income families. They must either pay more than they can afford for housing, or they cannot find housing at all.

The second way investment is penalized is through the limited ability to deduct one's capital losses. A capital loss deduction is limited to just $3,000 per year. Thus, if an investor loses $100,000 in a failed business, he is limited to deducting that loss at the rate of $3,000 per year over a period of 34 years.

The third way investment is penalized is through capital gains taxes. Prior to 1986, the law allowed a substantial exclusion from income of long term capital gain. That exclusion was removed in 1986. At present, long term capital gains are taxed as ordinary income, but with a cap at the 28 percent level.

The fact that capital gains are now taxed as ordinary income has caused much investment capital to be reinvested elsewhere. In most cases, such capital found its way into tax exempt bonds. Investment in government bonds only exacerbates a negative situation. Capital invested in private industry leads to the production of goods and services. However, capital invested in government leads to the production of *nothing*. Government does not produce; it only consumes. In *Costly Returns*, Dr. Payne suggests that for every dollar raised through capital gains taxes, it costs the economy $1.23 in lost production because of the disincentive nature of the tax.

The combination of these factors has had a profound negative impact on capital investment. In 1992, our rate of domestic investment was just 2 percent of net national product. Between 1980 and 1990, the investment rate averaged 5.6 percent annually. However, during the 1950's, 1960's and 1970's, the investment rate averaged 8.2, 7.9 and 7.9 percent respectively. Kotlikoff, page 4.

With the dangerous decrease in national savings and investment, it is not surprising that we have seen a marked decrease in the growth of real wages. Kotlikoff's report confirms that the growth of total compensation to employees, consisting of wages and benefits, grew by less than "3 percent per year" each year since 1975. By contrast, compensation grew at the rate of "35 percent" each year for the 15 years preceding 1975. Kotlikoff, page 5.

When business cannot obtain the funds it needs to make investments in machinery, labor, facilities and raw materials, productivity suffers. When productivity goes down, real wages follow directly in its path. Add to that fact the reality that *all employers* are severely penalized for hiring workers and we can begin to understand the rising unemployment rates we now see.

With each worker comes a hefty burden, both in terms of paperwork and money. We addressed the compliance problems associated with employment tax withholding, reporting and payment. Do not forget, however, that for each dollar paid in wages, the employer bears a 7.65 percent burden for social security taxes. That is in addition to unemployment compensation taxes, which rates vary depending upon the state rate. Now mix in workers' compensation taxes, which can be substantial depending upon the nature of the job. In all, an employer's tax burden can approach 20 percent of gross wages paid.

The current employment tax hit is just the beginning. Clinton plans an additional employment tax of 7-10 percent to fund socialist health care, and another employment tax of 1.5 percent to "educate and train workers." *Putting People First*, Clinton and Gore, 1992, pages 110 and 70.

The impact on employment is substantial when measured against this yardstick. Under the present structure, employers with just five employees pay enough in taxes to compensate a sixth worker. If Clinton has his way, the employment tax burden could increase by 33 percent. With any increase in the employment tax burden, you will see a correlative increase in the *unemployment* rate *directly proportional* to the tax rate increase. Remember, what you tax, you get less of. When you tax employment, you simply end up with fewer employees. When capital investment is limited and the priority tax rate on workers is so high, the first thing businesses do is lay off workers.

Dr. Payne draws a succinct correlation between tax rates, available capital, the growth of business and ultimately, the creation of jobs. He writes the following:

> "The combined effect of the 'inflation tax' along with the capital gains
> tax discourages individuals from investing in new business opportunities.
> For example, when higher tax rates for capital gains were adopted in
> 1976, *the flow of capital to new ventures practically stopped.* Whereas
> in 1968 more than 300 new high-technology companies were founded,
> in 1976 *none were formed.* One calculation made by Chase Econometrics
> Associates showed that a capital gains tax rate of 49 percent would cost
> the economy 440,000 jobs, compared with the number of jobs that
> would be created under a capital gains tax of 25 percent." *Costly
> Returns*, page 92 (Emphasis added; footnotes omitted.)

In order to make a garden grow, one must have good soil, adequate water
and proper fertilizer. Reduce one of these elements and you negatively impact
the harvest. Eliminate one of these elements and you eliminate your crop. An
economy is no different. To make it grow you need savings, which is not unlike
soil. You need capital, which is the economy's water. And you need productivity
which acts as fertilizer. When these elements are taxed, you get less of them. This
is basic economic truth. With fewer available essential elements, the economy,
like the garden, produces fewer crops. To make the nation's economic garden
grow, we must free the essential elements from the burdens of the income tax.

Conclusion

Do you want more jobs and a stronger economy? Would you like to see
businesses flourishing once more? Would you welcome an opportunity to start
your own business and be successful at it? The answer is simple. Eliminate the
income tax.

If we did nothing but change the manner in which the nation's revenues are
collected, but did not reduce the tax burden by *one dime*, we would free $720
billion annually. This is just the cost of complying with the current tax law. It is
incurred over and above the rate of the tax itself. Ask yourself what the nation's
business community could do with $720 billion in new-found capital. That kind
of infusion of capital into the economy would cause a flurry of research,
development, expansion, production and of course, *hiring*.

If America were not burdened with the confusion, complexity and cost of
the current tax system, our nation's economy would get a shot in the arm such as
it has probably never seen. Reductions in the tax burden help us all. Make no
mistake about it. Increases in the burden hurt us all. This is economic reality. The
leaders in Washington have made every effort to disguise this truth but our
nation's entire economy is being hurt in the process.

Referring to the state of our current income tax system, Paul R. Huard, a
senior vice president with the National Association of Manufacturers, was
quoted in the September, 1992, *Forbes Magazine* article as saying, "You'll never
be able to dismantle what we have done to the system. You need to throw it in the
can and come up with something new."

The *American Reconstruction Act* is the viable alternative to what we now have.

14 How **NOT** to Fix the Problem

By now, we can agree on two points. First, we need a system of taxation which provides government the funding needed to support its legitimate functions. Secondly, the IRS and the present income tax system is the world's worst way to do it. We need a system which meets the criteria set forth in my opening remarks to Chapter 13. Before we examine what such a system must be, let us examine the various proposals for alternative tax systems that do not hit the mark.

THE FLAT RATE INCOME TAX

A flat rate income tax (flat tax) has been pushed around as an alternative for a number of years. Proponents claim a flat tax rate of anywhere between 10 to 20 percent would raise as much money as the current, complex system, but with far greater simplicity and less cost to individual citizens. On the question of simplicity alone, the flat tax idea has merits. It also has serious problems.

The tax reforms of the 1980's were designed to push us in the direction of a flat tax. Our income tax system was at one time laden with a myriad of tax rates going as high as 90 percent. The 1986 act reduced the number of brackets to just three, with the top bracket of 31 percent. At the same time, it began hacking away at the deductions one could claim again such income.

The recent history of tax law changes points up my principle concern with the idea of a flat tax. Years ago I explained we could not trust Congress to hold the line on tax rates. I envisioned the elimination of all deductions, followed by an increase in the rates. The result would be a substantial increase in the effective tax rates we all pay, especially the middle class. This group generally has only its Schedule A deductions to act as any kind of tax shelter. With these deductions eliminated, the amount they pay would rise radically.

The passage of 1990 budget compromise and the 1993 Clinton tax plan evidence that this is precisely what Congress intends. While the attack on remaining deductions continues, the rates have started up the other way. We now have five tax brackets, the top rate being 39.6 percent. At the same time, we have precious fewer deductions than ever before.

Most people do not recognize that a 15 percent flat income tax represents a substantial tax increase for the average family. Would you be surprised if I told you, that even today, we have a totally flat rate income tax system in operation in this country? The tax I speak of collects as much money as the income tax, but no deductions are taken, no returns are filed and no refunds issued. You guessed it, the social security tax collection system is the one I speak of.

The flat rate of tax charged to the wage earner under this system is 7.65 percent. The rate applies to all wages beginning with the first dollar, up to and including income of $57,600 (for 1993). Under this flat tax system, wage earners pay as much or more in taxes, *at half the rate*, as they do in income taxes. On the average salary of $26,000 per year, total social security tax of $1,989 is withheld directly from the paycheck.

Let me illustrate the income tax liability of that same person, under 1993 rules. If that person is married with two children, he is entitled to four dependent exemptions worth a total of $9,400 (2,350 x 4). We will assume he is entitled to just a standard deduction, not itemized deductions. The standard deduction for married persons filing jointly is $6,200.

Thus, on gross income of $26,000, that person would have taxable income of $10,400 (26,000 - 6,200 - 9,400 = 10,400). The tax rate of 15 percent applies to all income up to $36,900 for joint filers. Therefore, the *income tax liability* under this scenario is $1,560 (10,400 x .15). If that same person incurred itemized deductions in excess of the standard deduction amount ($6,200), his income tax would be even less.

We clearly see that the *flat social security tax* at a rate one-half that of the lowest *income tax* rate costs the average person more money than does the income tax. We clearly see that a flat income tax of, say 15 percent, is actually a substantial tax increase for the average person. In fact, under the above assumed facts, our family's income tax liability under a 15 percent flat rate system would be $3,900 (26,000 x. 15). That represents an income tax hike of *250 percent!*

To be revenue neutral for the average person, a flat income tax rate would have to be just six percent. That is far below the rates proposed. The conclusion is that a flat rate income tax provides no financial relief to citizens.

Furthermore, as history has proven with both the social security tax rates and income tax rates since 1986, Congress will not leave them alone. Without a comprehensive financial plan such as proposed in this book, a flat tax might well begin at an acceptable rate, but will surely rise as Congress sees a greater and greater need for more of your money.

Proof of this has been provided as we witness each year the uncontrollable rise in Social Security tax witholding. If we as taxpayers were to surrender all control over our tax liability, as is proposed in the plan to install a flat tax, it would be like putting the fox in charge of the henhouse.

The larger concern with the flat tax system, however, is the remaining IRS presence. True, a flat tax greatly simplifies our tax collection system. But it does not eliminate the IRS. It does not eliminate the potential for tax audits, penalties and arbitrary determinations. Worst of all, it does not eliminate the potential for IRS liens, levies and seizures. All these enforcement practices cost America a fortune. To adequately restore our economy and Constitutional guarantees, they must be eliminated, not just reduced in scope.

You may ask, how can the IRS audit an income tax return if we operated on a flat tax with no deductions? What is there to audit? Keep in mind the lessons of Chapters One and Two of this book. The question of deductions is just *half* the equation when tax audits are performed. The other half is the question of income. The IRS may have no cause to audit deductions under a flat tax system, but they would certainly have a claim to audit income.

A major aspect of the IRS examination program already focuses upon unreported income. It uses the DIF program, 1099's, W-2's and other computer matching schemes to discover unreported income. Each year, it mails millions of notices to citizens claiming they either did not file a return or underreported the income on a return they did file. Each year, exactly half those notices are dead wrong.

As a consequence, millions of citizens are forced to deal with computer notices, challenge penalty assessments, contest audit decisions, appeal examination findings and go to Tax Court to prove their innocence. Those who are unable or unaware of how to pursue their rights are stuck with a bill they likely do not owe. Further penalties and interest are added and enforced collection processes begin.

Let me illustrate how serious a problem this can be. In 1992, Americans filed some 43.43 million 1040A - Short Forms. These forms claimed gross income from all sources of under $25,000 and *no itemized deductions*. The only adjustment to income one may claim on 1040A is certain IRA contributions. As a result, the form is very simple.

Nevertheless, the IRS found a way to audit 300,480 of these returns. As a percentage of the total, there were *more audits* of short forms with under $25,000 gross income than of regular 1040's with the same income! 1992 Highlights, page 34, Table 11. Of those audited, just 12.5 percent were given a clean bill of health. Those found to owe additional taxes were assessed, on the average, a total of $2,599. This was in addition to the tax paid at the time of filing the return.

We see clearly the risk of continued audits, assessments and enforced collection remains very real, even under a flat tax system. The incredible burdens of time, expense, hassle, lost productivity, and emotional and physical drain are not eliminated with any flat tax proposal I have yet seen.

Another important factor is a flat rate income tax is still an *income tax*. It presents the same general economic burdens of the current income tax system. Income taxes, regardless of how assessed, discourage savings and investment. We know this is bad for the entire economy, but it hits the poor and middle class the hardest.

Flat Tax System? Two Thumbs Down.

THE VALUE ADDED TAX

The Value Added Tax (VAT) is a tax on consumption, as opposed to income. Income is defined by economists as savings increases plus consumption. Thus, a consumption tax does not reach savings or investment. Whereas an income tax discourages savings and investment, a consumption tax encourages savings and investment. Kotlikoff describes the essential difference between an income tax and a consumption tax in this fashion:

> ". . .a consumption tax provides more incentive to save (invest) than does an income tax. . .Economists view savings, not as an end in itself, but as a means of financing future consumption. By taxing consumption and saving, an income tax effectively taxes future consumption twice, once when households save funds for future consumption and again when they engage in that consumption. Since current consumption is taxed only once, an income tax provides an incentive, at any point in time, to consume more now and save less for the future." Kotlikoff, Cato Institute Policy Analysis Report No. 193, pages 6-7.

This element of the VAT makes it far more desirable than the current income tax system. The benefits to the economy of increasing the rates of saving and investment will reach everybody.

Operationally, a VAT is a tax on the increase in value added to a product or service as it moves through each stage of production. Hence the appellation, "Value Added Tax." To illustrate how a 10 percent VAT operates, CCH provides an example using the production and sale of a book.

> "Stage One-Lumber. Say that the chain of production begins with the harvesting of lumber, which, for one book, costs one dollar. The tax on the lumber would be 10 cents, which is collected when it is sold to a paper mill for $1.10.

> "Stage Two-Paper Processing costs and profit require the paper mill to charge one dollar over its materials cost. This dollar is the value added by the mill and is subject to a 10-cent tax. No tax is charged on the lumber since that has already been taxed. When the paper is sold, the price is $2.20, two dollars for the value of the paper plus 20 cents - 10 cents collected at each of the first two stages.

> "Stage Three-Publication. This is where the greatest value is added to the book. Royalties to the author, editing, and printing plus publisher profit added five dollars to its cost. This means 50 cents must be collected from the book seller, which brings the total wholesale cost of the book to $7.70.

> "Stage Four-Book Seller. Retail sales adds an additional three dollars of value to the book and an additional 30 cents of tax. The end consumer, therefore, pays $11 for the book - $10 going to the various businesses in the chain of production and one dollar going to the government as value added tax." *Is There a VAT in Your Future?*, CCH 1993, page 5.

My chief rap against the VAT is its potential for complexity. Just for starters, the VAT accomplishes in four steps what a simple retail sales tax would do in just one. Now mix in the probability that social engineers may wish to build a progressivity feature into the tax to "tax the rich." A VAT is made progressive with a series of exemptions on certain products or services. Examples might be food or housing. With exemptions factored into the equation, the question of interpretations arises. The net effect could well be a system not much different than what we presently have.

True, under a VAT, individual income tax returns will be a thing of the past. That of course is a major, positive attribute. However, business will continue to carry a heavy compliance burden, considering the paperwork and calculations necessary to determine value added at each stage of production. Do not forget that tax return filing requirements and information reporting cost business a fortune each year. That burden will not be reduced under the VAT.

Of course, the IRS will not be eliminated. It will take on the role of policing business more closely to ensure compliance with the law. This means the potential for audit, assessment, penalties, and enforced collection exists. We are also left with the potential for IRS errors and abuse.

A chief consideration in the architecture of a tax system is simplicity. When this element is lost, the remaining positive aspects lose their attractiveness. Another chief consideration is the efficiency of the system. In this regard, I examine whether the system proposed is the least invasive method of raising revenue. In both these important categories, the VAT fails in my opinion.

Consider this. Since the example provided by CCH of how a VAT works, coincidently involved the manufacture and sale of a book, I shared the example with my publisher, Dave Engstrom. He observed:

> "No worse example could be provided to support the workings of a VAT than that of book production. Beginning with the purchase of raw lumber, the complexity of such a system hits us squarely between the eyes. While a papermill may buy a train load of hemlock trees, all of the same origin and type, those trees may be turned into hundreds of different types and weights of paper, all with a unique purpose and use and subsequently different values. The imposition of a VAT in this scenario would create the need for hundreds of different information returns to be filed, one for each type and quality of paper produced."

Our discussion led us further down this new winding trail of not-so-free enterprise. A VAT assumes products of all types, trains, planes automobiles and books, follow the same path through the marketplace from raw materials provider to end user. Along the path we'll find a raw materials provider (lumberjack), fabricator (paper mill), manufacturer (printer), and then through chains of distribution. In the case of a book, that begins with publisher then wholesale distributor on to retailer and finally the reader.

In all, seven steps through the marketplace could be taken. However, distribution of products is not so scientific as to rely on seven stages of production and distribtuion. In the case of a book, for example, the stages could be cut to four.

First, the publisher, who is in charge of all marketing including advertising and establshment of distribution but generally does not print the book, could print the book. On the other hand, the printer of this book, will print books for many publishers of which a few also have printing abilities but may currently be operating beyond their own capacity.

This slight twist in the free-market path traveled by books on their way to readers, now requires eight variations of VAT assessment to accomodate the singular roles of printer and publisher and the dual role each may play as well.

As you enter the distribution stages anything can happen cause anything goes. At any point in our example, from publisher on through to reader, each entity may play all remaining roles. For example publisher may sell directly to the reader, thus eliminating wholesaler and retailer participation in the distribution process.

On through the process the wholesaler could sell direct to the reader or the retailer could buy direct from publisher. At all stages, there will be several different pricing levels depending largely on the size of each order and total volume purchased.

If that isn't confusing enough, royalites to authors could be paid in accordance with a thousand different formulas to determine the amount. Royalties could be based on a flat fee (like the one paid to General Schwarzkopf), gross wholesale and retail sales, net sales to each based on untold variations of profit determination, per copy sold regardless of to whom and on and on. All this leads to the placement of a government expert in your business, within your business, to help you determine how your business can be run and taxed.

In addition numerous opportunites arise to limit the tax collected hence paid. Within our example, the advantages of a publisher to sell exclusively to the reader at a lower price than the retailer could, are greatly amplified. Currently, fair trade laws are designed to prevent each level of distributor from taking unfair advantage of their position in the distribution chain.

For example, wholesalers are restricted from selling the same product at the same price to both retailer and end user regardless of quantity. The imposition of a VAT would provide every manufacturer great incentive to shift his role of selling through the chain of distribution to that of selling direct to the end user. In so doing the end user could be charged less than the retailer or wholesaler would charge and be doubly rewarded by paying less tax as well.

In return the manufacturer would get paid more because he has eliminated the middleman and reduced the cut of the only remaining middle-man, government. What that means is VAT rates must increase to cover the revenue loss. Which, by the way, is exactly what is happening within every country that presently has a VAT.

Value Added Tax System? VAT chance! Two Thumbs Down.

BUSINESS OR PAYROLL TAXES

Given the bad light into which businesses, especially corporations, have been thrust as of late, increased business taxes are a high priority for social planners. Business is seen as a bottomless source of revenue obtained through evil means in the first place. Profit is scorned and business is looked upon as unfairly exploiting the wage earner. (Doesn't that sound like a Karl Marx speech?)

These sentiments make business taxes, generally assessed in the form of payroll taxes, quite politically attractive. A payroll tax is assessed on the gross amount of wages paid. As I point out in Chapter 13, payroll tax assessments at present approach 20 percent of a company's gross payroll. Payroll taxes fund social security, medicare, medicaid and unemployment compensation. These four aspects of federal spending constitute the largest element of the federal budget by a long shot. Defense spending, commonly looked upon by the political left as the principle beneficiary of federal funds, is second by a country mile. In addition to existing payroll taxes, Clinton proposes two new assessments. One to fund the socialist health care plan, the other to retrain workers.

My opposition to higher business taxes in general, and payroll taxes in particular, is based upon economic considerations. Remember, what you tax you get less of. Tax employment - end up with fewer employees. The formula is simple and quantifiable. If, as Clinton wishes, employment tax assessments are increased by as much as 33 percent, we will see unemployment rise by a corresponding rate. No magic, just simple mathematics based upon elementary economic principles.

Washington ignores another elementary economic principle because to do so is politically advantageous. The principle is this, corporations *do not pay taxes*. Regardless of the financial burden placed upon it, the corporation itself does not carry the load. It is passed in one or more of three directions, those being the economic elements of corporate existence. They pay the load.

All corporations exist based upon three elements. First, they have owners, known legally as shareholders. Second, they have employees, those who handle day-to-day business functions. Third, they have customers, those who purchase the goods or services offered by the company. Economically speaking, corporations are not nameless, faceless, legal fictions which exist purely to exploit workers and consumers. Corporations are a consortium of people falling into one of those three categories.

When corporate taxes are raised, the tax must necessarily be paid at the expense of one or more of three corporate economic elements. If the tax is paid through higher prices, the customer suffers by having to pay more for the same product or service. If the tax is paid by reducing payroll, employees suffer by experiencing either a reduction in salary or loss of jobs. If the tax is paid by reducing corporate profits, the owners suffer through reduced dividends.

Dividends, of course, represent return on investment for the owners. When return on investment is reduced arbitrarily through tax increases, the incentive to invest is also reduced. We know from the last chapter what happens to the economy in general with reduced investment incentive.

The current Washington opinion machine would have you believe that fat-cat rich people own all the corporations anyway, so why not tax them more? The reality of the situation is quite different. Remember the owners of a corporation are its shareholders. Investment in corporate shares, known as equities, is the number one way common working people invest their savings to build a retirement nest egg. This is done primarily through vehicles known as mutual funds. A mutual fund pools the resources of several thousand investors, then hires a professional money manager to investment it and make it grow. Profits in the form of dividends, interest and capital gains are then paid to the investors on a pro rata basis.

Since the early 1980's when mutual fund investing became popular, there has been an explosion in the growth of these funds. At present, there are over 2,500 different mutual funds managed by hundreds of different companies. They invest domestically and internationally, all seeking the best return possible.

Also beginning in the early 1980's, there was an explosion of revenue flowing into mutual funds. The reason is the popularity of the Individual Retirement Arrangement (IRA). The tax favored IRA allows a person to invest now and take a current deduction for the money invested. He is allowed to build the value of the investment tax free during his lifetime. He pays taxes on IRA distributions only when he begins drawing them at age 59.5 or thereafter.

Virtually every retirement plan in America is invested in a mutual fund of some kind. If any portion of your retirement plan, however small, is invested in a mutual fund, you are the likely owner of *no less than* 25 different corporations. Some small, some large, all in business to make a profit and pay a return to *you* on your investment. The return makes your savings grow, ensuring your comfort and security upon retirement. If you would like to tax the pants off corporations, the reality is you do so at the peril of middle income Americans struggling to sock away retirement money.

Another consideration is the fact that like rich people, there simply are not enough corporations with big bucks to make a difference. For example, if you simply confiscated the wealth (not annual profit, *all the assets*) of the nation's Fortune 500 corporations, you would not acquire enough revenue to pay the deficit for *just one year*.

Think about that. Annual federal budget deficits, before imposing Clinton's spending package, amount to about $300 billion, or 5 percent of Gross Domestic Product (GDP). The total federal debt is now in excess of $4.5 trillion. *Stealing* all the assets of all the biggest corporations would *not* pay one-tenth of the national debt. It would, however, cause economic turmoil and panic. Raising taxes on corporations does the same thing, only on a smaller scale.

Increase Payroll Taxes? Two Thumbs Down.

Estate, Gift and Inheritance Taxes

Taxing estates is specifically designed to redistribute wealth. The Clinton tax package increased the estate and gift rates substantially. Under the Clinton measure, two additional estate tax brackets were added. The top rate is now 55 percent of the net estate, up from 50 percent. The second new rate is a 53 percent bracket. The top rate applies to estates in excess of $3 million. Add to this the fact that Congress regularly moves to reduce the estate tax exemption. The last move came in 1992, but failed. It would have reduced the exemption from $600,000 to just $200,000.

Some time ago, the *St. Paul Pioneer Press*, my local newspaper, carried an editorial which observed that within the next decade, some $8 trillion will become available to pass on to the next generation. The editorial declared, "Not only is the potential for inheritance unprecedented; the ability to *transfer this wealth* without giving a dime to the greater community is also unprecedented." (Emphasis added.)

The author proclaimed the transfer of assets from one generation to the next to be a "virtually untaxed transfer of wealth." He deplored the notion that one should be allowed to transmit any of his assets, earned during his productive years, to his children or grandchildren, at a time when "hard-working Americans see their standard of living decline."

President Clinton began a new attack on the accumulated wealth of older Americans. This is a politically attractive way to raise revenue because estates, like corporations, are thought of as nameless, faceless, bottomless money pits. Politicians do not see estates for what they are - the tangible results of honest effort put forth by a decedent during his productive years.

What social planners fail to understand is the "untaxed wealth" to which they so contemptuously refer is not untaxed at all. While working his *entire life*, a decedent paid *income taxes* his entire life. Citizens with acquired wealth generally did not cheat the government to obtain it. Those who manage to preserve a few dollars until the time they die, pass assets to their family which remain *only after* all other tax burdens have been met.

Do not forget that one pays income and social security taxes on wages and business profits *as earned*. To the extent that anything is left upon which to build a nest egg, interest and dividends are taxed *as earned*. Should one decide to sell accumulated assets to reap the benefit of appreciation, capital gains are taxed *as realized*. In short, the profits earned by a given citizen are taxed at every turn.

The estate and gift tax concept is not satisfied with this. Under the concept, you should not be allowed to pass the remainder of your assets, that which is left after all previous taxes are paid, to the next generation. The estate and gift tax concept goes one step further in the process of harvesting wealth. Rather than merely taxing the fruit of the tree, its goal is to dig up the tree itself and move it to the property of some less fortunate citizen whose own tree died.

Let us put into perspective the financial impact of such a tax. The newspaper editorial suggests that by imposing a 50 percent inheritance tax on *all estates*, the sum of $100 billion could be generated within just "10 years." In 1992, the IRS collected $1.1 billion in estate and gift tax proceeds. Thus, the plan would increase annual federal estate and gift tax collections by *1100 percent!* Quite an impressive hike. This certainly seems to be an aggressive move toward balancing the budget and imposing financial social order. We shall see.

On October 29, 1992, the government announced that the fiscal 1992 federal budget deficit was $290 billion. This, please understand, was the operating deficit for just *one year*. The combined federal debt is now in excess of $4.5 trillion. By increasing estate tax assessments by *1100 percent*, we can hope to collect in *10 years* roughly *one-third* of what Congress overspends in *one year*.

The estate tax is a woefully insufficient way of raising money. There is simply not enough value in the average estate, nor are there sufficient numbers to make any difference. In short, there is no tax base from which to draw revenue. In 1992, just 235,000 estate and gift tax returns were filed.

The estate tax does not raise revenue, but it does reduce the standard of living of the next generation. That happens by depriving the nation's children and grandchildren of their rightful inheritance. This tax, more than any other, constitutes outright theft. It attacks the tree, not just the fruit of the tree.

Estate, Gift and Inheritance Taxes? Two Thumbs Down.

CONCLUSION

Our alternative tax system must be simple, fair and efficient. It must also respect the Constitutional rights of the individual and not impose the crippling effects of taxation as means to usher in somebody's notion of social equity. The Constitutional premise of taxation is to raise revenue to support the legitimate functions of government - period. There is no Constitutional mandate to redistribute wealth, favor one social group over another, or subsidize one business at the expense of another. Our tax system must therefore be balanced.

If it is to be fair, balanced, simple, efficient and Constitutional, it must necessarily eliminate the IRS. Embodied within the Internal Revenue Service we find the potential for the disruption of all the essential criteria I list. The Internal Revenue Service is often arbitrary, capricious, and acts without foundation. It imposes a police-state like presence upon all Americans which cannot be tolerated in a free society. Under our proposed alternative tax system, the IRS must go.

15 THE SOLUTION TO AMERICA'S TAX PROBLEM

In a free market economic system operating under a limited government, the only legitimate function of a tax structure is to raise revenue. But our present tax system has been transformed into much more than a source of revenue. It is now widely utilized as a means to achieve somebody's notion of social justice and other goals unrelated to the business of finance.

Let me illustrate with very poignant examples. They come to us courtesy of the Clinton Administration. In Clinton's first State of the Union Address in February of 1993, he explains how his proposed Btu tax would raise revenue to "balance the budget." However, *A Vision of Change for America*, the Administration's written explanation, tells a much different story.

According to it, the proposed tax had very little to do with raising revenue. The overriding concern in proposing the tax was to *make energy more expensive*. Despite Clinton's flowery assurances to the contrary, the tax was designed to lower the standard of living of all Americans, since that is the ultimate result of any tax increase. Please consider carefully this explanation from Clinton's own lips, found at page 105 of *A Vision of Change for America*:

"* * *The tax is *designed to promote* energy conservation and to reduce harm to the environment...The higher rate on oil is intended to *promote* energy security and the use of cleaner burning fuels.* * *

"Energy taxes will encourage conservation *by making energy more expensive*, reducing pollution, and decreasing the country's dependence on foreign energy suppliers.* * *" Ibid, page 105 (Emphasis added.)

As you see, the tax is a social measure, not a financial one. Clinton intended to use the taxing power of the United States to affect his own social agenda. In the process, he intended to reduce your standard of living. Hardest hit would have been those Americans on the lowest rungs of the economic ladder.

Not only would this have been the direct result of his energy social agenda, but he knows it. He knows more Americans would have been impoverished by the move. He knows the life-styles of all would have been adversely effected. Consider this statement, again from page 105 of *A Vision*:

"Without some form of adjustment or offset, the broad-based energy tax would impose a *particularly heavy burden* on low-income households. To avoid such an outcome, the energy tax is accompanied by proposed *increases in transfers* [read, "welfare." Author.] under the Low-Income Home Energy Assistance (LIHEAP) and Food Stamp Programs. Since many low-income households are outside the labor force and the tax system, these programs are needed to alleviate the burden of the energy tax." (Emphasis added.)

Clinton called for "radical welfare reform" in his speech. He said we must break the cycle of welfare to end it as a way of life for so many families. However, his tax plan would have had precisely the opposite effect. By hitting the lower income segments the hardest, he drives them deeper into the jaws of poverty. Rather than offer a way out, he would heighten their dependence by broadening the scope of the food stamp and home energy assistance programs.

Clinton's tax program is designed to accomplish precisely what every socialist dreams of. First, it destroys the ability of the middle class to earn an adequate living on its own. Next, it provides "assistance" programs to "replace" what was taken by the government. By slowly increasing its grip on the nation's finances through steadily rising taxes, more and more people are made dependent upon the government for their very existence. I described the government's social policies as follows: They tax the pants off you to pay for social programs designed to provide the goods and services you cannot afford because your taxes are too high!

You of course know the Btu tax did not pass. However, a substantial hike in the gasoline tax of 4.3 cents per gallon passed in its place. The purpose of the gasoline tax increase is no different. Consider this language from the Senate Finance Committee's report on the tax bill. At page 379, the committee states the following:

"The committee also believes that a transportation fuels tax should further other important objectives. The committee understands that in 1992, approximately two-thirds of domestic consumption of petroleum was for transportation uses. By providing an incentive to reduce motor fuel consumption, this tax should tend to improve environmental problems that result from the transport, storage and burning of petroleum products to power motor vehicles, vessels, and aircraft. In addition, reduced consumption of petroleum products should decrease U.S. reliance on imported oil." Senate Finance Committee, *Reconciliation Submissions of the Instructed Committees Pursuant to the Concurrent Resolution on the Budget*, June 23, 1993, page 379.

There you have it. There are few economic considerations involved here, *other than* to make motor fuels *more expensive*. By their own words we know that they know, increasing taxes on energy will reduce consumption. Consequently when consumption is reduced, there is no real increase in tax collected. In fact tax collections could decrease, vitiating the intended effect of raising the tax. All that is left in the balance, then, is social change.

This tax, like the Btu tax, is nothing more than a social program designed to reduce your standard of living because the present administration harbors a social objection to fossil fuels.

Whether you personally agree or disagree with these environmental goals *is not the issue*. The issue is whether the United States Government has the legitimate right to use its taxing power for a means other than that intended. Our Forefathers handed Congress the power to raise taxes to fund the legitimate functions of the government as outlined in the Constitution itself. I challenge any Constitutional scholar to demonstrate that the taxing authority of Congress may be lawfully used to artificially reduce one's standard of living solely to impose social change.

Congress' legitimate power to tax derives from Article 1, section 8 of the Constitution. The power to tax, like all power delegated to the federal government under the Constitution, is limited. The section reads, in relevant part, as follows:

"The Congress shall have Power To lay and collect Taxes, Duties, Imposts and Excises, to pay the Debts and provide for the common Defense and general Welfare of the United States;..." U.S. Constitution, Article 1, Section 8, clause 1.

The taxing power, as you see, is limited to just three purposes. Paying the debts of the nation, providing a national defense, and ensuring the general welfare (read, "soundness") of the United States. As you can plainly see, there exists no power to employ the taxing authority for social purposes.

The Founding Fathers never intended such a power to exist for one simple, very logical reason. The social goals of the nation are subject to change with each change of power in Washington. Each group has its own idea of "what should be." Each individual election *at every level* represents, at least ideologically, a shift in that power. If each group were allowed to use your standard of living as the means of affecting its social agenda, you are deprived of the most basic rights guaranteed by the Constitution. You are deprived of your property and the pursuit of happiness so that others may impose their notions of social utopia upon you without your consent.

It makes no difference that you may happen to agree with those ideals. In a society with free elections, it is inevitable that sooner or later, some group will come to power proposing ideals with which you do not agree. Is it your contention that the economy *may* be falsely manipulated provided you support the social agenda, but may not be so manipulated if you *do not* support it? You cannot have it both ways! You either support a free economy, in which case no social agenda may be furthered at the economic expense of others, or, *you are a socialist*.

The idea of using the power of taxation to accomplish purely social goals was espoused by Karl Marx himself. The Marx philosophy of socialism was designed to create an all-powerful state and to eliminate individual property rights. As we know from experience in Eastern Europe and the former Soviet Union, socialism does not work. With all incentive to produce removed from their economies, Soviet nations and their satellites simply stagnated. All citizens but the ruling class were reduced to abject poverty with no hope of bettering their conditions.

In Marx's *Manifesto*, he described the process of achieving the destruction of individual property rights. He writes:

> "The proletariat [defined by Marx as the "wage-labor working class." Author.] will use its political supremacy to wrest, by degrees, all capital from the bourgeois [defined as "middle-class property owners." Author.]; to centralize all instruments of production in the hands of the State, i.e., of the proletariat organized as the ruling class; and to increase the total of productive forces as rapidly as possible. Of course, in the beginning this cannot be affected except by means of *despotic inroads on the rights of property, and on the conditions of bourgeois production. . ."
> *The Communist Manifesto*, Karl Marx, 1848, (Emphasis added).

To achieve the transfer of wealth he envisioned, Marx developed a 10-point plan to impose in "advanced countries" through the process of legislation. Points two and three read as follows:

"2. A heavy progressive or graduated income tax.
"3. Abolition of all right of inheritance."

Without question, the concept of transferring wealth to impose a social agenda is an idea repugnant to the Constitution and our system of limited government. To solve America's fiscal problems, we must therefore abandon this practice in favor of a politically and socially *neutral* system of taxation. To satisfy the financial needs of the nation and remain true to our heritage, our tax system must be broad based. It must not favor particular industries, factions or individuals at the expense of others. It must not fall more or less heavily upon one faction or industry solely because of the social standing of that faction or industry.

You may be inclined to suggest, as many have in the past, that the "general welfare" clause of Article 1, section 8, seems to impart broad authority on Congress to enact funding measures which it alone deems appropriate. Indeed, does not the use of the phrase "general welfare" itself grant license to utilize taxing powers to achieve social goals? After all, is not "welfare" the quintessential social undertaking? This certainly has been the contemporary interpretation of the phrase. However, to ascertain its true meaning, we must visit the opinions of those who wrote it.

The *Federalist Papers* provide great insight to the thinking of the time. They are a series of essays by Alexander Hamilton, James Madison and John Jay. The articles were written in response to opposition to the Constitution offered from various quarters. The essays responded specifically to challenges and claims arguing against its adoption. Hamilton and Madison addressed specifically the taxing power under the Constitution and the "general welfare" clause of Article 1, section 8.

Madison expressed the conservative view. He reasoned that since the specific powers of the federal legislature were limited to but six narrow areas, the taxing power of Article 1, section 8 could be no broader. Congress has the power to raise an army and provide a common defense. It is empowered to maintain domestic tranquility and facilitate intercourse among the several states and with foreign governments. Certain utilitarian functions are imparted to the national legislature, such as the maintenance of post offices and post roads. Madison affirmed that the federal government enjoyed no power which was not expressly delegated under the Constitution.

During the public debate, some claimed that Article 1, section 8 would impart unlimited taxing powers to the federal government because of the undefined "general welfare" clause. Responding in *Federalist* No. 41, Madison retorted, "No stronger proof could be given of the distress under which these writers labour for objections, than to their stooping to such a misconception." He explained there was no authority for Congress to rely upon the "general welfare" expression to expand its taxing power, if in so doing, it disregarded "the specifications which ascertain and limit" its authority. *Federalist*, No 41.

Hamilton, on the other hand, asserted a much more liberal view of the Constitution's taxing authority. Like all our Founding Fathers, he recognized the powers imparted were limited, but clearly aspired to create a more proactive federal government. In *Federalist* No. 34, he explained the taxing power was "indefinite." He viewed the clause as imparting to Congress "the discretion to pronounce" the objects of taxation which "concern the general welfare." *The Basic Ideas of Alexander Hamilton*, page 220.

Despite the broad divergence of opinion of the two authors on the topic, both were in agreement that the power of taxation did not involve the power to redistribute wealth. The "general welfare" clause does not grant license to establish a welfare state under which largess is distributed to one class of citizens at the expense of another. Even in Hamilton's very liberal view of matters, he cautioned:

"The only qualification of the generality of the phrase in question, which seems to be admissible, is this: That the object of which an appropriation of money is to be made be general, and not local; its operation extending in fact or by possibility throughout the Union, and not being confined to a particular spot." Ibid, page 221.

If Madison represented the conservative view, and Hamilton the liberal view, then Jefferson must have expressed the *correct view*. Of all our nation's founders, Jefferson's influence was clearly the strongest. He sheds further light upon the issue, remarking:

"The laying of taxes is the power, and the general welfare is the purpose for which the power is to be exercised. They [Congress] are not to lay taxes *ad libitum* [defined, "at pleasure." Author.] for any purpose they please; but only to pay the debts or provide for the *welfare of the Union*. In like manner, they are not to do anything they please to provide for the general welfare, but only to lay taxes for that purpose." *Writings of Thomas Jefferson*, Library Edition, page 147 (emphasis added).

These remarks clearly indicate that taxation and government spending is intended for the welfare of the *nation* as a whole, not individual inhabitants thereof or locations therein. The authority to tax exists only to further the greater concerns of the Union itself. We can therefore conclude that the power to provide for the "general welfare" does not authorize distributions from the treasury to the benefit of private interests, individual concerns, or purely local pursuits.

More importantly, there plainly exists no authority to employ the power to tax as a means to bring about perceived social order, or to correct perceived social injustice. In this regard, Hamilton, the liberal, speaks quite clearly:

"* * *No tax can be laid on land which will not affect the proprietor of millions of acres as well as the proprietor of a single acre. *Federalist* No. 35.

Taxation under our Constitution, *even from the liberal view*, was never designed to favor one business over another, or one property interest over another. Taxation is nothing more than the simple expedient of raising money for the operation of the legitimate functions of government - period.

Whether politically conservative or liberal, all our founding fathers shared a common goal. As seen from the juxtaposition of Madison and Hamilton, they may have approached it differently, but their purpose was the same. Each possessed a burning desire to establish and ensure the greatest measure of individual liberty possible. Both recognized that unlimited taxing power is a direct threat to such liberty.

A NATIONAL SALES TAX SOLVES OUR TAX COLLECTION PROBLEMS

The framers of our Constitution wrestled with two major concerns in structuring tax policy. First was the issue of fairness; the other being the power of the federal government to sufficiently raise revenue without crushing the citizenry under the weight of taxation. They had, after all, instigated independence from England precipitated by her imposition of despotic tax policies.

Consumption taxes represented the best possible way to address those concerns. As to fairness, consumption taxes raise revenue while imposing as little adverse economic impact as possible. Even more attractive was the *indirect* nature of consumption taxes. As such, they keep the federal government from direct contact with the citizenry. The founders were greatly concerned the power of direct taxation would degenerate to a political despotism not unlike that which they had just freed themselves from at great cost.

The heart and soul of the *American Reconstruction Act* is to dismantle the current structure of federal taxation in its entirety. By that I mean, employment taxes, social security taxes, personal and corporate income taxes, and estate and gift taxes. In their place I propose to build a national sales tax set at a sufficient rate to provide the needed revenue to fund the federal government's legitimate operations. For reasons stated later, I propose to leave in place all excise taxes and import duties.

Of all the possibilities, a broad based sales tax meets all the essential elements of an effective system of taxation. It is very simple. Liability is determined based on the amount of the purchase. It is very efficient, requiring little in the way of record keeping or reporting burdens. It is extremely fair. The burden is distributed proportionally, with no particular class of citizens being punished or favored at the expense of another.

Just as importantly, a national sales tax will eliminate the IRS as we know it. No longer will citizens bear the burden of keeping a mountain of records of every financial transaction. They will not have to suffer through the nightmare of tax return preparation and information reporting which presently costs Americans hundreds of billions each year.

Even beyond that, the IRS will no longer conduct audits, execute enforced collection action, or otherwise drag citizens through the quagmire of tax law administration. Under the national sales tax system I propose, the federal government's right of direct contact with citizens vis-a-vis taxation will be a thing of the past.

One chief benefit of the national sales tax is its presentation of solution to a problem which has driven the IRS crazy for 50 years. I refer, of course, to the underground economy. Each year, billions are said to escape the tax collector because citizens deal in cash or otherwise evade or avoid income taxes. At last estimate, Treasury officials place the gross value of the underground economy at $176 billion. Some private economists fix it much higher. Much of the power handed the IRS over the years was specifically pointed at capturing taxes on those funds. If all consumption were taxed at the retail level, such tax evasion would be a thing of the past. A person will be taxed on the level of his consumption, not on the level of his income. Tax charged and collected at the retail level would reach revenue which now escapes the income tax.

Specifically exempted from the consumption tax will be savings and investment. Thus, if a person purchases any type of investment product, such as stocks, bonds, CD's, money market instruments including gold or silver coin or bullion, no tax will attach to such sale. But as Kotlikoff suggests, people save now to spend later. When they spend savings at a later time, the sales tax will then attach to that consumption.

Investments made by business into capital assets would not be taxed. An example would be the purchase of equipment to retool an assembly line. Part of the reason American industry is so unproductive compared to other developed nations is the aging condition of its production facilities. We want these facilities to be upgraded because as productivity increases, so does the rate of employment and the level of real wages paid to employees.

We would also exempt interest payments. At present, gross domestic debt amounts to about $12 trillion. This includes government debt, corporate debt, home mortgage debt and consumer debt. The sales tax would attach to all consumption purchases at the time of purchase, but would not apply to interest on loans to make such a purchase. For example, if you receive a loan to buy an automobile, the tax will be charged only on the sale price of the automobile.

Interest paid to the lender will be paid free of sales tax.

Likewise, there will be no tax on gifts or inheritance. The mere passing of funds from one person to another does not constitute consumption. Consumption occurs when the revenue is spent in the marketplace by the beneficiary of the gift or inheritance.

The principle rap against a consumption tax is it is seen as being *regressive*, not *progressive*. A regressive tax is one which hits lower income groups harder than higher income groups. A progressive tax is the opposite, hitting higher income groups harder. This supposition leads social planners to reject consumption taxes in favor of the graduated income tax.

Socialists are fundamentally wrong in their characterization of consumption taxes as regressive. In fact, a consumption tax is neither regressive nor progressive. It has no socialist characteristic whatsoever. That is precisely why it is so desirable as opposed to a graduated income tax.

Consumption taxes are *proportional*. The extent to which a person is affected by the level of taxation is in direct proportion to his financial standing. Higher income citizens pay more because they consume more. Lower income citizens pay less because they consume less.

The fact is, the one tax which presently operates to collect nearly half of all federal revenue is the classic example of a *regressive* tax. I propose to eliminate this tax under my plan. I speak of the social security tax. That tax is assessed against employees at the rate of 7.65 percent on the first dollar earned. Employers pay a matching share. The total hit is therefore 15.3 percent. However, there is a cap that increases annually for inflation, at which the tax no longer applies. In 1993, social security taxes are capped at $57,600 of wages. Under this system, social security taxes clearly hit lower income citizens much harder than higher income citizens. The higher the income one earns, the lower his effective rate of tax. This is not fair.

Please remember our Constitutional mandate is to avoid employing the power of taxation for anything other than raising revenue. As such, the founders sought only to create a fair system of taxation. Hamilton, the liberal, said, "Taxes on consumable articles have, upon the whole, better pretensions to equality than any other." *The Basic Ideas of Alexander Hamilton*, page 259-60. Expounding upon this premise, Hamilton, the liberal, observed:

> "The consequence of the principle laid down is that every class of the community bears its share of the duty in *proportion to its consumption*; which last is regulated by the comparative wealth of the respective classes, in conjunction with their habits of expense or frugality. The rich and luxurious pay in proportion to the their riches and luxury; the poor and parsimonious, in proportion to their poverty and parsimony." Ibid, page 257 (Emphasis added.)

In the business of raising revenue, there is nothing more fair than proportion. In fact, Hamilton, the liberal, insisted the incidents of taxation fall "not too heavily upon particular parts of the community." He called for a "judicious distribution" of the burden. Ibid, page 258. The Marxist idea of a progressive income tax was not introduced for revenue raising purposes. It was inaugurated for social planning purposes, a notion alien to our system of Constitutional limited government.

That is precisely why the founders turned to consumption taxes as virtually their only source of revenue. Hamilton specifically rejected taxing the "articles of our own growth and manufacturer" because such taxes are "more prejudicial to trade" than are consumption taxes. Ibid, page 258. It was not until 1913, when the 16th Amendment was added to the Constitution, that we began to tax income in earnest.

Prior to 1913, all revenue was raised through customs duties and manufacturer's excise taxes. Because of our vast service economy, such taxes are no longer feasible as the only way of raising revenue. The sales tax, on the other hand, enjoys the same feature of proportionality, and can be readily applied to services as well as products.

We know consumption taxes afford the least amount of economic distortion. They encourage savings and investment, and hence will increase the nation's productivity. A national sales tax affords the greatest revenue base and offers the greatest equality of all consumption taxes. I therefore assert it is time we abandon all other forms of taxation in favor of a national sales tax.

INSURING THE ELIMINATION OF THE IRS

Readers know that eliminating the IRS is of paramount importance to this rebuilding plan. I will not count the effort successful if, even after restructuring an equitable tax system, we face the prospect of audits, liens, levies and general disruption at the hands of the IRS. I therefore built a feature into the *American Reconstruction Act* insuring the elimination of the IRS.

The national sales tax I propose will not be collected by the IRS. Indeed no agency of the federal government will have the right or authority to enforce the national sales tax law *vis-a-vis* the public. Rather, the sales tax will be collected by the *states* alone. It will in turn be paid to the federal government pursuant to regulations established by the Treasury for that purpose. To the extent the national Treasury has any claim to audit books and records to ensure compliance with the law, the target of such enforcement will be *state governments only*. In this way, the federal collection mechanism as we presently know it will be completely dismantled.

This will add no greater burden to either the state governments or to citizens. Each of the 50 states in the union already has its own sales tax. It is no more costly for such state to collect, say, a 20 percent tax than it is to collect a six or eight percent tax. Whatever the national rate may be, the states simply add it to their existing rate and collect the gross amount. In terms of enforcement *vis-a-vis* the public, states currently enforce their own sales tax laws with sufficient vigor. The mere fact that the rate is higher will impart no greater cost of enforcement to the states.

Ironically, the greatest beneficiary under this system is the federal government itself. From its vantage point, its 125,000 member IRS police force is reduced to just the handful necessary to police the various state governments. The $7 billion annual IRS budget is eliminated, as are the vast sums spent on enforcing tax laws through other aspects of government, such as the judiciary. Its space age computers and the projected $21 billion expenditure for same is unnecessary as all information reporting laws will be eliminated.

Most importantly, the various tax collection points are reduced tremendously. At present, the federal government collects $1.1 trillion annually from *204 million* different sources. That represents the total number of tax returns filed in 1992. It includes all personal and corporate income tax returns, estate and gift tax returns, and employment tax returns. By making the states responsible to collect the national sales tax, federal collection points are reduced to *just 50*. The cost in administering a federal tax system with just 50 collection points is virtually non-existent.

It is true that business will retain the burden of collecting the sales tax and paying it to the states. But they have that burden now. This plan does not add to their costs. Just as it is no more costly for the states to collect at a higher rate, it is no more costly for businesses to collect and pay at a higher rate. *At the very least*, this plan will free 114 million families of the staggering burden of compliance with the federal laws they now face.

An added benefit to the federal government is the reduction and perhaps elimination of tax evasion. At present, billions in taxes are evaded each year, both through dealing in cash and through other methods. Under a sales tax system, very little evasion is possible. To evade income taxes, the would-be criminal likely completes just one criminal act in a given year. That is the act of either filing a false return or filing no return at all. To defeat the sales tax, however, he must engage in hundreds of criminal acts, one each time he attempts to make a purchase. This is not likely to happen on a broad scale.

Opponents of a sales tax claim the higher rate required to fund both federal and state activities would encourage evasion. This assertion ignores the economics of the situation. At present, some citizens are able to induce merchants to make a cash sale, thus avoiding the sales tax. This is possible only because the merchant has something to gain in the process as well. What he gains is the fact that the cash he receives does not show up on his books. Consequently, he avoids the income tax on his profit.

However, with the elimination of the income tax, the merchant has nothing to gain from assisting in the act of evading sales tax. In fact, he has everything to lose. State enforcement procedures allow an assessment of uncollected sales taxes to be made against the merchant who failed to collect it. These assessments occur much the same as IRS assessments for unpaid employees' withholding taxes. The unpaid sales tax, therefore, is collectible by the state directly from the merchant who fails to collect or pay it. Furthermore, sales taxes are classified as "trust fund" taxes for bankruptcy purposes. The significance is that a debt for trust fund taxes cannot be discharged in bankruptcy.

Given this structure, and given the fact that a merchant will have nothing to gain and everything to lose by assisting in sales tax evasion, reason and common sense suggests sales tax evasion will be extremely minimal. In all events, given the fact that we reach the underground economy and eliminate the incentive to cheat on the income tax, the federal government comes out well ahead of the game.

THE ECONOMIC RESULTS OF A NATIONAL SALES TAX

The greatest benefit to the private sector is the elimination of the cost of complying with our present system. With a compliance cost of 65 percent of revenue, the present system syphoned $720 billion out of the economy, in 1992 alone. Even if a national sales tax was set at a rate sufficient to produce precisely the same gross revenue for the federal government, it does so virtually without cost to society. Remember, businesses already have a sales tax compliance cost which will not increase under my system. Individuals will have no cost to comply whatsoever under my system.

Imagine what the private sector could and would do with $720 billion annually in new-found capital. What new products and services would be developed? What new jobs and industries would be created? How much would the cost of existing products and services drop because of radically increased productivity? One way to answer these questions is to measure the direct impact a national sales tax would have on the economy.

Kotlikoff designed a computer simulation module to test the economy's response to replacing all federal personal and corporate income taxes with a national sales tax. Even with no reduction in the net tax collected under a sales tax, the economy would reap the following important benefits:

* "An immediate and dramatic" increase in the national savings rate, which could rise as high as 7.6 percent;

* A substantial increase in investment;

* A rise in productivity as a result of increased investment. Consequently, workers experience substantial growth in "real wages."

* Interest rates fall "by almost 2 percentage points."

* Interestingly, the sales tax rate itself actually falls over time. Because of the increase in productivity and the ability of all citizens to consume more, the rate actually falls while meeting all government revenue demands. See Cato Institute Policy Analysis Report No. 193, *The Economic Impact of Replacing Federal Income Taxes with a National Sales Tax*, pages 11-13.

Kotlikoff's simulation was done with both a progressive and proportional sales tax. Under a progressive sales tax system, growth in every category outlined above was substantially reduced. This proves Hamilton's observations of 200 years ago, that a proportional system is far better for *everybody* than a socialist conceived progressive system. Ibid, page 15. We all benefit when the tax is fair and equitable. We all lose when it is artificially imbalanced for socialistic reasons.

THE RATE OF TAX

There should be no doubt that a national sales tax is far more desirable in every regard to personal and corporate income taxes. The only question now is, at what rate must we set the sales tax if it is to replace current sources of federal revenue.

After refunds, the IRS collected a total of $1.01 trillion from 204 million corporate, individual, estate and gift, employment and excise tax returns in 1992. Giving government the benefit of the doubt, *for the moment*, and assuming it needs all current revenue to function, the sum of $1.01 trillion is our collection target. In the next chapter, I address the aspects of my plan which reduce government spending and eliminate the debt.

According to Department of Commerce's *Survey of Current Business*, August, 1993, the consumption component of the GDP for 1993 is about $3.776 trillion. Another $243 billion represents the housing component of the GDP. The housing component is that portion which is spent on housing. We do not intend to tax either rent or mortgage payments. The tax on the housing component will attach at the time of building and is therefore added to the final cost.

The two elements together equal $4.019 trillion. That amount becomes the tax base for the national sales tax.

To collect $1.01 trillion from a base of $4.019 trillion, we need a rate of 25 percent. With that rate, we collect as much money as the current system collects, but without any of the costs of the current system. Be aware, the 25 percent sales tax rate is *not a tax increase*. It collects precisely the same revenue as does our current system. The difference is the levy is measured by consumption, not income.

The tax collected under the national sales tax would be deposited to the general account of the United States Treasury. It would be available to fund the various appropriations of Congress. You will note, however, that while government *collects* $1.01 trillion in revenue, it spends much more. In 1993, the federal government will spend $1.4 trillion. This deficit, occurring year after year, must stop without further delay. What's more, the accumulated debt must be paid.

For that reason, the *American Reconstruction Act* proposes to leave in place all customs duties and manufacturer's excise taxes. During 1992, the IRS collected $32.108 billion in excise taxes. In the same period, the U.S. Customs Service collected $20.16 billion from import duties. This equals $52.268 billion. Those revenues will be specifically earmarked for application to the principle amount of national debt. This would allow us to at least begin to pay off the debt, something which is not happening now. Once the debt is retired as suggested in the next chapter, manufacturer's excise taxes can also be eliminated.

A major aspect of the *American Reconstruction Act*, discussed in more detail in Chapter 16, is the fact that deficit spending will no longer be permitted. Through deficit spending, Congress has managed to accumulate a $4.5 trillion debt in just 14 years. This must stop if America is ever to regain its status as a world economic leader. There is no moral, religious, constitutional, economic or legal reasoning to justify deficit spending. The only justification is expedience, and that is something no responsible nation can tolerate in the formation of public policy. It must end now.

Conclusion

In the course of development of the American Reconstruction Act, I discussed its various features with numerous economists both in and out of government. One person whose counsel I sought was none other than Professor Milton Friedman. Professor Friedman is a Nobel Prize winner and the nation's, if not the world's, leading free market economist.

In a personal letter to me, Professor Friedman explained, "Your proposal has a great deal of appeal, but I am skeptical that there is any possibility of having it adopted in a form that would be acceptable to either you or me." The source of Professor Friedman's skepticism is his faith, or rather, *lack of faith* in Congress' willingness to do the right thing. He points out that our current tax laws perform more of a "political function" than they do a revenue raising one. This I elaborated on earlier, when I discussed the social element of taxation.

The solution, therefore, is to take the fight to the people. Just as I have done with the issue of taxpayers' rights and IRS abuse, I shall take the cause of the *American Reconstruction Act* directly to America. In the final chapter of this book, I explain how you can help push for a system that will:

* Increase your spendable income;

* Increase jobs and benefits;

* Increase savings, investment and production;

* Increase everyone's opportunity for success;

* Control government spending;

* Decrease federal debt; and best of all

* *Eliminate the IRS!*

16

THE SOLUTION TO AMERICA'S FINANCIAL PROBLEMS

Whether you are conservative or liberal, Republican or Democrat, there is no arguing the fact that America is in trouble financially. The nation is sinking further and further into debt each day with no provision to retire it. With federal debt at $4.5 trillion and rising as I write, the inevitable seems only that it will be passed on to our children. In my opinion, this is criminally irresponsible.

Alexander Hamilton, the strongest liberal voice of all our Founding Fathers, while in favor of a national debt, explained that it "should not be excessive." More specifically, he warned, ". . .the creation of debt should always be accompanied with the means of extinguishment." *The Basic Ideas of Alexander Hamilton*, page 232.

Jefferson, on the other hand, saw a national debt in a more grave light. He feared such a debt would be looked upon by the government as a means of increasing taxes to despotic levels. He cautioned:

"* * *But if the debt should once more be swelled to formidable size, its entire discharge will be despaired of, and we shall be committed to the English career of debt, corruption, and rottenness, closing with revolution. *The discharge of debt, therefore, is vital to the destinies of our government. . ."* *The Essence of Jefferson*, Martin A. Larson, page 178 (Emphasis added).

Our contemporary leaders have ignored the warnings of the brightest political minds in history. Our national debt is not only excessive, it is crushing. Total domestic debt is now at $12 trillion and the federal government owns more than one-third of it. Worse, it has provided absolutely no means to extinguish it, save the continued call to raise taxes. This, of course, leads us directly to the place envisioned by Jefferson. Already we see the rapid deterioration of Constitutional safeguards brought about by the need to raise revenue. As the debt problem escalates, we can expect only further assaults on those basic liberties. In this regard, Jefferson said:

". . .we must not let our rulers load us with perpetual debt. We must make our election between economy and liberty or profusion and servitude. If we run into such debts, as that we must be taxed in our meat and in our drink, in our necessaries and our comforts, in our labors and our amusements, for our calling and our creeds...we [will] have no time to think, no means of calling our mismanagers to account but be glad to obtain subsistance by hiring ourselves to rivet their chains on the necks of our fellow-sufferers. And this is the tendency of all human government. A departure from principle in one instance becomes a precedent...till the bulk of society is reduced to be mere automatons of misery. *And the forehorse of this frightful team is public debt. Taxation follows that, and in its train wretchedness and oppression.*" Ibid. (Emphasis added.)

Debt saps productive strength from the nation by diverting capital which would otherwise be available to fund business expansion and employment. *Every dollar loaned to the federal government is one dollar which cannot be loaned to business and industry.*

We learned in Chapter 14 that as investment shrinks, so does productivity and employment. America needs a plan to first control its debt, then extinguish it. Without such a plan, our children will never share the same opportunities for success and independence as we did. In his letter to me, Professor Friedman wrote, "The only long-term effective reform of the federal tax system, in my opinion, is to reduce government spending and reduce the amount of taxes collected." I agree fully with that statement. That is why I have built into the *American Reconstruction Act* provisions which limit both federal spending and taxation.

If it can be said that there is a flaw in our Constitution, it is that no express limit is placed either on the federal government's power to borrow or spend money. Why would such an oversight have occurred? Our Founding Fathers, in their wildest imaginations, never perceived future politicians would adopt such short-sighted, irresponsible views as those we now see. The Founding Fathers never believed future politicians would search for every opportunity to twist the meaning of the Constitution into conclusions it never intended.

Why is the Constitution silent on such limits? The answer is provided, once again, from Hamilton, the liberal. He said, "...why declare that things shall not be done which there is no power to do?" Common sense dictates that a massive federal debt cannot be tolerated. It would be entirely contrary to the very nature and purpose of the limited government they created. Why declare that such a debt cannot be created when no person in his right mind would attempt to create one? Why declare that such a debt cannot be created when the Constitution did not authorize one in the first place? Unfortunately, our contemporary leaders have abandoned both common sense and Constitutional principles in furtherance of their own personal agenda.

WHY WE HAVE A BUDGET DEFICIT

Do you know how the federal budget and appropriations process operates? Most people do not. When you understand how the system operates, you can better appreciate two things. First, why the budget is out of control. Second, why nobody seems to know the difference between a *budget cut* and a *spending increase.*

Politicians often describe the federal budget as being on "automatic pilot." What is budgetary "auto pilot?" Simply stated, it is the process by which federal spending increases automatically, based only upon an inflationary index. The system is referred to as the "baseline" funding system. It was created by the *Congressional Budget Act of 1974.* Under that law, funding to specific programs increases regardless of the level of *need* for that program. Increases are based upon inflationary growth.

For example, suppose program A spends $10 billion during 1991 to provide finger painting supplies to underprivileged, inner city children. Suppose further the inflationary index is 10 percent in that year. Under the terms of the *Congressional Budget Act of 1974*, the level of funding to the program *automatically* increases in 1992 by 10 percent from the *baseline.* The baseline was last year's appropriation of $10 billion.

Consequently, the program receives $11 billion in funding for 1992. The added billion in funding is provided regardless of whether the program needs (or wants) it. Further, it is provided without respect to funds actually spent by the program during 1991.

It is easy to see how a budget can grow wildly using such a system. However, we cannot lose sight of the fact that our elected officials are responsible for both the baseline system and appropriating funds to a given program. In other words, baseline increases or not, the finger painting program would never receive a dime in federal money if enough elected representatives had the guts to say that inner city children do not need a finger painting program to enjoy an equal opportunity for success in life.

Under the baseline, autopilot program, there are two ways to cut the federal budget. Substantial deception arises, however, when the methods are presented to the public as identical. Clearly they are not. The first method of cutting the budget is to either reduce or eliminate the finger painting program. If funding is reduced, the program is appropriated, for example, just $6 billion. In that case, taxpayers actually save (as in, *put back* into their pockets) $4 billion. If the program is eliminated, taxpayers save $10 billion.

The second method of "cutting the budget" is what we have seen happening over the past 10-plus years. That method is to make "baseline" cuts. While such cuts are offered up by politicians as budget cuts, in fact, they are not cuts at all.

A baseline cut works this way: The finger painting program was slated for a funding increase of 10 percent over its $10 billion budget. But rather than receiving $11 billion, as called for by the "baseline," the program receives just $10.5 billion. As you can plainly see, the program receives *more money* than in the prior year, but not as much as it *would have* under the "baseline." This is referred to as funding "below the baseline." Congressmen refer to these as "budget cuts."

Let me provided a clearer analogy. Imagine you are walking through the local mall, window shopping. You pass a clothing store featuring raincoats at 50 percent off the regular price. You do not currently need or want a raincoat at any price. However, the store clerk persuades you this is a once in a life time deal, so you buy the coat. The normal price was $120, but you paid just $60. Upon leaving the mall carrying the coat you did not need or want, you convince yourself you *saved* $60. The reality, however, is you *spent* $60 more than you intended to, and perhaps, $60 more than you could *afford*.

This process went on throughout the decade of the 1980's. The Democrats accused Republicans and the Reagan and Bush Administrations of decimating social programs with "deep cuts." In reality, spending on social programs *increased* during 1980 to 1990 from about $350 billion to well over $700 billion annually. However, because they did not grow at the pace called for by the "baseline," Democrats assert the programs were "cut."

In actuality, not a dime was cut from the federal budget the entire decade. Spending increased steadily, leading to *annual* deficits which have grown from around $50 billion in the early 1980's, to well over $300 billion today. Total federal debt is fast approaching $4.5 trillion as I write.

To see just how our deficits have grown throughout the extended period of "budget cuts," please refer to Chart 2-11, taken from page 19 of Clinton's *A Vision for Change for America*.

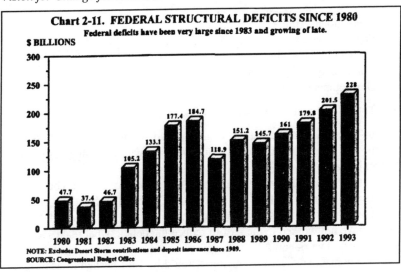

Chart 2-11. FEDERAL STRUCTURAL DEFICITS SINCE 1980

Federal deficits have been very large since 1983 and growing of late.

NOTE: Excludes Desert Storm contributions and deposit insurance since 1989.
SOURCE: Congressional Budget Office

CAN PRESIDENT CLINTON'S ECONOMIC PLAN SOLVE THE DEFICIT?

During his State of the Union address in February of 1993, Clinton insisted over 150 specific budget cuts were in store for the nation. Total federal spending cuts, he insisted, would equal $240 billion. He insisted a combination of major budget cuts and tax increases on only the very rich would solve the deficit problem in four years. However, while the President spent over an hour detailing the manner in which he intended to *spend* more money, he did not dedicate three minutes to describing the ways in which he intended to *cut* excess from the budget.

In an effort to find out just what these cuts were, I did a little research. In February of 1993, I spoke at length with analysts from the Office of Management and Budget (OMB) on the issue. The men I talked with were personally familiar with Clinton's plan and studied the numbers that appear in *A Vision of Change For America*, the 145-page text of the President's proposal to Congress.

What I learned did not surprise me. When I phoned the OMB to research the 150 budget cuts, I asked a simple question. "Are these cuts true, honest-to-God spending reductions, or are they baseline cuts?" You should now be fully aware of the fact that a baseline cut is not a cut at all. Rather it is a spending increase, albeit at a slower rate than would otherwise occur.

I was told, "For the most part, all the cuts are in the baseline sense."

I then asked my contact whether the proposal contained *any* legitimate reductions in actual spending (i.e., not baseline cuts, real cuts)?" I learned of a few - *five* to be exact. These are what he called "absolute cuts," in billions over four years:

> Defense $33.0
> International Affairs 1.3
> Energy Programs 7
> Agriculture Subsidies 11.0
> Community and Regional
> Development Grants 1.4

Total *Real* Spending Reductions = $47.4 Billion

In his speech to the nation, Clinton asked whether we would continue "business as usual," or whether this truly was "a new day." I suggest to you the answer is plain.

In my conversation with OMB, I pointed out that Congress has been taxing and spending for the past 15 years (at LEAST), and all it has done is lead to staggering annual deficits and a $4-plus trillion federal debt. I asked, "If such tactics have not worked in the past to reduce the deficit, what makes anybody think they will work now?"

My contact answered by saying, "You'd be hard pushed to achieve any (deficit) reductions" under this proposal.

I then asked, "Isn't it true that without substantial, real spending cuts, the deficit cannot be reduced?" His response was, "I think that's correct." He then went on to explain that the deficit "may grow more slowly, but it will continue to grow." Included here you will find a copy of Table 7 reproduced from page 140 of *A Vision of Change for America*. It shows what really is happening with America's federal expenditures. As you can see, they *rise* (not fall) from $1.475 trillion in 1993 to an estimated $1.767 trillion by 1998. That, my friends, indicates substantial spending increases, *not cuts*.

TABLE 7. BUDGET OUTLAYS BY FUNCTION

(In billions of dollars)

Function	1993	1994	1995	1996	1997	1998
			Estimate			
National defense	292.9	277.3	272.3	264.9	249.2	252.7
International affairs	19.3	18.7	18.7	18.2	18.0	18.4
General science, space and technology	17.2	18.1	19.7	20.7	21.6	22.2
Energy	4.9	3.4	4.1	4.5	4.2	4.0
Natural resources and environment	22.1	21.9	22.8	23.3	23.7	23.7
Agriculture	21.6	18.1	13.8	12.2	10.9	11.5
Commerce and housing credit	13.6	14.0	0.6	-10.5	-10.2	-7.0
Transportation	36.9	39.8	40.4	41.3	42.7	43.7
Community and regional development	10.8	11.1	10.4	9.7	9.5	9.7
Education, training, employment, and social services	53.4	53.8	56.6	56.1	62.7	65.5
Health	105.3	118.3	133.3	149.6	166.8	185.4
Medicare	132.7	147.2	162.8	179.0	195.2	213.6
Income security	208.8	214.3	221.5	229.7	240.4	249.1
Social security	305.0	321.0	336.7	351.3	367.4	383.1
Veterans benefits and services	35.7	37.8	37.5	37.0	39.1	40.0
Administration of justice	15.3	15.9	17.2	17.4	17.7	18.2
General government	14.8	14.4	15.6	15.5	15.7	15.8
Net interest	202.1	212.0	227.2	243.3	257.4	272.7
Allowances	*	-3.3	-6.1	-7.2	-8.9	-9.1
Undistributed offsetting receipts	-37.3	-39.0	-40.7	-43.2	-45.6	-46.1
Total outlays	1,475.1	1,513.0	1,564.5	1,612.8	1,677.5	1,767.0

* $50 million or less.

It seems plain that our contemporary leaders in both the White House and Congress have absolutely no intention of ever eliminating federal deficit spending. Despite assurances to the public that Clinton can get the job done, the words of his own plan defy the notion. Listen to this:

"This Administration believes that its policies of deficit reduction and public and private investment will increase the growth of productivity and incomes, thereby increasing Federal revenues, retarding the expansion of Federal spending, and forcing the deficit down. *If the economic outcome is more favorable than we have assumed, the deficit will grow more slowly.* Under the more optimistic assumptions, the deficit will be stabilized as a percentage of the GDP (Gross Domestic Product). * * *" *A Vision of Change for America*, page 116 (Emphasis added).

If I understand this statement, Clinton says, "If all goes according to plan, the deficit *will grow*, but more slowly than at present rates." Clinton says, "We will continue to have annual deficits, but when measured against GDP, those annual deficits will be a stable percentage." Clinton's deficit reduction plan assures us that while we will continue to see annual deficits, they will not grow from year to year as measured against GDP, and will not increase faster than the rate of domestic productivity.

I have only one question. What good is that? If you run an annual deficit of just one dollar, you are still spending more than you collect. If you borrow just one dollar, your total liabilities for principal and interest increase, thereby reducing your spendable income. When you continue to borrow year after year, even if you borrow just one dollar at a time, future taxpayers are burdened with a growing demand for taxes just to service the debt, however small or stable it may be. This saps capital from the economy and we know from history what happens as a result. The entire nation suffers. More critically, this policy ignores Hamilton's warning, that government must have a plan to extinguish a national debt before amassing one.

Debt is debt. It is never good. It bears compound interest which slowly but steadily eats the substance of your wealth. It steadily reduces your capacity to get ahead. Steadily increasing debt will eventually - inevitably - crush you. It does so to businesses and individuals, and it will do so to the federal government as well.

A stable or more slowly rising annual deficit is no more acceptable than an unstable or quickly rising annual deficit. In either case, the overall burden to the taxpayer is greatly and mindlessly increased and *it must stop*. In Clinton's own words, his plan does not propose to stop it.

The question of the integrity of Congress and Clinton on the issue of solving the deficit problem can be answered very simply. The question is, will they stop spending more money than they collect? Tax increases or not, will they stop driving YOU and your CHILDREN deeper and deeper into debt? In my midwestern naivete', the issue is that simple. If they stop pushing you deeper into debt, they can begin to pay off the debt that now exists. If they continue to push you deeper into debt, there is no way to pay off existing obligations.

On May 13, 1993, I believe we obtained an answer to this very simple question. At that time, the Congress voted to *increase* the federal debt ceiling. The debt ceiling is the amount of money the Congress is authorized to borrow. It is very much like the spending limit you have on your credit card. When you reach the limit, you can no longer use it to spend money. However, the Congress enjoys a luxury you and I do not. They can vote to increase the spending limit and nobody can stop them!

At the time of Clinton's first State of the Union address, the debt ceiling was set at $4.145 trillion. Congress voted to increase the debt ceiling to a whopping $4.9 trillion! In the words of the Senate, the debt was increased to "facilitate the smooth functioning of the Federal government. . ." Mind you, they made no effort to cut spending, as you or I would if our credit ran out.

In the March, 1993 issue of my newsletter, I explained that Clinton's plan would increase total federal debt by 28 percent. If all goes according to Clinton's plan, total debt will *grow* from $4.145 trillion (the debt as of March, 1993) to $5.302 trillion by 1998. However, the recent increase in the debt limit represents an *18 percent* hike in total federal debt. This hike occurred within the first *six months* of Clinton's Presidency. At this rate, we are likely to blow through the 28 percent level long before Clinton's projected date of 1998.

True, the Congress has not yet spent its new found credit. According to historical spending patterns, it typically takes Congress about 18 months to max out its latest credit card. If that pattern continues throughout the remainder of Clinton's term, we will see the federal debt increase by something closer to 54 percent. There is no telling what may be the resulting effect on the economy and individual liberty if Congress attempts tax increases to solve *that kind* of debt problem.

We must face it. We are being lied to and our economy is being falsely manipulated. We must gather the courage to face this reality and do something to stop it. If we do not, and Congress continues as it has for the past two decades, our childrens' future will be lost.

WHY TAX INCREASES WON'T CUT THE DEFICIT?

The logical solution to the debt problem seems to be that we need a combination of spending cuts *and* tax increases. Spending cuts alone, it is often suggested, will not solve the problem. Advocates of this seemingly reasonable suggestion point out that during the 1980's, federal spending ran at the rate of about 23 percent of GDP, while federal taxes were levied at the rate of just 18 percent of GDP. It seems quite plausible that a few percentage point decrease in spending, coupled with a few percentage point increase in taxation, will end deficits forthwith.

Unfortunately, there are two very important reasons why this otherwise perfectly reasonable proposal will not work. First, Congress simply will not stop spending money. In fact, the Clinton Administration originally sought $2 in spending cuts (baseline cuts, of course) for every dollar in tax increases. That is not the way it worked out, however. Powerful liberal leaders well entrenched in Congress presented formidable opposition to broad based "cuts," even of a baseline nature.

James Payne discusses this phenomenon in his book, *The Culture of Spending*, (ICS Press, 1993). Dr. Payne explains that throughout the Reagan Administration, while the President attempted to cut various useless, outdated or wasteful programs from the budget, Congressional leaders simply refused to eliminate the appropriations.

Dr. Payne documents the fact that in hearings on appropriations for the various programs, Congress is simply inundated with beggars seeking one form of government handout after another. Any time a proposal is made to cut a particular appropriation, the program's supporters come out of the woodwork. As Payne stated:

"Congress does not hold *hearings* on government programs and expenditures; it holds *rump hearings*, proceedings overwhelmingly dominated by the advocates of federal action. Of the witnesses it hears, 97.7 percent speak for the programs, and only 0.7 percent oppose them." *The Culture of Spending*, page 12 (emphasis in original).

As a result of what Payne calls "an opinion climate so one-sided that it amounts to indoctrination," no real cuts in spending are ever made.

I assert that no cuts will likely be made unless the people of this nation stop looking to Washington for their daily bread. The Constitution did not intend to create Santa Clause when it gave Congress the power to appropriate funds for the "general welfare" of the nation. As we learned in the last chapter, that power is to be used solely to benefit the nation *as a whole*, not individuals, their businesses, organizations or social interests.

If you asked a thousand people whether federal spending in general is too high, 999 of them would likely tell you it is. However, if you asked those same thousand people whether a particular program should be cut, 999 would likely say no, the program is good and should continue. The cold truth the public does not seem to grasp is that you cannot cut spending in general, unless you cut spending to specific programs. Until the body politic accepts that proposition and is willing to live with it, no amount of tax increases will be sufficient to solve the budget crisis.

The second major problem with using tax increases to raise revenue is the strange paradox that tax increases often do not raise revenue. Tax increases often cause a reduction in the flow of revenue to the Treasury. The reason is that taxes influence economic behavior. As we learned earlier, what you tax you get less of. When you tax production and growth in general, you end up with less production and growth. In short, you shrink your tax base and tax revenue shrinks with it. The reality is that you cannot increase tax revenue by raising *tax rates*. You increase tax revenue only by increasing the *tax base*.

William C. Dunkelberg, Temple University's dean of the School of Business and Management, and John Skorburg, chief economist for the Chicago Association of Commerce and Industry, combined to produce a study proving this point. Cato Institute Policy Analysis Report No. 148, *How Rising Tax Burdens Can Produce Recession*. February 21, 1993. Their study finds that each one percent rise in the federal tax burden leads to a 1.8 percent reduction in economic growth. Similarly, each one percent rise in the federal tax burden leads to a 1.14 percent decline in national employment. Everybody knows government revenue does not increase when the nation is facing rising unemployment and reduced economic growth. The decline in revenue occurs because of a cut in the tax base, brought on by higher tax rates.

Let me illustrate this point with a clear example. I want you to look back to the *Revenue Reconciliation Act of 1990*, passed on October 27, 1990. This was the act Bush signed into law despite his promise of "no new taxes." It was a pure "tax the rich" proposal designed to get even with rich people who do not pay their "fair share."

A major aspect of the 1990 budget act, among higher tax rates, was several provisions imposing excise taxes on "luxury items." The "luxury taxes," as they came to be called, were announced as a sure-fire way to get into the pockets of the rich without affecting the middle class. A ten percent surtax was added to boats in excess of $100,000 in value, aircraft in excess of $100,000, autos in excess of $30,000, jewelry in excess of $10,000, and furs in excess of $10,000, and high priced airplanes.

Congress believed there was no way for the rich to "get around" paying these taxes. When they purchase the opulent products rich people are known for and cannot resist, *POW*, they would be hit with the tax! They wont even see it coming! The federal coffers, it was believed, would be filled with excise taxes extracted from rich people caught *in the very act of being rich*. What could be better than that?

Just one little problem our social engineers in Washington overlooked. While they *could* tax the pants off the purchase of such a product, they neglected to understand that they *could not* force somebody to *buy* such a product. Thus, in the face these new taxes, the rich did what everybody does when confronted with higher prices on non-essential products. They simply *stopped buying* them!

During the time these taxes were in effect, industry sold virtually no boats or aircraft in excess of $100,000, motor vehicles in excess of $30,000, jewelry in excess of $10,000 or furs in excess of $10,000. The result of this has been, as you should have guessed by now, massive layoffs in these industries. In particular, the boat building industry has lost thousands of jobs as a direct result of the luxury tax.

Just for the record, who do you suppose built those $100,000 boats? Do you suppose they were built by rich people who could afford to lose their jobs? Or, do you think they were built by people earning $10 to $20 per hour and needed the jobs to support their families? Of course, it was the latter. As unemployment in these industries rose, the government's revenue stream from taxes on their wages fell dramatically.

So we have an irrefutable correlation between increased taxes and lost jobs. We also have an irrefutable correlation between increased taxes and an overall adverse effect on the economy. Ironically, Congress knows this is a proximate result of increasing tax burdens. To prove it, let me point to the Clinton tax act:

You may or may not be aware that the act *repealed* the luxury excise taxes. Why did they repeal the luxury taxes?, you ask. The answer is found in the committee reports released by the House Ways and Means and Senate Finance Committees. At page 188 of the Ways and Means Report entitled, *Fiscal Year 1994 Budget Reconciliation Recommendations*, dated May 18, 1993, we find the following statement supporting the committee's repeal recommendation:

> "During the recent recession, the boat, aircraft, jewelry, and fur industries have suffered job losses and increased unemployment. The committee believes that it is appropriate to eliminate the burden these taxes impose in the interests of fostering economic recovery in those and related industries."

Precisely the same language is found in the report of the Senate Finance Committee, dated June 23, 1993, and entitled, *Reconciliation Submissions of the Instructed Committees Pursuant to the Concurrent Resolution on the Budget*, at page 213.

When the luxury taxes were passed, they were purely "tax the rich" proposals which could in no way harm the middle class or the economy. However, these same taxes are now referred to as "burdens" imposed on specific industries. Furthermore, these "burdens" must be "eliminated" in order to "foster economic recovery" in those and "related industries." Why must "economic recovery" be "fostered?" Because the industries "burdened" with these taxes "have suffered job losses and increased unemployment."

If it is true that one small excise tax, pointed at a very tiny fraction of the public - the most rich - caused undue economic burdens and unemployment within certain industries, what will happen when Congress imposes any type of broad based tax impacting all citizens and all industries? Are you saying that taxes will cause economic turmoil when imposed sparingly, but will not cause such turmoil when handed out across the board? Such a suggestion is simply preposterous!

There is no question but that increased, broad based taxes have a negative impact on the economy. As a result, revenues to the Treasury do not increase. If that is true, then the contrary assertion must also be true, i.e., reduced tax rates actually increase the flow of revenue to the Treasury. Bruce Bartlett, former Deputy Assistant Treasury Secretary produced a well-documented historical analysis proving such is exactly the case. Cato Institute Policy Analysis Report No. 192, *The Futility of Raising Tax Rates*, April 8, 1993. Bartlett writes:

> "The history of tax-rate increases shows that they seldom produce much revenue. *Their principle effect is to make higher taxes on the poor and middle class more palatable.* In fact, because of inflation and real growth of the economy, in just a few years tax rates originally imposed on the rich often apply to those with middle incomes.* * *" Policy Analysis Report No. 192, page 1 (emphasis added).

President John F. Kennedy recognized the truth in Bartlett's observation. Some 30 years prior to the issuance of Bartlett's report, President Kennedy, speaking to the Economic Club of New York, observed:

> "Our true choice is not between tax reduction, on the one hand, and the avoidance of large federal deficits on the other. It is increasingly clear that no matter what party is in power, so long as our national security needs keep rising, an economy hampered by restrictive tax rates will never produce enough revenue to balance our budget, just as it will never produce enough jobs or enough profits.* * *

> "In short, it is a paradoxical truth that tax rates are too high today and tax revenues are too low, and the soundest way to raise the revenue in the long run is to cut the rates now. The experience of a number of European countries and Japan has borne this out. This country's own experience with tax reduction in 1954 has borne this out. *And the reason is that only full employment can balance the budget, and tax reduction can pave the way to that employment.* The purpose of cutting taxes now is not to incur a budget deficit, but to achieve the more prosperous, expanding economy which can bring about budget surplus." Kennedy, quoted in Cato Institute Policy Analysis Report No. 192, page 15 (emphasis added).

During the period from World War II to the end of America's involvement in Korea in 1953, taxpayers were burdened with confiscatory income tax rates. In 1953, the highest marginal rate was 91 percent. A person in that bracket was not permitted to retain a single dime of each dollar he earned.

During the Kennedy Administration, consistent with his expressed intentions, marginal rates dropped substantially. The top marginal rate by 1964 was 77 percent, and by 1967, it was 70 percent. During the same period, unemployment in the United States went from 6.7 percent to 3.5 percent.

During the 1970's, rates began to rise again, hitting the 72 percent level by 1980. You may also recall that the economy bounced through many sluggish periods during the 1970's. By the end of the decade, America was mired in the worst recession in modern history. Interest rates were above 20 percent, the Dow was holding on to 700 by its fingernails with unemployment and inflation rates in double digits.

With the election of Ronald Reagan in 1980, marginal rates were slashed. They went from 72 percent to a top rate of 50 percent by 1986. With the *Tax Reform Act of 1986*, top rates were cut again, this time to 28 percent by 1990. During the same period, interest rates fell to their current 30-year low, inflation is virtually non-existent, the Dow flew through the 3300 mark, and unemployment rates went from 7.6 to 5.3 percent.

Beginning in 1990, however, the trend reversed. With the 1990 Democratic budget compromise, the top marginal rate climbed again to 32 percent. At the time, the 1990 tax increase package of $150 billion was the highest tax increase in history. With it, the unemployment rate climbed back to over 7 percent. Clinton's 1993 tax increase pushed the top tax rate to 39.6 percent. At $326 billion, it now holds the record for the single largest tax increase in our nation's history. Surely we shall see even further declines in the employment rate and consequently, federal revenue.

Based upon this irrefutable historical evidence, the solution to America's budget problem is not to employ a combination of higher taxes and less spending. The solution is to slash both taxes and spending. By slashing taxes, we infuse the economy with revenue which otherwise would largely be wasted by the government. With that influx of capital, we would see an increase in savings, investment and employment. The economy would flourish and consumption would naturally follow suit. With a consumption based sales tax, revenue to the federal government would flow in more than sufficient quantity to fund its legitimate functions. Deficits would be a thing of the past.

California's experience with Proposition 13 in the late 1970's provides further proof of truth of this assertion. Proposition 13 was the "Tax Revolt" spearheaded by Howard Jarvis and Paul Gann. It slashed California's property tax rate by 57 percent in one year. The result was $7 billion in revenue pumped in the economy in that same period.

The opponents of Proposition 13 predicted doomsday if the measure passed. They claimed vital services would be cut, massive layoffs of teachers, fire and police forces would occur, libraries would close, and in general, life as we knew it would end. As Rabushka writes, "One had to be living in California to fully experience the degree to which the voters were warned, intimidated, threatened, or bribed by the ever shriller hysteria, dishonesty, and hypocrisy of

13's opponents." Alvin Rabushka, *The Tax Revolt*, Hoover Press, 1982, page 24.

The effects of 13 were precisely the opposite. While there were no measurable reductions in any of California's vital services, California saw an increase of 935,000 private sector jobs within just three years of Proposition 13 passing. Rabushka observes, "Between July 1978 [date 13 was passed] and July 1980, California added nearly three in every ten new jobs" created nationally, "almost a doubling of its prior share." Ibid, page 86. Going on, "These gains constituted an increase of 7.4 percent in the state's civilian labor force, compared with an overall increase in the nation's total civilian employment of only 2.7 percent in the same two-year interval." Ibid, pages 86-87.

The general effect of 13 on California's business environment was positive. The Advisory Council of the State Department of Economic and Business Development conducted a survey of 4,500 California business. The findings: "84 percent of the companies that responded said they felt 13 had improved the state's business climate." Ibid, page 89.

Proposition 13 opponents threatened, among other things, that $7 billion in property tax cuts would lead to a sharp jump in the state's inflation rate. Wrong again. California's Consumer Price Index, the government's measure of inflation, fell by one full percentage point as a result of 13. Ibid, page 89.

The road to America's future economic security is plainly marked. We must cut taxes and we must cut government spending. Dr. Friedman himself echoes this important point. In his book *Tax Limitation, Inflation and the Role of Government*, the Nobel Prize winner declares:

> "Every step we take to strengthen the tax system, whether by getting people to accept payroll taxes they otherwise would not accept, or by cooperating in enacting higher income taxes and excise taxes, or whatnot, fosters a higher level of government spending. That's why I am in favor of cutting taxes under any circumstances, for whatever excuse, for whatever reasons." Friedman (Fisher Institute 1978) pg. 19.

It is clear our present leaders in Washington do not wish to be guided by the plain historical facts. They seem guided by the platitudes of socialism designed to reduce the productive strength of the nation and the standard of living of its inhabitants. We are at a crossroads. Should the nation stay on its present course, we shall be crushed under the parasitic weight of government which will all but eliminate the productive qualities of our economy. Imagine the pain of recovering from such a debacle.

On the other hand, if we change directions now, we can rebuild our economy with as little pain and disruption as possible. As Senator Phil Gramm says, "Everybody wants to go to heaven, but nobody wants to die." To correct our national course, we all must die to the idea that government, through tax and spend federal policies, can provide our every need. Governments can do no such thing. They can merely create a suitable environment in which the people themselves can produce the things they need.

THE FOLLY OF THE RHETORIC OF ENVY

For years, socialists have justified their tax increases as a means of making the rich "pay their fair share." As though rich people pay nothing, increased rates are used by social planners as a means of getting even with those who have managed to get ahead financially. The inevitable impact of those policies upon the poor and middle class, however, are never explored. If the body politic was remotely aware of the economic realities of those policies, surely no such increases would be tolerated.

At no time, however, do socialist planners ever suggest to us what one's "fair share" actually is. Whatever the rich are paying in taxes, that is not enough. Therefore, they cannot be paying their fair share. Tax rate increases must then be used to even the odds with those less fortunate.

If the current top rate of tax is 31 percent, as it was in 1990, then it seems more fair to raise it to 36 percent, as recently happened under Clinton's plan. But if it is fair to raise the rate to 36 percent, why not 40 percent, or 50, or even 60 percent? Surely 60 percent is more fair than 40, if 36 percent is more fair than 31 percent. And if 60 percent is fair, why not 70 or 80 percent? In fact, if it is unfair for rich people to be rich, why not tax them at the rate of 100 percent?

As you can see, the "fair share" logic is strained at best. When tested, it cannot stand up to the yardstick of common sense. The truth is, it is absolutely fraudulent to suggest that rich people received a tax break during the 1980's at the expense of the poor and middle class. While Clinton and other liberals insist on this time and again, such is simply not the case.

Treasury statistics bear this out. In the January, 1991, issue of my newsletter, I explained that during the period of 1980 to 1990, the share of income tax paid by the richest five percent of the population *grew* from 36.8 percent in 1980, to 44.1 percent in 1990. The share of tax for the richest one percent of all American's went from 19 percent in 1980 to 25.6 percent in 1990. The report was issued by the Treasury on November 2, 1990.

Bruce Bartlett, one time Treasury Official whom I quoted earlier, produced a chart of the percentiles of tax liabilities paid by the richest members of our society. In each of the five categories listed, the members' saw an increase in their tax burden during the years in which they allegedly received a free ride. I borrow Bartlett's chart, drawn from Internal Revenue Statistic of Income data:

Share of Total Federal Income Tax Burden by Adjusted Gross Income Percentile (Percent)

Tax Year	Top 1%	Top 5%	Top 10%	Top 25%	Top 50%
1980	19.0	36.8	49.3	73.0	92.9
1981	17.6	35.0	48.0	72.3	92.5
1982	19.0	36.1	48.6	72.5	92.6
1983	20.3	37.3	49.7	73.1	92.8
1984	21.1	38.0	50.6	73.5	92.6
1985	21.8	38.8	51.5	74.1	92.8
1986	25.0	41.8	54.0	75.6	93.4
1987	24.6	43.1	55.5	76.8	93.9
1988	27.5	45.5	57.2	77.8	94.3
1989	25.2	44.0	55.9	77.4	94.3
1990	25.6	44.1	55.8	77.4	94.4

To correct our national financial situation, we must reject the rhetoric of envy as a lie. I shall define what constitutes a person's fair share of the tax burden. One's fair share is measured in *proportion* to his consumption. Those who consume more because of their comparative riches shall pay more. Those who consume less because of their comparative poverty shall pay less. That and that alone is the only reasonable measure of one's fair share.

How to Limit Government Spending and Taxation

The departure of our contemporary leaders from the principles of sound economic policy and individual liberty have left us with no alternative but to expressly limit their tax and spend powers. Without such limits, recent history has proven that our liberties will be cast aside as the government takes more and more drastic measures to support its habit. The *American Reconstruction Act* proposes specific limits on these powers. In addition, we propose a plan to pay down the debt. Let us address the elements.

1. Absolute Cap on Government Spending. First, I propose an absolute cap on government spending. It is not sufficient to enact a balanced budget amendment to solve our financial problems. True, the federal debt is a matter of grave concern, but it is just half the problem. The level of taxation is the other half. Without firm spending limits, the Congress will simply continue to raise taxes to support its spending. "You want a balanced budget? Fine. We'll just raise the tax rate another five percent this year to accommodate spending."

Unchecked increases in federal spending, with or without a balanced budget amendment, will surely lead to despotic levels of taxation. This must be avoided. I am in favor of a balanced budget requirement, but in addition, I propose to solve the problem by placing absolute limits on government spending.

To begin with, we freeze government spending at the current level of revenue collection. You will recall that our 25 percent sales tax rate nets about $1 trillion in 1993 and slightly more in 1994. No further deficit spending is permitted. That means government will simply have to find a way to roll back spending to 1986 levels.

That will not be so hard to do if government implements the suggestions of the Grace Commission and cuts waste, duplication, inefficiency, fraud, and incompetence. In its 24-volume report, the commission made literally thousands of recommendations on that regard, absolutely none of which were heeded. Secondly, when the social component of spending is removed and government concentrates on spending for the "general welfare" as we now understand that phrase, there is no question but that spending can be reduced to the still quite high level of $1 trillion.

The fact of the matter is this provision asks nothing of Congress which it has not, on its own, declared to be perfectly feasible. In 1985, Congress passed the *Balanced Budget and Emergency Deficit Control Act*, commonly called the Gramm-Rudman-Hollings Act. In passing the act, Congress recognized the importance of deficit reduction and the need to balance the budget. The terms of the original act would have balanced the federal budget by 1991. If Congress thought it necessary and desirable to balance the budget in 1985, so much so that it passed a law to that effect, certainly it should have no quarrel with such a proposal now.

Those who most benefit from high government spending will, as was the case in California, likely predict massive, traumatic economic fallout if this policy is adopted. They will call it irresponsible, short-sighted, or insensitive to the social needs of society. Such a spending limit is precisely the opposite in every regard. Continuing on our present path will surely lead to great economic hardship. Growing unemployment and a faltering economic base is what we have to look forward to. Which is more irresponsible or insensitive, to abandon such a course or lead the nation headlong into serious trouble?

Each dollar not consumed by the government is one dollar available to the private sector to create jobs and wealth. As the job base grows, the need for federal assistance programs falls in direct proportion. As our economy becomes stronger, more and more citizens will work their way off the lower rungs of the economic ladder. The marketplace, not the government, provides the only opportunity for this to happen.

2. Implement a Plan to Pay Down the Debt. At present, there are no provisions to pay the principle on the $4.5 trillion debt. Government currently spends about $250 billion annually paying interest on the debt. Many economists fear that if something is not done about continued borrowing and the fact that principle debt is not being retired, there will soon come a time when one hundred percent of federal revenue will go to pay just the interest on the debt. If that happens, not a dime will be spent on any other federal concern, including defense.

My plan involves a steady, progressive approach to retiring the debt. It is based upon the natural growth of the economy, plus the added growth we can expect from infusing at least $720 billion annually in the form of income tax law compliance savings. With the income tax laws dismantled, the costs of compliance will immediately be transmitted into savings and investment. Over time, that increase will show itself in the form of greater employment, higher real wages, cheaper goods and services, and increased sale of goods internationally. There is no telling just how dynamic an increase we could see in GDP over say, five years, as a result of this move. Without question, however it will be substantial.

We do know that GDP grows naturally (in present sluggish conditions) at about two percent annually. We also know that we will add $720 billion annually from the compliance component. Reasonable estimates are it may take the marketplace two years to convert $720 billion in capital to GDP. Let us assume the GDP sales tax base begins at the 1993 level of about $4 trillion. Within two years, we will see GDP increase to $4.88 trillion (two percent per year, plus $720 billion).

With the nation's GDP sales tax base raised to $4.88 trillion, the government collects $1.22 trillion in revenue (4.88 x .25, the national sales tax rate). So while we have grown federal revenue by 22 percent in just two years, we have frozen spending at the $1 trillion level. Therefore, the additional $220 billion is applied directly against outstanding debt.

Under this program, we pay off the national debt in a maximum of *12 years*, even if GDP grows no faster than two percent annually. The reality is, the economy will grow much faster because of the rapid increase in productivity. The California Proposition 13 case study proves that. As productivity grows, so does the number of wage earners and consequently, their consumption. Consumption is, of course, our tax base. Therefore, federal revenue will also increase rapidly. Consequently, it is perfectly feasible to reduce the debt in fewer than 12 years.

Under this plan, government has an important incentive to keep its hands off the economy and allow it to grow. As the debt is paid down in larger and larger amounts, the amount of interest the government must pay from its fixed budget is also reduced. As non-discretionary spending is reduced, there is a proportional increase in funds available for discretionary spending.

At such time as the debt is paid in full, the spending freeze is to be lifted. However, we continue to limit federal spending to a specific percentage of GDP. With a balanced budget requirement and a spending limit, Congress will never again be able to accumulate an irresponsible debt such as we have now. Furthermore, it will not be able to inflict despotic tax rates upon the people.

My proposal is to limit spending to 15 percent of GDP. That would give government equal benefit of all economic growth and would cut the national sales tax rate by 40 percent, from 25 percent to 15. That in turn will spur more economic growth and even more revenue to the government. The cycle of growth and expansion will start all over again.

Under our very conservative assumptions, our national debt will be retired in year 12. At that time, the consumption component of GDP will have risen from its present level of $4 trillion, to $6.19 trillion. At 15 percent, government revenue amounts to $928 billion. You may ask why government should accept a reduction in its revenue? In reality, its spendable revenue is higher at $928 billion in the 12th year than it was at $1 trillion in the first. The reason is there are no longer any interest payments to be made. Therefore, $920 billion without an interest obligation is the same as $1.17 trillion with an interest obligation. In any event, each year thereafter, federal revenues are allowed to increase as GDP increases.

3. Revise the Appropriations Process. We must revise a revenue appropriations process which has become a disgrace. At present, any group, cause, organization or special interest which can persuade a few members of a Senate or House Appropriations Committee as to the merits of their program, can receive federal funds. As you learned from this book, federal spending was never designed to accommodate any one group or individual at the expense of another.

But that is precisely where we are today.

To ensure the test of spending propriety is met, we shall require all appropriations be passed by a vote of two-thirds majority of all members of Congress. At present, it takes but a simple majority of those voting to spend your money. This is why special interest groups have had so much success with Congress. My proposal ends this nonsense.

In addition, we shall give the President the same tool enjoyed by a majority of the governors of the various states - a line item veto. This way, a President can veto specific spending proposals which do not meet the test of Constitutional propriety without vetoing an entire appropriations bill.

4. Absolute Cap on Level of Taxation. With spending under control and the debt retired, we can cap the level at which the federal government taxes the nation. At present, federal taxes take some 23 percent of total GDP. As we saw in the historical analysis of taxation, this kind of tax rate can cripple an economy. Like spending, I propose to limit the level of taxation at 15 percent of GDP. Since Congress is limited to what it can spend, there is no need to collect revenue beyond that point once the debt is retired.

5. Borrowing only in case of Emergency. Since borrowing got us into trouble, I propose to limit the federal government's authority to borrow funds. Under my plan, the government shall have the authority to borrow funds in only the four following specific circumstances: rebellion, insurrection, invasion or declared war. The existence of one of the four conditions shall be affirmed by a two-thirds vote of Congress before borrowing can commence.

Moveover, as part of the Congressional Resolution on the matter, Congress shall specify the time and manner in which such loan shall be repaid. Congress shall be authorized to raise taxes during such national emergency, but the tax increase shall be considered automatically repealed when the emergency passes. The emergency is considered resolved when a simple majority of Congress voting adopts a resolution so stating.

6. No Phase In of Plan. This plan shall not be phased in. When the *American Reconstruction Act* is approved by Congress, it shall take immediate effect. History has proven that when plans are phased in over time, Congress has an opportunity to muddle things. Former four-term Texas Congressman Ron Paul personally explained to me that phased-in tax programs do not work. Congress may begin eliminating one tax when it starts to adopt another, but once it sees the revenue stream grow, it abandons the phase-in and turns the crank on both taxes. The elimination of the original tax never occurs and the people are left to contend with two taxes, not one.

7. No Use of Estimates to Determine GDP. In ascertaining Congress' tax and spending authority, it shall not be entitled to make estimates of GDP. Tax and spend levels for a given year shall be determined by GDP, less government

CONCLUSION

spending, *for the prior year*. Therefore, when ascertaining its spending authority for 1993, Congress shall be mandated to use 1992 GDP levels. This builds in a protection against false or erroneous economic estimates which might defeat the tax and spending limits. Plus, it builds in incentive for the government to leave its hands off the economy so it may flourish naturally. The higher the economy soars, the greater the benefit to the federal government.

Conclusion

There is no question this plan will work, but similarly, there is no question it will encounter great opposition. The greatest opposition will likely come from those with a vested interest in maintaining the tax and spend culture Congress has created. It is unquestionable that our nation will undergo a period of difficult adjustment if this measure is enacted. That is unavoidable. It is like the process an alcoholic must endure to get sober. It may be uncomfortable–but necessary– to avoid self-destruction.

Do not lose sight of the fact that we are going through a difficult economic period now, and it will only get worse if something is not done. In the past several years, our nation's largest and most stable employers have down-sized considerably. We have seen massive layoffs in the auto industry, oil industry, computer industry, aero space industry and even in the service sectors of the economy. Giants such as IBM and Boeing, previously thought immune to the ebb and flow of the economy, have cut costs by eliminating 10's of thousands of jobs. These workers are now largely displaced, but because American companies are barely profitable, they cannot afford to retrain them for other work.

The only way massive numbers of workers will be retained is if industry can once more become profitable. This can happen only when the hand of government is removed form the pockets of American business, industry and consumers. Major reconstruction of our tax system will certainly cause some disruption, but failure to rebuild it will just as surely lead to disaster.

To illustrate how sincere and serious I am about the *American Reconstruction Act*, you should know that when it is adopted, I will be one of those workers cast out of a job! With the elimination of the IRS, the personal income tax and IRS abuse, my career as a tax litigation consultant will come to an end.

What's worse, I have no other training but that of tax law.

I should think that constitutes putting one's money where his mouth is.

17

SUMMARY AND CALL TO ARMS

The American Reconstruction Act
A Summary

The *American Reconstruction Act* may be summarized as follows:

1. Eliminate all personal and corporate income taxes, employment taxes, estate and gift taxes, and social security taxes. In short, repeal the Internal Revenue Code.

2. The Act does not eliminate manufacturer's excise taxes or import duties.

3. Eliminate the Internal Revenue Service, the nation's present tax collection vehicle.

4. Replace the above stated taxes with one national sales tax levied upon retail sales of goods and services.

a. The sales tax rate shall be based upon the consumption and housing components of the Gross Domestic Product (GDP).

b. The sales tax shall not attach to payments of interest, or the purchase of any savings vehicle such as stocks, bonds, CD's, money market instruments, gold or silver coin or bullion, or the like.

c. The sales tax shall not attach to the purchase by any person of any capital asset, with the exception of housing.

5. The tax shall initially be levied at the rate of 25 percent of GDP as defined above.

6. The tax shall be collected by the various state governments throughout the nation, and paid to the national Treasury upon demand pursuant to regulations established for that purpose.

7. The federal government shall have no legal claim whatsoever to audit or prosecute any person, business or entity regarding his compliance with this act. The enforcement of the tax assessed by the Act will be the function of the various states using the machinery currently in place to enforce their own sales tax laws.

8. Immediately upon the adoption of this act, Congressional spending shall be fixed at a level equal to its revenue that exists in the year passed.

a. The spending freeze shall remain in effect until such time as the total accumulated federal debt is paid in full.

b. The amount of revenue existing in the year this act is adopted shall be considered the government's maximum spending authority until such time as the total accumulated federal debt is paid in full.

c. During the period of such freeze, all tax revenue paid to the government in excess of its spending authority shall be applied to the principal amount of federal debt.

d. All revenue obtained through manufacturer's excise taxes and import duties shall be applied to the principal amount of federal debt.

9. At such time as the national debt is paid in full, the spending freeze shall be dissolved.

10. Upon dissolution of the spending freeze, the government's spending authority shall be adjusted to 15 percent of GDP as defined above.

11. Upon dissolution of the spending freeze, the national sales tax rate shall likewise be reduced to 15 percent of GDP as defined above.

12. Deficit spending shall be illegal.

13. Upon passage of this act, the President of the United States shall be empowered with line item veto authority.

14. Upon passage of this act, specific appropriations shall take effect only when authorized by a two-thirds vote of all Congressmen, subject to the veto power of the President.

15. The national sales tax levy shall not be increased above 15 percent except by vote of two-thirds majority of all Congressmen, subject to the veto power of the President, but even then, only in time of a defined national emergency.

a. A national emergency exists only in time of insurrection, rebellion, invasion or declared war. The emergency must be affirmed by Congressional resolution passed by two-thirds vote of all Congressmen.

16. Upon resolution of the emergency situation, any tax increase shall be considered immediately and automatically repealed, at which time the rate shall return to 15 percent.

a. The national emergency is considered resolved upon the affirmative vote of a simple majority of Congressmen.

17. Congress shall have no authority to borrow money, except in time of national emergency as defined above, upon the vote of two-thirds majority of all Congressmen.

a. The Congressional resolution authorizing the borrowing of funds for emergency purposes shall specify the time and manner in which such funds are to be repaid.

18. For purposes of ascertaining GDP, no estimates of any kind shall be permitted. Rather, the GDP base for current levies shall be GDP as recorded for the previous year.

19. The act shall take full effect immediately upon ratification by Congress. It shall not be phased in.

The plan, as you see, is very simple. Through its structure, we can solve the tax and spending problems we now face.

A CALL TO ARMS

In his books, Dr. James Payne explains that Congress' isolation from the people of this country, and its continued exposure to tax and spend interests, both in and out of government, has created a Washington culture simply out of touch with the real needs of the nation. It's difficult to argue with Dr. Payne's conclusion.

When considering whether to impose a tax increase or somehow increase the compliance burden on citizens, Congressmen hear from Treasury officials, IRS officials, and OMB officials, but not citizens. Congressmen are told of only how the proposals will help solve this or that administrative problem, how they might increase federal revenue, or decrease tax avoidance. They are not told how the measure might impose additional, costly burdens upon citizens and business, or how they might further distort economic conditions.

When considering whether to commence, continue or expand a government spending program, Congressmen hear from the bureaucrats who administer the program and from the beneficiaries of the program. They do not hear from taxpayers who must pay the bill to support it. They hear only of the "good things" the program is doing or could do, but not how taxpayers in general will have their standard of living reduced to pay for those "good things."

Each time money is transferred by the government to a citizen to help him pay for food, education, home energy, or medical care, there is somebody out there who now has less of his own money to pay for food, education, home energy, or medical care. This is the fact the Congress seems to have lost sight of. They seem to think that federal money is free. That it simply materializes without causing hardship to the citizens who must provide it through tax payments. Payne explains that the "underlying attitude" of Congressmen "is that it doesn't hurt anybody to spend government funds." *The Culture of Spending*, page 60.

Former Congressman Ron Paul confirms Payne's observation, that most members of Congress are simply out of touch with reality. In his book, *Freedom Under Seige* (1987), Congressman Paul writes that members of Congress promote tax and spend policies "with the best of intentions, believing that economic conditions can be improved through government spending and control." Ibid, page 129. They simply do not realize the harm they visit upon the nation and its people through these policies. They do not see it because all they hear, day in and day out, is how good, helpful, noble or necessary are their various spending endeavors.

What this means is We, the People of the United States, must make our voices heard to the body which we have elected. Middle income taxpayers have been silent too long on matters which affect them the most. They are largely unrepresented in Congress in terms of lobbying groups or associations, while every other special interest has an army of professionals knocking on the doors of Senators and Representatives each day.

Events of recent history prove that when America is mobilized, Congress does listen. Recall in the spring of 1993, when President Clinton nominated Zowie Baird, then Kimba Woods to the position of U.S. Attorney General.

During the confirmation process, it came to light that both nominees had failed to pay social security taxes on their domestic help. The media quickly dubbed the scandal "Nannygate."

Outraged that two high powered and high paid attorneys either did not know of, or chose to ignore a provision of tax law imposing a liability on them, American citizens phoned their Congressmen and the Senate Judiciary Committee by the thousands. Their message was quite simple. If this person is going to be the Unites States Attorney, our nation's chief law enforcement officer, it seems only reasonable that such person should actually *obey the law!* An aide to Senator Joseph Biden, Chairman of the Senate Judiciary Committee, told me that calls were coming into his office at a rate of 900 to 1 against Baird's confirmation.

As you know, Clinton quickly withdrew her nomination. Shortly thereafter, it came to light that his second nominee, Kimba Woods, had precisely the same problem. The scenario played itself out all over again.

What this proves is, our elected officials do listen to the public if they are forced to. They do take into consideration the realities of the situation, so long as a sufficient number of Americans stuff the facts down Congress' collective throat. This is what we must do to force Congress to address the merits of the *American Reconstruction Act.*

According to James Davidson of the National Taxpayers' Union, each sincerely written letter to Congress is considered to represent 5,000 similar opinions on a given topic. You must write your Representative and Senator and implore him to adopt the *American Reconstruction Act.* Your sincerely written letter is worth 5,000 votes on this issue. We have been taught to believe that we are powerless when it comes to influencing Congressional opinion, but such is not the case. Our nation's future is at stake. There is no more opportune time to prove the people still have a voice in the operation of their own government.

My specific plan to carry the day on the *American Reconstruction Act* involves you. You must be willing to carry part of the burden to help push this measure through Congress. Do not look for somebody else to do it. There is nobody else. You must be willing to stand up for your own interests; you must be willing to defend the future of your own children, or surely you have no interests remaining and your children will have no future.

There are five things I want you to do. You can do them without expending much time, and certainly without expending much money, *but you must do them.*

1. Write your Congressmen and implore him to ratify the *American Reconstruction Act.* You can write your Representative at: The Hon. (name)_____, U.S. House of Representatives, Washington, D.C. 20515. Your Senator is reached at: The Hon. (name)_____, U.S. Senate, Washington, D.C. 20510. You can also phone your Congressman. The switchboard number is 202-224-3121. Make your voice heard! When you write your letter, please send me a copy of it. Send it to me in care of Winning Publications. Mark the envelop "ARA Letter."

2. Spread the word about this book and the *American Reconstruction Act.*